Running
Free

A Book for Women Runners
and Their Friends

by
Joan L. Ullyot, M.D.

G. P. PUTNAM'S SONS, NEW YORK

Library of Congress Cataloging in Publication Data

Ullyot, Joan, date.
  Running free.

  Bibliography: p.
  1. Running. 2. Sports for women. I. Title.
GV1061.U42   796.4'26   79-25048
ISBN 0-399-12492-6

PRINTED IN THE UNITED STATES OF AMERICA

CONTENTS

To Teddy, Jonny and Bill

PREFACE

Several years ago, I wrote a "how-to" book about running. The book was undertaken in response to numerous letters, mostly from women, with very practical questions about training, running gear, injuries and the like. In the book I answered these questions in detail, and gave advice to those who could not consult me in person.

Contrary from what one might assume from the present glut of books on the market, there is not much to learn about the "how" of running. A local columnist, disgusted by the growing piles of instruction manuals, remarked that if you're suddenly face to face with a tiger, you don't need a book on how to run, you just do it—and quickly. Though I seldom agree with this particular columnist, I think he's right in this instance. If you avoid blatant style faults, get in some mileage and learn the basic principles of training, you know enough to run a marathon.

So, once my "practical" guide appeared, I figured I wouldn't write anything else about running. I also assumed the letters would stop and I would be spared future years of writer's cramp. The assumptions were wrong. The same readers who had learned, quickly enough, *how* to run, were doubly eager to explore the *why* and *what* of running. The letters multiplied.

Runners are like converts to religion. The sport begins to dominate their schedules and their lives. They love to talk about running, read about it, explore goals, methods, and results. Non-runners are bored, but other runners are fascinated.

The truth is, of course, that running, perhaps because it's so very natural to the human species, causes profound changes in new converts. The runner finds herself undergoing a transformation which affects her body, her mind, her entire social life. Usually pleased, but puzzled and often apprehensive, she wants to know if these changes are unique to her, or are experienced by other runners. Most of the letters I have received in recent years discussed these changes, both physical and mental. Some women just want to share their experiences, others ask for reassurance. Universally, they feel excited, pleased with their new self-image, and optimistic about future development.

So this book is about the changes that running can induce, not only in the individual, but also in old established institutions—the family, the medical establishment, even perhaps, if we're lucky, the International Olympic Committee!

I wish to thank all those women who have spoken or written to me about the changes in their lives these past few years, for sharing with me their concerns, their excitement, and their future hopes, which they will find reflected here.

Glossary

Runners' Terms

aerobic: "With oxygen." Any vigorous exercise in which the uptake and utilization of oxygen are sufficient to meet the needs of the working muscles. Capitalized, as "Aerobics," refers to the system of exercise devised by Dr. Kenneth Cooper, which improves oxygen uptake and thus conditions the heart and lungs.

fartlek: From the Swedish "speed-play." An unstructured, playful workout combining fast runs of varying distances with recovery jogs, hill-bounding, and (sometimes) exercise.

intervals: Sets of repeated fast runs on a track, with recovery jogs in between. Examples: 12 x 440 yards (with 220 yards jogs), 20 x 220 (with 220 yards jogs), 6 x 880 (with 440 yards jogs).

pace-work: Practice running at the pace you wish to maintain in a race. If your goal is to run a 6-minute mile, doing "quarters" in 90 seconds each would be pace-work (whereas 80-second quarters would be speed-work).

P. R.: Personal record. The most significant kind of record to most runners, far outclassing world records. Your own best time for any distance. Note: P.W. = "personal worst."

quarter: One lap around a standard track, equivalent to 440 yards, or ¼ mile. Half a lap is a 220, 2 laps an 880.

11

In Europe, the standard track is 400 meters in circumference—437.4 yards.

speed-work: Any running at a pace faster than you intend to race, so, of necessity, done over a shorter distance. Intervals and fartlek are two common types of speed-work.

the Wall: Abrupt slowdown at about 20 miles in a marathon, believed to reflect glycogen depletion.

wind-sprints: A type of schoolboy torture frequently used for track runners in the 50s, now usually reserved for football players. You sprint across the field so fast that you are winded, repeat frequently. Designed to "build wind."

Medical/Physiological Terms

bradycardia: Slow pulse, usually under 60.

catheterization: A type of "invasive" heart examination, in which a thin flexible tube (catheter) is threaded into the heart chambers and used to take pressure readings and blood samples. Important diagnostic tool in congenital heart disease.

cholesterol: A blood lipid. Excess amounts are thought to contribute to coronary artery disease and atherosclerosis. Desirable levels are 110–180.

chondromalacia: "Runner's knee," or pain under the kneecap, associated with soft, thickened cartilage, and inflammation.

hematocrit: Percent of a blood sample that is occupied by red cells; thus, a measure of anemia. Should be at least 40 percent in males, 38 percent in females.

lipids: Various kinds of fat that circulate in the blood (or serum). Includes cholesterol, triglycerides, free fatty acids (FFA), and lipoprotein particles of various sizes: VLDL (very low density lipoprotein), LDL (low density lipoprotein), and HDL (high density lipoprotein).

oxygen debt: Occurs whenever oxygen needs of working muscles exceed the available supply, causing feelings of breathlessness and extreme muscular fatigue. Exercise which results in oxygen debt is called "anaerobic."

shin splints: Pain in the muscles along the front of the leg, below the knee. Can have various causes, most commonly hard shoes or improper running style.

stress fracture: A "fatigue" fracture, usually hairline (but painful), caused by overuse rather than trauma. Common sites in runners include the foot and shinbone (tibia).

tachycardia: Fast pulse, usually over 90. Normal during exercise, abnormal at rest.

tendinitis: Inflammation of a tendon, causing pain and/or swelling. Common in the heel-cord (Achilles tendon), around the ankle and the knee.

$\dot{V}_E$: Pulmonary ventilation: the volume of air that is moved in and out of the lungs (liters/minute).

$\dot{V}O_2$ **max.:** Maximal oxygen consumption. The amount of oxygen that can be utilized during a maximal (all-out) exercise test. Expressed as milliliters of O_2 kilograms of body weight/minute. Considered the best single measurement of aerobic capacity, or "fitness."

I: RUNNING FREE

Chapter One: Why Run?

Many non-runners tend to equate running and jogging, and a few "serious" runners are offended at being asked, "Oh, do you jog?" after they have just finished the Boston Marathon. They think that the word "jogger" connotes slow, plodding, and dull—someone shuffling around the block, wheezing. Anyone who runs under 8 minutes a mile, they suggest, is a runner, not a mere "jogger."

I disagree with this distinction. After all, effort and speed are relative measures. My 8-minute training pace would have been an all-out effort when I first started running, but is comfortable now. Top male runners can "jog" along easily at a 6-minute pace. In the Western States 100-mile Endurance Run, through the rugged Sierra Nevada, top finishers averaged 12 minutes/mile. Was this a jog, a run, or a hike? In any event, it was a "serious" race for "serious" runners.

Motivation. My own distinction between jogging and running is based on motivation rather than speed. To me, a "jogger" is concerned primarily with her health, her figure, or her appearance. She may not like the activity at all, but feels it is good for her, or a duty. The runner, by contrast, likes to run. The sport is enjoyable in itself, leads to a warm glow, a sense of relaxation and contentment. Whether she moves along at 12 minutes/mile, or 8; whether she runs in the Olympic games, or just down a rural road to the mailbox, the woman who loves to run is a runner.

By this definition, most of us started out as joggers. We didn't see runners pound past us in a road race, eyes slightly glazed, mouths open, obviously straining to win, and think to ourselves, "Gee, that looks like a lot of fun, I think I'll try it." I remember my own reaction when I inadvertently saw the Boston Marathon leaders flash past me 10 years ago. I thought, "Why would grown men run through the streets of Boston in their underwear, obviously inflicting pain on themselves?" I shuddered with distaste and turned away. The runner's mentality was a mystery to me. I wasn't even a jogger yet—I had a prejogger's scorn of road runners.

People who start jogging do so for a variety of motives, but anticipated pleasure has not been on the list, at least not till recent years. Most of us are driven by vague guilt, fear, or vanity. The list of specific reasons for taking up jogging is extensive. Here are some of the most common responses to the question, "Why run?"

Fad. "Everyone else is doing it, so I thought I'd see what all the fuss is about." The fad jogger is usually recognizable

16

by her bright, fashionable, velour "warm-up suit," in which she is actually jogging—not just standing around keeping warm, before or after the run. Even if the weather is cold, a runner who plans to sweat would not wear a lovely velour outfit—she'd save it for the post-run party. Fad runners also tend to wear expensive running shoes selected to match the velour outfit. Their hair and makeup are suspiciously well preserved. They prefer to run in fashionable areas, where all the "in" people can be observed. Most of them are into roller-skating, by now, so their numbers are diminishing. But a few, who jogged their first miles because of the fad, got hooked on the feeling, changed their velour jumpsuit for nylon shorts, and are now runners—indistinguishable from the rest, disheveled, and happy.

Health. As a doctor who recommends aerobic exercise for everyone, I naturally consider health a far more valid motivation for jogging. There is no doubt that general health is improved by jogging; even those few doctors who frown upon running sports as too "strenuous" recommend brisk walking—which produces many of the same changes. Women around age 30, and men around age 40, who may have been sedentary for close to 20 years, usually have a nagging feeling that they're not as energetic, as resilient, as . . . *young* as they used to be. This slight malaise can get them out the door on their first tentative jogging run. It's not the specter of genuine ill health that drives them, so much as a dissatisfaction with a less-than-optimal condition. They jog off in search of WELLNESS.

To Prevent Heart Disease. This is a specific variant of the vague urge toward health; it often motivates men who have relatives or close friends that succumbed to heart attacks. (Since women are far less susceptible to heart disease, they rarely take up jogging out of this particular fear.) There is considerable controversy among doctors as

17

to whether running prolongs your life, or helps ward off coronary artery disease. Almost all would agree, however, that it won't hurt, and *may* help. The jogger who jogs to help his heart should realize that there are no absolute guarantees, and he would be wise to stop smoking and adhere to a low-fat diet for greater insurance. Jogging does tend to reduce weight and blood pressure, alleviate the urge to smoke, and curb "Type A," time-pressured behavior—thus it eliminates several high-risk factors in one blow, and is definitely more healthful than the sedentary life-style.

Vanity. More women than men start jogging in the hopes of improving their appearance. The majority of women, myself included, take up running to lose weight, or inches—in general, to "shape up." It seems so much more bearable than dieting, requiring less willpower. Of course, those who lose fastest have counted calories as well, but almost all women joggers slim down visibly within a short time. Men lose their paunches, too. There are more subtle changes in appearance that may lure some—clear skin, lustrous hair, a general aura of energy around runners. Vanity is a valid reason to take up jogging, but you shouldn't expect overnight miracles. Changes take time, and a mile jog daily for 1 month will not eliminate cellulite (after a few years, it might!).

Fitness. Many joggers are already interested in a sport—tennis, soccer, swimming, handball—and wish to improve their stamina or endurance. Running is considered to be the easiest and fastest way to get into condition. Some of these joggers who hope to improve their game get so hooked on running that they end up as ex-swimmers, ex-golfers, etc. Or they end up only playing sporadically. Others start whipping all their former tennis buddies, who then take up jogging, too, to get back on the same competitive level.

Competition. Very few adults begin running in order to enter or win races. If the fruits of victory were a new Jaguar or a vacation in Tahiti, rather than a medal or a trophy, this kind of motivation might assume more significance. Generally, though, the only runners around now, who started as racers, are those who ran track or cross-country at the school or college level. The hard work, frequent overtraining, and "pain ethic" associated with such competition can actually discourage participants from running later on in life.

Conversely, for runners past the beginning level, competition can provide a healthful and welcome spice to running, and lure joggers into new challenges. The Bonne Bell series of 10 km. races for women only, in cities scattered throughout the country (over thirty in 1979), has provided such a competitive spur for thousands of women. It is estimated that 80 percent of Bonne Bell participants are running either their first race, or their longest run to date. The experience tends to "hook" them into further road racing and convert them from joggers to runners.

The motivation to change one's life patterns, to take those first running steps, has to be quite powerful to overcome physical inertia and mental resistance in the non-athlete. The inertia can be far more striking in women than in men, since women have the added barrier of social expectations to hurdle—that is, until the last few years, women were not expected or encouraged to be active or to actually *sweat.* So the combined motives of health, appearance, and curiosity must usually be linked with *opportunity,* to make the vital transition from spectator to jogger. Once the individual has started jogging, for whatever obscure motives, the hardest part is over. The jogger gradually evolves into the runner, who finds other, more subtle rewards from the activity.

Ask any regular runner why she is out there on the roads or trails, and you will get a variety of answers, none of which are linked much to health or appearance. Except, of course, for the joking, "I run so I can eat what I like without getting fat." It's true that 80 miles/week gives a runner carte-blanche at chow time, but it's easier to exercise a modicum of self-restraint than to run 80 hard miles. So this "excuse" is merely a humorous red herring.

Enjoyment. Though it's hard for the beginning jogger to comprehend, running can actually be a pleasurable experience. Only the most masochistic individual would continue to pursue an activity that was painful. If you run aerobically, without building up any oxygen debt (which sears the throat and leadens the legs), the sensation of movement is enjoyable—especially downhill! Running through scenic, cool, sweet-smelling terrain naturally enhances the pleasure.

Mental Refreshment. Almost universally, runners report that the run allows relaxation, calms tensions, helps settle the mind after a tough day. Many writers (myself included) deliberately use the time alone, in motion, to organize their thoughts. Once the "head work" has been completed, usually in the first half-hour, the mind drifts on naturally to other things. It is said that philosopher Immanuel Kant composed his entire *Critique of Pure Reason* in his head, during 8 years of daily strolling through the woods near his home. A huge book, the *Critique* must have required correspondingly great amounts of activity. Once Kant had worked out the details while he was in motion, he sat down and put it all down on paper.

Until I started running, I never believed this story (especially after reading Kant in college). Now I see that this is a natural way for the mind to work. As Dr. Sheehan says, "You never have a sound thought unless you're in motion."

Self-Esteem. Running builds pride in one's own abilities, through experience. For most of us, who once doubted our capacity to run a single mile nonstop, the progression to 3-mile runs, to hills, to races at longer distances, is a way to build confidence step by step. Each new challenge met pushes back the frontiers of the possible. Today, the Pikes Peak Marathon; tomorrow, the World! Seventy-one-year-old Walt Stack, president of San Francisco's DSE (Dolphin South End) Runners, has used this ploy for years, in luring women (from ages 7 to 83) to make the 14-mile Pikes Peak ascent, from 7,000 to 14,110 feet. "After you do this," he assures them, "you'll feel ten feet tall! You'll be able to tackle anything!" The Peak Busters, the association of women who have accomplished this feat, now number over 300.

Self-Exploration. Many runners have already achieved remarkable levels of fitness, have climbed the peaks (including Pikes), and couldn't slim down more if they tried. They may have no realistic chance of setting world records, or winning Olympic medals. Most of them will seldom beat out the field even in a local age-group race. So why do they continue to run? All the conventional motivations would seem to be left far behind, and even enjoyment isn't always possible, for most of these veteran runners push themselves hard on occasion, or try to overcome new barriers.

Musing on this question one summer morning at running camp, I asked Dick Taylor, director of Devil's Thumb Ranch, why *he* runs. Dick is primarily a cross-country skier and could have given me a simple answer, such as "Because there's no snow." Instead, he put his continued fascination with running and skiing in metaphysical terms. "It's the eternal conflict between human power and human frailty," he explained helpfully. Dick sees running and skiing as a kind of interface between the physical

21

actuality and potential. The point is not so much to overcome limits, to fight past barriers, as to explore these unknown areas, to play with one's unknown capabilities, to test the waters of stress. It all sounded rather existential to me—"I run, therefore I am." It verged on Transcendental Running, which I discuss further on. But I understood clearly what Dick was trying to put into words. Most runners would agree that running is a means of exploring the natural world and their own selves. The miles run each day add up to a continuous voyage of discovery. And they enjoy it.

Transcendental Running.

Certain running advocates have confided to reporters that they consider running a "religion." Bob Anderson, who possesses considerable clout as the publisher of *Runner's World,* dismissed critics of his burgeoning "fun-runs" in Los Altos, California, as unenlightened non-believers, incapable of understanding the needs of the semimystical community of runners. Naturally, this sentiment did not help in settling the very real car versus runner confrontations along the Los Altos roads. About the same time (1978), *Runner's World* featured an article "Is Running a Religious Experience?" by Hal Higdon. According to Hal, some people feel they "find God" on the run. Since others claim to achieve this experience with LSD, or sky-diving, or skiing, I doubt that running is the only path to enlightenment.

Personally, I must confess that after 8 years of fairly steady running, I have yet to find God along the path. Birds, beautiful scenery, uplifting thoughts, fragrant flowers, occasional startled rabbits—even, once, a fox— these I have encountered. They add considerable enjoyment and color to my runs, and are the main reason that I prefer running on wooded trails to city streets. But a mystical experience, as I would define it, has thus far eluded me. Perhaps I am just too earthbound, too practical. Perhaps I am running too fast, or too slow. I suspect that a large oxygen debt, or a metabolic alkalosis caused by puffing out too much CO_2, may induce peculiar mental states—whether these are interpreted as hallucinations or revelations. The more frequent outcome is a faint, however. I never run myself hard enough to faint. Perhaps I lack sufficient religious commitment to running.

I feel that too much publicity about various mystical states and/or "Runner's High" can be misleading. Your average beginning runner is more worried about getting around the block on a daily basis than about enlightenment. Search for meaning "beyond jogging" may be fine, but not before you can handle the jogging alone without undue strain. The beginner is going through profound physiological and anatomical changes. Muscles unused for years are protesting. The would-be runner wonders if this pain is normal and if it will ever pass. She is not in a "religious" mood. And she will only be discouraged to read ecstatic accounts of transcendental experiences on the run. She may even quit, convinced that running can't be for her, because of the pain and effort she feels.

As a doctor, trained in human biology, I prefer to consider running as our natural means of locomotion. Our species survived for several million years by its ability to walk and run. The running may have been more like "shambling" for our earliest ancestors, but it still was their fastest way of moving around. Sometimes I have great sympathy for these early ancestors as I myself shamble out the door on my morning run. It may not be very fast, but it gets me around—as it did them.

Our modern dependence on wheels and engines to move us around lies at the root of the view that running is something esoteric, to be either admired or condemned by "outsiders." If the oil shortage persists, and we're forced to revert to muscle power, to abandon our cars, you'll suddenly see a whole nation of runners—and walkers. People will no longer boast of being runners, or assume a "holier-than-thou" attitude because they can use their legs and lungs. We'll all recognize again that we are animals, physical creatures.

The knowledge that the physical can go hand in hand with the spiritual self is not new. The ancient Greeks devoted their efforts to training both the body and the mind. Among modern groups, the Seventh-Day Adventists condemn abuse or neglect of the body because they consider the body the "Temple of God" or of the spirit, if you prefer more secular phraseology. Even this latter formulation may not be appreciated in some circles—a San Francisco sportscaster, Jan Hutchins, confided to me that he used to sign off with the reminder that "the body is the temple of the spirit" until he received a nasty letter from his TV bosses. They told him to cool it; that his role was to give the news, not personal opinion. "What do they think the news is?" complained Jan.

Speaking from a physician's viewpoint, I am increasingly convinced that it is impossible for an isolated part of the body—heart, liver or brain—to function optimally in an underexercised or otherwise abused environment. The "mental giant" who is weighted down by mounds of flesh, or is polluting his cellular structure with cigarettes and similar poisons, is not working to his highest potential. Since our society has been sedentary and self-abusing for so long, many of us who become runners in our middle years experience for the first time what it is to be physically fit. This fitness, this daily oxygenation of the entire body, can lead to a new sense of harmony with nature and the universe. I believe it is this feeling of harmony, very natural to physical beings, which can overwhelm the runner at unexpected moments and lead to the experiences that some call "religious." But please, don't ask the struggling, panting beginner, who may have just given up cigarettes the previous week, if she runs for the "high." If she can summon up enough energy, she may kick you. And I wouldn't blame her.

24

Chapter Two: The Transformation of a Cream Puff: My Own Story

When I give lectures these days and am introduced as some sort of an athlete, when women come up to me and wonder what my training secrets are, I become aware that they see me as someone quite different from the person I feel I am. They see me as tall (almost 5 feet, 10 inches), slender, a (once-upon-a-time) world-ranked marathoner, a natural athlete with a physique and talent beyond the reach of ordinary women.

In my own eyes, I am still tall (hard to change that), but there the resemblance stops. I am perpetually 10 pounds or more overweight compared to my aspirations; my 2:51 marathon best leaves me miles behind the world's top women runners, and I am the least athletic person ever to tie on a pair of running shoes. In short, my natural talent is zilch. The fact that I have achieved some success in my running career, despite these handicaps, is the ultimate proof that *anyone* can do it. Perseverance and stubbornness must be the key, rather than innate ability. If running involved hitting or kicking a ball, for instance, I would never have made it.

I explain my lack of talent at every opportunity—convincingly, I think. But the· audience usually remains skeptical. At a Dallas talk, one listener interrupted my disclaimers with the drawled comment, "Bul-l-l-shit." Still, it's true. I would have been voted least likely to succeed, athletically, in high school. The only ones who understand this are my former classmates, from Westridge School in Pasadena. When I spoke to them at a class reunion recently, they were rolling in the aisles from the start. They are the only ones who realized how ludicrous it was for Joan, the bookworm, to be lecturing them on running!

My Unathletic Past. For those who can't quite believe it yet, I will recount the dismal details of my unathletic youth. The purpose of this memoir is twofold. First, to reassert that virtually anyone in normal health can become a good runner. Second, to demonstrate how foreign, how unimaginable, the idea of running could be to a woman, less than 10 years ago. If I was one of the first to stumble into the sport (which now makes me a "pioneer"), it was purely accidental—a quirk of fate. I would never have thought of running.

Physical Education. Looking back, I can see that I was shunted away from sports at an early age. I think I was born nearsighted; by age 4, I noticed that the world was generally fuzzy, but I didn't get my first glasses till age 7, after I had tripped and bashed my head open a few times.

Most of our school sports involved balls—kicking, catching, throwing, hitting or dodging them. With my poor eyesight, I could hardly see the ball, much less dodge it. Naturally, I was one of the last chosen for teams. Knowing I was unathletic, I turned to books. At least I didn't get my glasses knocked off in the library.

26

Outside of school I was more active, as are most kids. I was fairly strong and agile, so I liked to climb trees, swing on ropes, and wrestle. Until puberty, my sister and I together could outwrestle any two boys in the neighborhood. But these outdoor activities were considered tomboyish, not athletic. By age 12, I had succumbed to growing social pressure and tried to behave like a proper young lady. No more wrestling or rope-climbing permitted. My arm muscles went into a decline.

At school, the games with balls continued, and my athletic self-image reached rock-bottom. In California, we all played tennis. I was perpetually in the lower half of the middle tennis ladder, sometimes dropping into the top of the bottom ladder. Gym classes were extremely uninspiring. In a 45-minute period, we would change into gym shorts, march out to the playing field, and stand around waiting for our turn at bat, or for the ball to come to our side in half-court basketball. Twenty minutes later, we'd return to the gym for unpopular showers. They weren't necessary, as no one had worked hard enough to sweat. There was no time to wash or dry our hair, and it was hard to pull on socks and shoes over damp feet. Gym was a dismal experience. After 4 years of high school games, I did earn my letter, but it was in swimming, an after-school sport that didn't require good eyesight, or *any* eyesight, actually. All I had to do was put my head down in the water and power along a few lengths of the pool. In the smog of Pasadena, anyone who could survive a few lengths without coughing and gasping too much was a shoo-in for the team. The athletic girls were out playing ball.

College was better, in that it only required 2 years of physical education, and there was some choice. I chose crew, canoeing, folk-dancing and life-saving. There was a compulsory course in body movement and relaxation, most of which was spent on our backs, asleep. "Girls! Girls! Wake up!" the instructor would admonish us. "You are supposed to be learning *conscious* relaxation, not *unconscious!*"

My years of "physical education" were over when I was 18. I had learned nothing at all except for the rules of a few ball games. I had, however, learned that I was "hopeless at sports." No one, in all those years, mentioned the Greek ideal of mind/body development, or that we were physical beings whose very nature demands activity and play. Running—as in track and field, cross-country, or general conditioning for other sports—was never offered as an activity, or even referred to. Some boys ran, but girls didn't, just as girls didn't do push-ups, or chin-ups, or wrestling. In some vague way, we had been warned that such activities would strain our female organs, as would overarm pitching, or full-court basketball. Girls were obviously inferior physical material. It is amazing how readily these ideas were transmitted, even though I went to all-female schools and college.

Some small part of me, some remnant of body wisdom, must have protested, as I look back. Although my daily life was entirely sedentary, exam periods in college drove me to a peculiar habit, which I never quite understood. During exam week I always got up an hour early, at six o'clock, and walked around the lake before breakfast. The walk took an hour, and would leave me refreshed and calmed, ready to face the exams. The rest of the year, however, I slept till seven o'clock, and avoided long walks. I smoked over a pack a day all through college, and couldn't walk very fast.

The Cream-Puff Years. "Physical education" having failed to educate me as to my physical needs, I continued to degenerate. My heart and lungs were "normal," i.e., flabby. If to be weak is to be feminine, I was very feminine. My bouts of exercise were sporadic and usually accidental. Once or twice I went skiing or snowshoeing. One year at medical school, I dated a fellow student who was an ardent cyclist; when we broke up, I still had the 10-speed bike he had encouraged me to buy, and I continued to use it as convenient transportation. In Boston, the bicycle got me to outlying hospitals, or to Harvard Square in Cambridge, much faster than my friends in cars. But after someone slashed my tires for the second time, my bike languished on the porch, gathering rust, and I traveled by MTA—bus or streetcar.

At age 25 I was married, and following graduation, we sailed off for a year in Scotland. I considered myself in good health, but the hardy Scots put me to shame. Their favorite recreation is "hill-walking," which means roaming over the low but rugged Cairngorms, through bogs, fog, and fields of heather. I was lured along on a few group "walks," but after the first, a 23-mile jaunt on which I was successively lost, cold, and semicrippled, I lost my enthusiasm. I remembered that I was not athletic, and thereafter met my husband and friends *after* their all-day hikes, by a cozy pub fire. Soon I was pregnant, which gave me a good excuse for staying home.

Several images from that miserable time, when I was both unfit and blimp-like (I got up to 176 pounds at my pregnant peak), stand out in my mind. One day my husband decided I needed fresh air, and took me for a stroll in the country through the usual bogs and heather. As he strode briskly ahead, whistling, I bogged down, literally, in my Desert-Boots, which were of ankle-high suede, and the only non-dress shoes I owned. I pulled each foot alternately out of the bog, leaving the boots behind, and braced myself in the heather to rescue the ruined suede boots. Meanwhile, the rain fell gently, and our Labrador puppy trotted back down the path, anxious about my fate. When my husband, Dan, also returned, he found me in tears, barefoot, and (naturally) nauseated. After one more outdoor adventure, a 5-mile hike through the snow, I resolved to abandon outdoor sports forever.

During the next few years, I was totally sedentary. I did

my internship, had two children, kept house (after a fashion), and limited my walks to trips to the corner grocery store. One day in 1969, I was returning from S.S. Pierce in Brookline, Massachusetts, my arms occupied with grocery bags. I found my way blocked by a crowd at Coolidge Corner, and had to shove my way through, muttering "excuse me." A burly Irish cop tried to hold me back, "You can't come through now, M'am," he said, "the Boston Marathon leaders are due." I growled something ungracious about the Boston Marathon and its leaders, and evaded the policeman. Reaching the other side of the street, I glanced back and saw a couple of hard-breathing men in shorts dash past, to wild cheers from the crowd. Shrugging, I went on home with my groceries, wondering how so many people could get excited about such a silly spectacle, physical freaks running through the streets. I didn't understand it at all.

Five years later, I was myself one of those oddballs, running past S.S. Pierce, in the Boston Marathon.

Early Exercise Attempts. I like to refer to myself, in those prerunning years, as a cream puff, because I still had an attractive surface, but was totally soft and mushy inside. No real substance, no fiber, just goo. My heart and skeletal muscles hadn't been exercised for years, any demand wore them out rapidly. I had no stamina, I tired easily. Like many young women trying to manage two preschoolers, a house, and a demanding job, I felt harassed and nervous. I suffered from constipation, migraine headaches, and insomnia. I bought sleeping pills in lots of 500 and used them almost nightly.

My husband tried to help. Occasionally, when we went ice-skating, he'd watch me circle the rink once or twice and turn beet-red with the effort. Even though I was a woman, and unathletic, this reaction worried him. He suggested that I needed more exercise, that fresh air would cure my

30

insomnia. This angered me. "I get plenty of exercise picking up after you and the kids," I snapped. So we dropped the subject. I had the nagging feeling, however, that Dan might be right. There were lots of books and articles that recommended exercise. So I got the *Royal Canadian Air Force Exercise Manual,* and. tried that program. Twelve minutes a day would work wonders, according to the book. Just do the leg lifts (female), push-ups, and other exercises, work up gradually, and you'll get fit. *Anyone,* surely, had enough willpower to spend 12 minutes a day with this simple program.

Alas, as always before in my life, I proved myself an exercise failure, a dropout. The 12 minutes were so *boring.* And while I got so I could touch my toes and do more push-ups, I didn't really feel any better. My migraine and insomnia persisted. I tried the RCAF program about once every 6 months, but always petered out after 2 to 6 weeks. The first part to be dropped was always the last 2 minutes, jogging-in-place. That was the dullest part of all.

I did try running once, in 1969, after reading about Cooper's Aerobics program. Dan and I went out to a local track and I tried to run around it once, with him. My throat burned, I coughed and spat for hours afterwards, and I decided "If that's running, forget it!"

When we moved from Boston to San Francisco, in 1969, our lives changed. Californians are all *outdoors* people. The outdoors is there—mountains, the ocean, rivers—and the weather is always good. No one stays inside except to work. After work and on weekends, everyone seems to do *something.* They swim, ski, fish, sail, hike, bike, ride horses, or if they're totally antiexercise, ride motorcycles. My family got swept along into the outdoors. We'd go for drives in the country, picnic, take walks, swim. Dan started running, he told me, with some doctors from U.C. Medical Center, where we both worked. They would come back, flushed, breathless and acting virtuous, from 1- to 3-

mile runs. It never occurred to me to join them. But on our weekend hikes, I was slowly building some endurance and learning to go longer—from 3 miles, initially, to 10 or 12. My bad knee, which had once given out on Mount Washington and forced me to be carried, humiliated, back down the trail, slowly grew stronger and stopped acting up. California life was beginning to toughen up the Boston Cream Puff—almost without my knowing it.

In 1970, when I turned 30, I began to realize that I was not really in optimum health. In fact, I noticed a downward trend in my condition. Primarily, I worried about middle-aged spread. My weight was as high as 145, though I could diet down to 135, my high school/wedding weight. But my hips kept getting larger. Previously a size 12, I now wore 14 and sometimes (shudder!) a 16. I could see the future progression—size 18, 20, and on into half-sizes and "matronly" styles. At 30 years old, I was degenerating, and felt myself doomed. Further deterioration seemed inevitable. I didn't know what I could do to halt the biological process. All the older women I knew, all my friends' mothers, had spread, had turned matronly, and had accepted their fate.

A running friend of mine who had known me in Boston in 1963, and met me again at this period in San Francisco, confirms that I was then indeed a mess. "Not fat, really," she says, "but sort of puffy. Pasty-faced. You looked tired, and as if you lived indoors." She is too polite to say I looked as if I had just crawled out from under a rock.

Moments of Decision. The idea of running came by accident. One day I was sitting on the grass in Golden Gate Park, talking to my friend Joella Utley, also a doctor. We were watching from the sidelines as our husbands, both heart surgeons, got their exercise in the traditional manner of American males. They were tossing a football back and forth, throwing "long bombs," leaping in the air, making spectacular efforts and catches. Joella and I were impressed and envious. "Look at those guys," I said gloomily, "getting all that exercise, while all we can do is just sit here, *spreading*." I knew that I, like all women, couldn't catch a football thrown that hard, much less throw a "long bomb." We were doomed, by age and sex.

Joella was sympathetic. She was several years older than I, and also worried about her hips. It was she who came up with a brilliant idea. "I know a woman who lost four inches around the hips by jogging in place," recalled Joella. Four inches! That was really impressive. But jogging in place didn't turn me on. That was always the part of the RCAF program that I dropped first. I cast about for an alternative that might accomplish the same miracle. I knew that our husbands ran in the park on occasion. Perhaps, I suggested, they could show us the one-mile course. Then, instead of jogging in place, we could cover a little ground with each step and jog around the mile. Surely the effect would be the same on our hips.

Notice that we didn't say we'd run. Women didn't run. Women were not capable of running. We didn't even think of it. We'd just be jogging in place, an acceptable activity, but moving a little bit at the same time, cheating a little. Not running.

Joella was agreeable to the idea. We'd start together when she returned to U.C., near the park, for the next stage of her residency. This was still 4 months in the future, so we didn't rush into anything. In fact, we dropped the subject.

We might never have carried out our plan without another accidental encounter. I still had this ingrained conviction that women couldn't run. I had never seen nor heard of a grown woman running. Except for Wilma Rudolph, who had won 3 gold medals in the 1960 Olympics—in running. Even I had heard of that. But I must have felt that Wilma was a physical wonder, trained from birth to run—not on the same plane with ordinary women like myself, who couldn't run.

Then one day, taking my kids to nursery school, I

bumped into Anneliese Snyder, wife of one of Dan's surgical colleagues, dropping off her kids at the same school. Anneliese was wearing (men's) cotton running shorts. This was in 1970, before such garb was chic. The shorts could only mean one thing. "Anneliese!" I said in astonishment. "Do you run?" "Only a mile, Joan," replied Anneliese modestly, disclaiming all athletic prowess. But I was amazed. "Only a mile!" A whole mile! How phenomenal! Here was Anneliese, an ordinary woman like me, in fact a few years older, with kids in nursery school. And she could run a mile! It was then that I had the thought all women must have before they start to run—"By gum, if she can do it, I can, too!"

In later years I learned that this was a false assumption. Anneliese, though in her 30s, was no "ordinary housewife" who just happened to jog. Her parents had both run in the 1936 Olympics, on the German team, and Anneliese herself had been a promising sprinter as a high school student in Germany, running 11.3 for 100 meters. Fortunately, I didn't know her athletic background in 1970. After that encounter at the nursery school, I went home inspired. I called Joella and reminded her about our plan to jog. She was still interested, and we agreed to meet at the gym after work. Not surprisingly, 5 months had elapsed between the original concept and our first try at running.

First Steps. Like many women, Joella and I felt a bit silly going out to jog. We changed into jeans, turtlenecks and sneakers—*canvas* sneakers—and set out, walking, for the park a few blocks away. A few male runners in shorts charged past us, puffing, looking as if they knew what they were doing. I felt increasingly awkward, and wished I were carrying a tennis racquet so no one would suspect I was going to try running. Joella and I acted a bit furtive, intruders into a man's world. We tried to be inconspicuous. Fortunately, it was dusk, and our faded jeans blended into

34

the background. Still, I had the impression that all the people driving past in cars were staring at us, pointing, giggling. If I hadn't been out with a friend, committed to this endeavor, I would have turned around and headed home.

Still, there we were, committed. We decided to go as slowly as we had to, but to keep jogging. Talking in little gasps, we set out. Fortunately, the mile route was virtually flat, a pleasant circle around the baseball fields, past trees and flowers, with little traffic. Soon we were halfway. We weren't going very fast. I vaguely recall being passed by some little old lady out walking her dog. But we were jogging, we didn't walk.

We made it! It was hard to believe. We had performed a feat of which only Wilma Rudolph was capable, or so we had thought. Two ordinary women in their 30s, we had actually jogged an entire mile nonstop.

Ecstatic, we walked back to the gym and called our husbands. Joella's responded appropriately. "A whole mile? Really? Joella, you're a gazelle!" A bit exaggerated, perhaps, but just what we wanted to hear.

My husband was more blasé. "A mile, eh?" he said. "How fast did you do it?" I had no idea, of course. And if I had known, "about fourteen minutes" would not have been an impressive answer. I felt a bit squashed, though still pleased with myself.

Moral for husbands: Be sure to act impressed with your wife's first mile. Ninety-nine percent of the women in America can't, or won't, jog an entire mile. A woman who does so deserves extravagant praise.

In the following 2 weeks, Joella and I met 4 or 5 more times to jog our mile. Slowly, it got easier. We even considered extending the distance a bit, but hesitated. We weren't sure whether to go farther or run faster. On the third or fourth occasion, we timed ourselves at about 8 minutes—but it was hard work.

In retrospect, we were doing things wrong. It's always advisable to run farther rather than faster, and very bad policy to time yourself over a standard course. Our running attire—jeans, heavy shirts and canvas sneakers—didn't make our jogs any easier.

Our bad habits took their toll before long. Joella got a cold. Probably she had overstressed herself, trying for greater speed (at my ignorant suggestion). I was faced with an unpleasant decision—stop running while Joella recovered, or go out alone—without my moral support and talking companion.

By that time, the mile was getting easier, and I could relax, smell the flowers and grass at dusk, listen to the birds. On our last run I had suddenly realized that this new exercise wasn't boring like all the others, it was actually sort of enjoyable. And we both felt exhilarated after each mile.

I was already hooked. So when Joella got sick, I went out alone. I didn't even stop to measure my hips. The original purpose of my jogging was already forgotten.

Early Mistakes and Progress.   I would never encourage anyone to run the way I did those first months. It was a wonder that I kept up the running. Sheer stubbornness must have been the root of my perseverance. Not knowing the first thing about jogging, I did everything wrong. For example:

Pace.   All the runs were timed, as soon as I could get hold of a stopwatch. Since I tried to go faster each run, I was always out of breath and straining. Several times, in a finishing sprint, I would almost run myself into a faint—my fingers would tingle and I'd see spots in front of my eyes. Naturally, running so hard, I didn't feel like extending the daily stint. I was a 1-mile runner for months.

Shoes. After 2 weeks of running in flat sneakers, without any arch, ankle support or cushioning, both my ankles hurt and swelled up. I hadn't twisted them, they just weren't accustomed to all that jarring. Finally, on the advice of a running friend, I invested $20 in a pair of Adidas jogging shoes—rather clumpy, all-leather Olympia's. They were far superior to anything I'd worn before, and my ankles healed quickly. However, I began to have bad arch pain, perhaps because the shoes were quite stiff, and before long I had also sustained painful stress fractures (hairline cracks) of both shinbones.

A few things worked to my advantage. Not all 30-year-old women can jog a mile the first time out, no matter how slowly they go. My weekend hikes had probably conditioned me enough to do this. Women who are extremely out of shape will have to use a jog-and-walk technique for the first few weeks.

I was also an "early addict," that is, I came to need the regular running activity very quickly, before I was set back by injury or illness. Joella, who caught cold before she was hooked, didn't return to jogging for a month. By then, I had progressed beyond her level, so she had lost the early companionship that is so vital to new runners. Joella gave up running and didn't start again for several years.

Dimly, I sensed that running would be much easier with a group than alone. So I persuaded a co-worker in our laboratory, Irene, to give running a try, in addition to her usual swimming and skiing. Soon we were joined by another swimmer, Gail. Starting with our 1 mile, the three of us gradually built up to 2- , then 3-mile runs. In 1974, our U.C. Medical Center team won the first National Women's Marathon Championship—a testimonial to the value of group encouragement and perseverance—for certainly, our speed was not blinding.

For perhaps a year, we all overdid the running and suffered the consequences. Our workouts were all races.

We'd walk to the hydrant that marked the start and finish of our training loops, start our stopwatches, and charge off, all trying to outrun each other. Irene was usually out in the lead early, while I would surge ahead and pass her in the last mile, as she tired. We'd stop at the hydrant, panting, after a final sprint, and wait for the others to finish. We never conversed or kept each other company during the run. And we rarely ran more than 20 minutes. It's embarrassing for me to remember those days—a bit like the Dark Ages. Sprained ankles, arch pains, pulled muscles, inflamed tendons and stress fractures plagued us most of the year.

I'm not sure how the change came, or when we switched to a more enjoyable and less injurious form of running. Perhaps we realized, as our runs grew longer than 20 minutes, that it was boring to race along without talking. Or perhaps it was reading that did the trick—we had discovered *Runner's World,* a whole magazine devoted to our newfound sport, and began to absorb the "run gently, run long" philosophy of editor Joe Henderson.

We also discovered that we were not the only three women in the world that ran, though we were still a rarity. At a local race I entered after about 6 months, a slim blond-haired woman popped up at the elbow. "Hi, I'm Elaine Pedersen, who are you?" she said all in one breath. "Pedie," as she is called, was the Number One local pioneer, a runner since 1966, a veteran of the Boston Marathon, distinguished by having been kicked out of local road races for years, before they were opened to women (in 1971–1972). Pedie, delighted to welcome new women into the running world, introduced us to the social running scene, and the "Scenic Runs" of San Francisco, sponsored by the DSE runners.

Before long, Gail, Irene and I were folding newsletters, helping at races, sharing in potluck supper-runs. We had met a host of new running friends, who all seemed to be fit, energetic and amusing. Instead of gathering for cocktails and getting bombed, these new friends like to run, picnic and talk. It was a whole new, playful way of life. At least in California, the "loneliness of the long distance runner" was only a myth.

The Further Education of a Jogger. People often ask how I decided to run my first marathon. Actually, I didn't decide anything, it just happened. Peer pressure can lure one into many wild escapades.

One day at a "scenic run," DSE president, Walt Stack, appeared in a T-shirt bearing the words "Camp Crockett" above the silhouette of a runner. "What's this camp, Walt?" I asked. Apparently it was some sort of YMCA camp in the Colorado Rockies, catering to _grown-ups_ who liked to run. It sounded like a nice vacation, and a good way to recuperate from my latest injury, a stress fracture of the hip. So off I went, the summer of 1972, a 3-mile/day jogger who had just been grounded for the past 3 months.

Camp was a revelation. From a daily 1- to 3-mile jog, I progressed to twice-a-day, 3-mile trail runs, interspersed with hikes, horseback rides and frisbee games—all at high altitude. More important, I heard two lectures a day on running. I was amazed that there was so much to learn about a sport—history, tactics, training methods, physiology, the great names. For the first time, I heard about Paavo Nurmi, Emil Zatopek, Ron Clarke, Arthur Lydiard, Percy Cerutty, and others—figures central to modern running. I learned that there were basic principles of training and racing, enabling one to build and improve on a predictable schedule. Ambition stirred within me.

But not too much. On a hike with Walt Stack, I was talked into running the 13-mile-uphill Pikes Peak Marathon. Walt waxed eloquent about my future. "After the Peak, Joan, you'll feel ten feet tall. Soon you'll be running full-length marathons." "No way, Walt," I assured him.

My longest run ever was 10 miles, and that had led directly to a stress fracture. Thirteen miles up Pikes Peak was goal enough for any sane person.

Of course, runners tend to be irrational, and when I got back to sea level and my San Francisco running friends, I found that they were also thinking about marathons. After all, "everyone else" ran them, so why not us? Gail and Irene had upped their mileage to 30+ miles/week. When I left for camp, they had still been doing a comfortable 15 to 20. I had to hustle to catch up with my peer-group.

Before long, I was the only non-marathoner in our group. When Irene, Gail, and newer women in our U.C. runners' club ran their first and later 26-milers, I was usually sitting out, injured, trying to work my way back to a daily 3- to 5-mile jog. Eventually, I too became a marathoner, but not until the summer of 1973, 2½ years after my first jogging mile. The long delay had allowed me to acquire racing experience and get in a couple of "twenty-milers," so I managed to run 3:17 in that first marathon. Not so remarkable these days, when there are plenty of young track-trained runners who can last a sub-3-hour marathon on their first try. But for a 32-year-old jogger-turned-racer, not bad. I was delighted.

Some women who have been running for years and trying to break 3:20 may be discouraged and feel that I have some talent they lack. I disagree. I feel that marathoning success is totally a function of experience and proper training, both of which I had. Here are my "secrets."

1. RUNNING BACKGROUND.

I had been running consistently for 2½ years (except for short interruptions due to injuries). Even when temporarily grounded by a stress fracture, say, I had kept in condition by vigorous swimming, walking and cycling.

2. RACING EXPERIENCE.

I had run over 30 races at distances from 3 to 15 miles.

The first few races were disasters, as I ran out too fast and "died," walking in. Gradually I learned what pace I could sustain comfortably over the required distance, and what effort would wreck me after the first mile. A good sense of pace is crucial in the marathon.

3. TRAINING.

From a long-term background of 30-mile weeks, I increased to 50 miles the last few weeks before the marathon. The increase was due primarily to the two 20-milers I did. The first of these 20-milers was far more tiring than the marathon itself!

4. PACING.

Convinced by camp lectures that an even pace was the key to a good marathon, I decided to run 7:30 miles from the start. The race course was flat, 5 times around a 5-mile loop, with a smaller loop at the end, so once I had settled into a comfortable 7:30 pace (aided by 1- and 3-mile "splits"—times called out) it was easy to maintain the same effort.

5. A GOOD DAY.

The marathon is an unpredictable race. Cool weather is a great help, as are well-organized aid stations. Both were present, as was that other vital ingredient—sheer good luck.

Any woman who makes use of the same training and racing "secrets" can do just as well. You have to have faith in your training, in the value of even pacing, and in your ability to maintain pace. The most common mistake is running out too fast, hoping to get "ahead" of your schedule. This mistake, more frequent in men than in women, leads to certain disaster—a drastic slowdown or "crash" later in the race.

So there I was, former cream puff, finally a full-fledged runner. Of course, one doesn't have to run marathons to be a runner, but for me, it was a recognizable rite of passage. I realized I had changed. I felt my legs tentatively—they were definitely firm. Somewhere in the past 2 years I had dropped from a size 14 to a size 10, though my scales still read around 135 pounds, not very different from cream-puff days. I felt younger. I could run circles around my children, exhaust our poor dog on runs, charge up the hills ahead of my husband on weekend hikes. For the first time in my adult years, I felt fit and energetic. I realized that at no previous time, not even age 10, when I was the neighborhood wrestling champ, had I felt so much in control of my body and my life. I had become a runner, even an athlete.

For a woman in her 30s, who has lived her whole life as a bookworm and a non-athlete, it is tremendously exciting to realize the change that has occurred.

I have told my own story in such relentless detail because it is the one I know best, not because it is unique. Every woman runner has a similar story. Cream puffs are being transformed daily.

No wonder we seem enthusiastic, even evangelistic! Our whole way of looking at ourselves, our potential, and the world around us changes as we become runners. We realize that we, too, are physical beings.

Chapter Three:
Women's Psychological Edge

In view of the tremendous psychological and social barriers which prevented women from running until recent years, it is surprising to see so many women out jogging in 1980. More surprisingly, most of them seem to be smiling, chatting, actually enjoying themselves. Gone is the stereotype of the middle-aged male jogger, who supposedly always puffed along sporting a painful, agonized expression. Non-running newspaper columnists used to write, with satisfaction, that they had never seen a happy-looking jogger. This boast obviously wouldn't apply to the women—perhaps they don't qualify as "joggers," in the columnists' eyes.

Athletic Machismo vs. Running for Oneself. My own feeling is that enjoyment is a natural part of running, and the only valid reason for spending so much time in play. It also appears to me that women, far from being handicapped by past "suppression" of their running careers, may actually benefit by coming to the sport with open minds and enthusiasm. Unlike men, who may have suffered through years of grueling, often misguided track training, women are not programmed to view running as an inevitably painful experience. "Why do it if it hurts?" they think, sensibly. Whereas the former 440-yard runner is more likely to conclude, "If it doesn't hurt, it's not doing me any good."

You can see the origin of this masculine "pain ethic" at any traditional track or cross-country meet at the junior high school level. Young boys, usually totally unconditioned, are encouraged to run their hearts out for school glory and for victory. Because the average 12-year-old has neither the time, the coaching, nor the knowledge to train effectively, this effort at fast running is painful in the extreme. I have seen many young children collapse at the finish of the race, in a faint, or vomiting. Some boys appear to feel they have let the team down if they *don't* vomit at the end of a workout. Physical agony and collapse are the badges of courage. They demonstrate that you have done your best, given your "all."

The truth is, of course, that fainting and nausea indicate inadequate conditioning. The training is insufficient for the race demands. More mature runners race within their effective limits. But track and cross-country experience in most American high schools has been slow to catch up with modern, physiologically sound methods. And the sole object of running has been competition, not participation or individual development. No wonder the hardest person to convince that running can be fun is the 40-year-old male who has gruesome memories of wind-sprints and "punishment laps" in high school.

Women, long considered too "delicate" to run, miraculously escaped this athletic brainwashing. They may have unpleasant or boring memories of gym classes and half-court basketball, as I do, but they see running as a new and different activity, one which offers freedom, self-exploration, and enjoyable movement. They can approach

44

the sport with an innocence and anticipation of pleasure which would be foreign to most men.

I have often had the experience of running with macho men who equate speed and breathlessness with ability. Since my ego is not involved in training fast, I keep telling them to slow down, take it easy. I don't *like* to run at speeds painfully close to my aerobic maximum. Save those efforts for races, I feel.

The reactions are amazing. Most men slow down reluctantly, sure that if the pace is comfortable, they are not working, not benefiting their cardiovascular system. The pain ethic runs deep. A few have acted condescending. "Do you girls always run this slow?" said one. "Maybe I should run with you more often, to get some *easy* miles." We smiled noncommittally at these remarks, but all of us took pleasure in beating him by minutes in that weekend's 10-mile race. All our slow, easy, enjoyable miles had gotten us into better shape than his few all-out training efforts.

The ability of most women to run at an enjoyable pace, without guilt, is probably responsible for the number of women flocking to running in recent years. The sport is unregulated and need not be competitive. It can be anything you choose to make of it. Each run can be fast or slow, relaxation or challenge, depending on your own wishes. A woman can grasp this concept on the first jog, when her own breathing tells her whether to run faster or to walk. The older male runner, taught to run hard and fast without regard to the feelings of his own body, may take months to overcome this early brainwashing. Some never learn how. Some continue to feel that enjoyment is somehow, well . . . *unmanly*. The average man who starts jogging has less chance, psychologically, of evolving into a true runner, than the average woman. If 100 men start, 20 may persist, whereas over 50 percent of women seem to keep on with their new hobby. This natural affinity of women for running accounts for the ever higher percentage of women in clubs and road runs. I was one of a handful of women, maybe 5 percent, when I joined San Francisco's DSE runners in 1971. By 1980, almost half the club's members were female. Women, who were officially forbidden to run marathons until 1973, are over 20 percent of the entrants in the Honolulu marathon. Their percentage is increasing rapidly. Some day soon, a majority of road runners may be female. This dominance of a previously all-male field undoubtedly reflects a psychological as well as physical suitability for running.

This suitability becomes especially notable in long-distance runs—the marathon and beyond. These races have traditionally been regarded as the ultimate test, the most grueling demonstration of manhood. Newspapers love to show pictures of the finishers—exhausted, drained men, stretched out on the grass, nearly unconscious after their supreme effort. The top male runners, of course, finish in good condition and looking fairly cheerful, but most of the rank-and-file male runners do look rather done-in.

Women finishers are a different story. Whether they complete the race in 3 hours, 4 hours, or more, they seem to finish smiling, happy, enthusiastic. After the 1978 Boston Marathon, I ran into both the male and female winners, and the contrast was astounding. Bill Rodgers, drained, white-faced and exhausted, was half-carried, half-supported past me by two burly Boston policemen. Gayle Barron, hair almost unruffled and laurel wreath perched jauntily on her head, bounced over toward me, gleefully hopping over a barrier rope. "Hey, I won, can you believe it?" she said in excitement. She appeared full of energy and in search of a party to celebrate.

Bill Rodgers, of course, had run the race a half-hour faster than Gayle, so skeptics may say he had worked harder and used up more of his resources. But in terms of speed and oxygen uptake relative to their maximal capacity, Bill and Gayle had put forth equivalent efforts. And Gayle undoubtedly looked fresher.

Male runners who have trained hard and long for their

marathon effort can be both puzzled and frustrated by the relative ease with which women cover the distance. I often train step by step with men who are basically much faster than I. I'm left yards behind when we run intervals, minutes behind in 10-km. races. But in the marathon, something peculiar often happens to these men. Inexplicably, after about 2½ hours or 20 miles, they begin to fade, and are left behind. Something other than speed and training must be involved.

Long races can be a heady experience for women, who generally start out slowly, while men and boys dash out as if they were in a mile race. One of the most satisfying races of this type is the annual "Pepsi Twenty-Miler" in Sacramento, which attracts huge numbers of high school boys competing for special divisional awards. Most of them have never run more than 6 to 10 miles, but they figure 20 can't be much harder. From 12 miles on, many of these naive teenagers are walking, and I must confess it does my heart good to pass them. One year, when I was the first woman, I saw a gangling young man up ahead, walking. As other runners passed him, he would look up briefly, then hang his head and walk on—obviously done in. But when I, a woman, ran past, it was too much for his macho self-image. I heard him give an incredulous, heartrending cry, "Oh, SHIT!" as he saw me, then he summoned his last strength and came galumphing past me. The burst was short-lived; 100 yards down the road he was walking again. This time he didn't even look up as I passed.

Women in the Honolulu Marathon have reported the same success in passing men, who have a tendency to start out too fast, and then fade. As Kenny Moore reported in *Sports Illustrated,* the presence of a large number of Marines in the Honolulu race results in a field day for the strong-finishing women, since Marines find it psychologically impossible to start slowly. They "die" in hordes after the 20-mile mark. One woman told Moore, "When a woman passes a Marine, it's like a knife twisting in his heart." A ghoulish but accurate observation. In any marathon or longer event, more of the men finish suffering and apparently in extremis, while more of the women finish smiling.

Various explanations have been advanced for this situation. Dr. Ernst Van Aaken, the German doctor and promoter of women's distance running, feels that women have a physiological advantage, namely, a better ability to utilize fat. They look better at the finish because long distances are physically easier for them than for men. Others feel that women just don't push themselves so hard as men, so they don't suffer as much. If women ran faster, they too would hurt, says this theory. Of course, anyone can run fast enough to hurt—a quarter mile will do it—but no one should run a marathon that way.

My own theory is more psychological, and was developed over several bottles of Rhine wine, after the 1976 International Women's Marathon Championship. Several of us relaxed with a steamer cruise down the Rhine, neatly timed to coincide with the wine festivals in various towns. Already deep in my cups one night, celebrating German–American friendship and marathoning, I had a revelation about female superiority at the longer distances. "You see," I explained to the interviewer, "women run realistically, whereas men run romantically."

Realistic vs. Romantic Running. Think about it. Almost all male runners have an idealized, romantic concept of the great marathon they should be able to run, given their own talent and the standards set by Rodgers, Shorter, et al. They run the first 10 or 20 miles fueled by this vision of themselves, which may have no foundation in reality. Reality hits somewhere around 20 miles, when the romantically set pace begins to hurt, and the infamous Wall appears.

Women are more levelheaded. They look at their past performances, try to figure out what kind of pace they can sustain, realistically, over 26 miles, and pace themselves accordingly. There are rules of thumb available in figuring out one's optimal marathon pace (½ minute/mile slower than your best 10-mile race pace, for instance), and it is well known that even effort gives the best results—for both men and women. All one needs is the common sense and realism to adhere to these guidelines.

The real mystery, to me, is not why women can run realistically and finish in good condition, but why so many men perversely refuse to do so. The last miles of the marathon are littered with the wrecked bodies of those men who gave lip service to the concept of even pacing, then dashed out at a 6:00 pace (2:37 marathon) when their stated intent was only to break 3 hours (6:50 pace). Time and again, running at 6:30 or 6:40 pace myself, I have passed these male friends who were supposed to be running 7-minute miles the first half. "What are you doing *here?*" I ask them, not unkindly, but with a certain exasperation. After all, we've discussed this question of proper pacing before. They usually sound a bit guilty, but still hopeful. "Well, those first miles, I thought I was running 7:00, and when I found out it was 6:20, I figured it felt okay, so . . . " etc., etc.

It just doesn't work that way. If you've judged your optimal pace properly, you should stick to it. If you're ahead of pace, you'll suffer for it in the last miles. Women seem to grasp this concept easily. Men, all but the most mature and experienced ones, can't seem to restrain themselves.

"But I thought women *liked* their men to be romantic," interjected my German interviewer at this point. "True," I replied, "but it doesn't help them in the marathon."

The truly amusing aspect of this psychological analysis is that the male and female attitudes are exactly the reverse of the accepted stereotypes. Traditionally, *women* are the romantics—emotional, dreamy, impulsive, useless in a crisis. Men think of themselves as the realists—strong, silent, levelheaded, basically macho.

In the marathon, women's true nature is brought to the fore. The psychological foremother of today's female distance runner is the pioneer woman—calm, dependable, self-reliant, tough and resilient, she held the frontier together. Running fosters these same traits, bringing them into sharp relief. In the non-runner, they may have been buried, hidden under the fluttery, emotional façade—for women still try to *appear* romantic, to live up to their accepted stereotype.

The longer, harder, and more challenging the race, the more obvious becomes the female doggedness and imperturbability. A good example is the Levi's Ride-and-Tie, a unique event that combines endurance horseback riding with cross-country running. Teams consist of two runners who share a horse, and the course is usually a hot, hilly 40 miles. Unpredictability is the keynote, and no one's carefully laid plans survive the first few exchanges. The horse may be held up, the runner may miss the horse, times may be miscalculated, etc. Because of the nature of the race, flexibility and persistence, as well as horsemanship, are as important as basic speed. An all-women's team has finished as high as fifth place overall, and man–woman teams score consistently in the top ten—even though male–male teams are theoretically fastest.

An endurance-horse trainer who has worked with both all-male and all-female teams told me he much prefers to work with the latter. "Look at Mary and Dawn," he said, referring to the two women who won their division 5 times in a row. "Neither is an especially fast runner, but when the unexpected happens, they aren't fazed. They just keep on going, and do their best. The men, faced with a change in plans, or a delay, go all to pieces. They get upset, dissipate their energies, and fall behind. Give me a good women's team anytime!"

The Ride-and-Tie, like endurance races, definitely favors the dogged over the flashy. The tenacious runner who makes the most of her abilities, who trains thoroughly and paces herself rationally, has a tremendous advantage over faster runners who depend on basic talent rather than conditioning, or who fail to utilize their energies coherently. Perhaps women, lacking brute strength and tremendous speed (which demands power), are more accustomed than men to using their wiles, to planning rationally. The longer races, then, permit them to exploit this psychological edge most effectively.

This same ability to convert a handicap (lack of strength) into an advantage (wiles) is seen in a variety of sports. Recently, the first woman to climb Yosemite's El Capitan solo admitted that she had to use different routes and techniques from the men. Unable to muscle her way up the most direct routes, she employed ingenuity, along with balance, grace, and that same doggedness which helps women excel in other endurance events. Similar style differences are seen in women's tennis, soccer, gymnastics—even rugby. Wherever raw power is lacking, the women compensate by using their heads and their carefully developed endurance.

The psychological differences between men and women runners are as profound as the physiological differences, and just as fascinating. When men and women compete in the same event, as in the marathon and other road races, the resulting interaction of styles and game plans leads to amazing discrepancies—the 70-year-old woman, for instance, finishes, while a strapping 20-year-old who runs a 4:30 mile has to drop out. Such a paradox occurred in Switzerland, where photographers took a touching picture of a little old lady apparently hugging and congratulating her grandson after a 100-km. road race. But when the reporters asked the young man his time, he said they were mistaken, he had only run the last 10 km. with his grandmother—she had run the whole race. Such distances, said the young Swiss, were beyond his capabilities.

Chapter Four: Changing Relationships

Divorce and the Runner. One day in 1976, I was running alone in Golden Gate Park when I spotted Pete Mattei, a friend from the East Bay. Pete is a tough, wiry man in his 50s who excels as a hill runner—one of the local "mountain goats." Not long before our encounter in the park, I had startled Pete and myself by passing him on the downhill stretch of a long, tough hill race. It was the first time I had ever finished ahead of Pete in a race, and he was still brooding about it. "You sure are running well these days, Joan," he said. "Are you getting divorced, by any chance?"

Surprised by this apparent non sequitur, I replied, "Why, yes, how did you know?" Pete shook his head glumly. "It never fails," he complained. "People split up, or are unhappy in their marriage, they start running all the time, training hard, and then they start beating me in races!" I laughed, but I have to admit I've observed the same pattern in many of my acquaintances.

Some of this apparent association between hard running and divorce proceedings may be misinterpreted. Non-runners, in particular, take a gloomy view of a sport that can break up marriages. "It was all that running she (he) was doing," they decide. "The family just couldn't put up with it any more."

I think it is more valid to see the running as a *response* to stress. This is the view that Pete took, and it is one readily understood by runners, both male and female. We all know that running has become our preferred way of dealing with anger, tension, hostility or depression—prime components of all domestic troubles. If you're angry, or hurt, or in tears, you know you can go out and run hard, for 20 miles if necessary, and dissipate your stress, or work through your concerns. The relief experienced is predictable and healthy. You don't have to go jump off the Golden Gate Bridge—a run across it and back will restore your spirits much better.

I remember one time when my husband, a surgeon, called up 2 hours before the annual party we used to have for his surgical colleagues and nurses. In 4 years of parties, he hadn't ever gotten to one in time to play host. Something always came up. So that final year, I was hardly surprised to hear that he had an emergency operation that would tie him up all night, leaving me to be hostess for a lot of people I had never met. But while I wasn't surprised, I *was* furious. I pulled on my running shoes and charged off to run 7 miles in the park. I don't think I've ever charged around that path so quickly, swearing under my breath the whole way. Near the end of the run I approached a short, steep hill near the hospital where my husband was awaiting the arrival (by helicopter) of his emergency case. Resentment and fury boiled up in my chest as I looked at the hospital, and I immediately transferred my anger to the hill—quite consciously, because here was a situation I could deal with. "I'm going to KILL that hill," I muttered to myself, and stomped up it with energy and great satisfaction. After wiping out that surrogate for my husband, I felt lightened, relieved, even cheerful. I whistled as I went back to host the party, which I enjoyed. How much better to trample a hill underfoot than to wipe out your spouse with a .38.

I remember how startled our running community was when one of our members committed suicide some years ago. Our immediate reaction was that he hadn't been running enough. The dismal facts, as we gossiped about them on the run, seemed to support this view. The unfortunate man had a fat, nagging wife who did not "approve" of his running. Husband X's running habits thus acquired a cyclical pattern. He would run a lot, lose weight, and look cheerful. Then he would be nagged, appear worried, cut back on the running to mollify his wife, and grow fat. Then, in self-disgust, he would start running again, grow lean, and realienate the wife. Finally, in a down phase (and fat), he shot himself. "I guess he just couldn't take the nagging," I remarked on a run, "Yes, but why shoot himself?" reasoned a friend, "he should have shot his wife instead." Not a very good solution, either, since his running time would have been severely curtailed in prison. Still, we all agreed, running more could have made him more resistant to nagging.

There's an old joke on this subject, that circulates every few years in the running community. I'll tell it here in case you've never heard it. An unhappy husband consults a psychiatrist about his marital problems. The doctor, a runner, suggests his patient start running 10 miles a day, to help relieve the strains. Ten days later the patient calls up and reports that he feels great, he's really pleased the doctor recommended running. The psychiatrist, delighted, asks if things have also improved between the patient and his wife. "Gee, I don't know yet, Doc," is the reply. "I'm a hundred miles from home!"

In Dr. George Sheehan's film, *Coping with life . . . on the run,* a real-life counterpart of this patient explains how he happened to run the Boston Marathon. He started running, he says cheerfully, to get away from a wife he couldn't stand. Later, getting divorced, he ran even more to help himself through a bleak and lonely period. Eventually he became a marathoner—and a happy one.

In most cases, it seems, runners see their activity as a solace for, not a cause of, marital discord. Many men, in particular, seem to be able to stay longer in an unhappy situation because they have a physical outlet. This outlet has, until recently, been closed to women. They often turned to eating or drinking excessively. (Then the husband would feel even more justified in running for hours.) Exercise is usually a far more healthful response to stress than alcohol, food or psychosomatic complaints.

In the 70s, with many women starting to run *before* their husbands, we often see the same pattern in reverse. The wife, often reluctant to leave an unhappy marriage because of security or inertia, becomes a "running nut." She begins to leave sweat clothes and muddy shoes in the entry way, reads and talks incessantly about running; goes off to runners' parties and potlucks. She runs long distances with *other men,* arousing suspicions in her husband, who can't imagine what they can be talking about—much less doing —on those 20-milers. When she is injured, the house reeks of Ben-Gay. The diet grows more vegetarian; steaks vanish from the table, to be replaced by sprouts and other rabbit food. The wife begins to look slim, even sexy. Her cheeks glow. So do suspicions.

At this point, the non-running husband doesn't know what to make of his wife, who he thought was a fragile, delicate klutz needing his eternal care and protection. Now this formerly flowerlike creature has turned into an *athlete.* He suspects, darkly, that she may be able to outrun him. If they enter a race together and she actually does so, he is shattered. He may act proud of her, but underneath, he feels the foundations of their relationship crumbling. He may retreat into boisterous beer-drinking sessions with the boys, making her seem more feminine again by contrast—"Dammit, I thought I married a sweet, quiet woman who always wore perfume," one husband complained. "Now, when I come home, she's out running, supper isn't even on the stove yet, and our house smells like my high-school locker room! If I'd wanted a jock, I'd have married one."

Though one has to sympathize with this agonized, if helpless, husband (why doesn't he start supper so his wife can eat as soon as she finishes her run and shower?), I don't think the real problem is her running. I think it lies in the shattering of his expectations. It's a very real problem. Women have always expected their men to be semi-athletes, or at least latent sports buffs. If he turns from spectating to participating, it doesn't require her to re-evaluate their marriage. But if she is transformed, as I was, from "cream puff" to marathoner, the world turns upside down for many husbands.

Let us look at this process in more detail. For the sake of argument, assume that the husband is a well-meaning, but "traditional" ex-jock. He may have starred in track or football in college. He still loves to watch football games and can talk knowledgeably on all sporting matters. His wife has always looked puzzled or bored when plays are discussed. She probably thinks a "flea-flicker" is a kind of miniature fly-swatter.

One day, fed up with middle-aged spread, she decides to run it off. The husband is a bit uneasy. He has heard that running can lead to marital stress, destroy a happy relationship. What can he do to discourage his wife, while appearing to support her?

A Cautionary Tale. One husband, entirely subconsciously, came up with a variety of interesting ploys.

Most of them fell under the heading of well-intentioned "advice from the expert." Here are his suggestions for the budding athlete:

1. ALWAYS RUN FASTER.

His wife had a tendency to shuffle along, talking. So the husband ran along, pushing the pace, reminding his wife that if she didn't talk, she could break 8 minutes a mile. To encourage her to make a good effort, he stayed 10 paces ahead at all times. He discouraged her from running with female friends, who tended to dawdle and chat.

2. TRAIN ON THE TRACK.

Observing his wife from the sidelines, this husband tried to correct the wife's "marathon shuffle." He showed her how to lift her knees and use her arms so as to run a good 440. Unfortunately, he forgot that his wife was training for a marathon, and not the 440. In fact, he was unaware that the desired style for distance runners is not that of a sprinter. The first time his wife tried out her "440" style for 2 miles on the road, she developed severe shin splints.

3. WEAR RACING SHOES.

The husband thought that the shin splints must be due to those thickly cushioned training shoes she wore. No track runners ever wore such things in his day. He went out and bought her two pairs of thin-soled, lightweight racers—one with spikes, for the track, the other flat, but equally thin-soled and shaped on a "track last." He had seen these fancy, striped models on all the best American sprinters in the Olympics, so he knew they were good.

4. TIME EACH RUN.

How else will you know if you're making progress? Unfortunately, his wife could only run a single 440 (quarter-mile) in 80 seconds. The husband gently pointed out that Francie Larrieu, the Olympic 1500-meter runner, could run 4 quarters in succession, and 23 percent faster.

Still, with more track work, and more concentration on style, he was sure his wife could improve.

5. KEEP RUNNING SEPARATE FROM THE REST OF YOUR LIFE.

It was unfortunate that his wife's continued shin splints and sore knees required the use of liniment, because it made the house smell a bit like a locker room. All liniment should be confined to the basement, along with running clothes, magazines and shoes. Better yet, perhaps his wife could run her workout, shower and wash her clothes *before* he came back from work. That way, running couldn't intrude on their time together, and supper would always be ready on time.

After several months of running according to the above rules, this wife decided it wasn't much fun after all—too boring, lonely, and hard work. And her legs hurt constantly. She hung up her running shoes and returned to her tennis and ballet.

The husband, unaware of his influence on this decision, was nonetheless pleased. He preferred the pleasant, graceful wife, who dabbled in tennis and ballet, to the competitive, lean athlete he had glimpsed in the budding runner. Though he had seldom mentioned it, he had hoped she wouldn't develop those "bulging, unsightly muscles" he had seen in Russian women who threw the discus. Track and field sports, he reflected, were really a *male* province.

This "jock husband" who so quietly and effectively discouraged his wife is a composite. No man I know has ever been guilty of all five misguided "rules," though numbers 1 and 4 are fairly common among former track athletes, and none of the rules was invented by me—I've heard them all, in various contexts.

You may notice an interesting evolution in attitudes in the "jock husband." The man starts out somewhat proud of his wife, though condescending. It's cute of her to want to

58

run, and healthful. She'll probably shape up tremendously, and he'll admire her appearance at parties.

A former "jock" himself, the husband naturally wishes to guide his sweet wife's footsteps. Having benefited from years of tough coaching and pain, he feels himself ideally suited to pass on the macho sport ideals he has absorbed in his youth. He does hope to make a star out of his wife, and may bask in reflected glory as her coach. Unfortunately, this competitive approach is totally at odds with the natural inclinations of his wife in most cases. So pressure from a jock husband simply sets up more strains in a marriage, and discourages the budding runner. Most wives subjected to rules 1 through 5 quit running within the first few weeks or months. Many get injured, others are simply discouraged.

If the wife gets to the point where she's no longer just a cute klutz trying to keep up with the boys, and actually gets into good condition, the husband's attitude often begins to shift again. No longer proud, or even patronizing, he becomes anxious and resentful. If the wife can outrun men (even untrained ones), she has overstepped the sub-conscious boundaries of appropriate behavior set up by many traditional husbands. She no longer fits his mental image of a wife, or even a woman. Hence the beginning of the pressure to fulfill her traditional sex role—to stick to "feminine" sports, and cooking. The husband, at the same time he is reproaching his wife for lack of femininity, becomes acutely aware of her growing appeal to other men. They obviously admire and are attracted to her. The husband grows increasingly anxious, even paranoid. He assumes the adversary role and *opposes* running. Sports are great for men, he concludes, but totally unsuitable for women. The former jock has become anti-jock!

There has been, of course, no fundamental shift in attitude at all, in such a husband. The truly tradition-bound male (who is fortunately rare since the 70s) defines and judges all women according to his own preset arbitrary notions of what is proper "feminine" behavior. And in general, for this type, "feminine" means whatever boosts his own ego and makes him feel more masculine and dominant. Obviously, outrunning a man like this in a race, even if you've trained much longer and harder than he has, will not be seen as a glorious expression of your femininity. It is more likely to be interpreted as a deliberate put-down, making you automatically a "man-hater."

My private opinion is that women who have the misfortune to be married to such men are lucky if they start running and come to an early realization of their true situation. Then they are in a position to decide what to do about it. Some will leave. Others, for reasons of security or moral commitment, will choose to stay with their tame MCP, but at least their eyes are opened. They can continue running quietly and inconspicuously, and hide the sweaty clothes, prize ribbons and other evidence from their husbands. The outlook is not totally bleak. Men, like all human beings, do grow, change, and modify their attitudes. As women athletes become more acceptable to society as a whole, even "traditionally" raised men will not have to feel threatened by a running wife.

I think it would be incorrect, should a divorce occur after a woman starts running, to claim that running caused the marital breakup. It seems more accurate to say that running helped to facilitate new insights about the basic premises on which the relationship was founded. A clearer understanding of these premises may or may not lead to divorce. But you can't blame the window washer if the view is bad after the windows are cleaned.

Running, while not the "cause" of divorce, may hasten a potential breakup if the wife is the "runner" of the family. I don't know if running is unique among sports in this regard, but one doesn't hear much about divorce occurring when the wife takes up tennis, bowling, swimming, or skiing. Perhaps the difference lies in the distinct mental changes that are often associated with running.

I had never really considered running to be a unique sport. I knew, of course, that it was the only one I myself had stuck to, or excelled at. And I knew it was becoming increasingly popular, but had never analyzed why.

On a trip to Washington, D.C., in 1978, I received a clue. I was being interviewed by Colman McCarthy, a marathoner who also writes for *The Washington Post* (typically, I list his running credentials before his occupation). Colman is a sensitive, philosophical Irishman who likes to probe the moral implications of living and playing. So he asked me if I considered runners *more moral* than other people. That stumped me. I considered runners I have known. They were not a particularly *moral* bunch, in conventional terms, but they did seem to share certain mental (spiritual?) traits. After a moment of reflection, I identified the elusive common bond. "Well, Colman," I said, "I'm not sure runners are moral, but they do seem to have more self-knowledge than non-runners."

It was obvious, once I had thought of it. Of *course* we had more self-knowledge than the average person. Most adult Americans dash through their days (and their lives) doing things, keeping busy, earning a living, caring for their families. They have little time for solitude and even less for introspection. Most of them are so busy they can't even find 15 minutes a day to run—or so they will tell you. "If only I had the time . . . , " they sigh.

Well, runners—the "addicted" ones, at least—*have* the time. They *make* the time, somehow. And for half-an-hour, or an hour, several times a week, they are essentially alone. Even if they run with friends, they are moving by themselves, thinking their own thoughts (between snatches of conversation), drifting off, getting to know their bodies.

Racing, especially marathoning, is a more dramatic self-confrontation. You get to know your own body—its aches, its limits, its unplumbed potential. You learn all about your competitive responses (or lack of them), your jealousy or generosity toward your friends, your goals. All running leads to introspection.

A man may not change much if he acquires self-knowledge this way. He may already have taken time for himself all his life, or have a clear concept of who he is. But a busy executive who begins running in later years may find radical changes occurring in his life-style and values. One such executive who claims that running "changed his life" is Jess Bell, president of Bonne Bell cosmetics. Since Jess's "conversion," he has become a tireless advocate of running, and sponsored the Bonne Bell 10-km. race series for women. Regardless of its commercial considerations (Bonne Bell's market is mainly female), by aiming this series at women, Jess has sensed another peculiarity about running: it seems to change women even more than men.

Psychological Changes in Women Runners. I noticed this when I taught running classes in the early-to-mid 70s. The men in my groups tended to lose weight, gain endurance and change their wardrobe. But aside from that, they were the same guys after conditioning as before. Not so with the women. Most of the ones in my classes were in their 30s, the ages ranging from 20 to 66. Nearly all of them changed so remarkably that I began to feel like Pygmalion, creating new and beautiful forms (it was quite a heady experience). These amiable, but quiet housewives, with slightly puffy faces, and pale skin, were transformed as they became runners. Their eyes sparkled, their cheeks glowed with ·internal energy, they slimmed down and became fit. Even more strikingly, their personalities changed. Those who started out somewhat insecure, and self-deprecating, acquired a new confidence. First, they could run 1 mile, then 3! A former impossibility had become a reality. They began to wonder what else they could do that they had always considered impossible.

A mood of exploration and assertiveness, along with increased energy and laughter, suffused the group. The men and women got along beautifully, but domestic relationships were not always affected so positively. There were several divorces. By then, I wasn't surprised.

It is hard for most men to comprehend the profound impact that physical accomplishment can have on the average American woman. Those of my generation (born in the 30s or 40s) were raised on the *dogma* that we were not capable of most physical performances expected of men. In gym classes, we did push-ups from the knees only—"girls' push-ups"—so as not to "damage our female organs." Similarly, because our arms were ostensibly weak or improperly formed, we couldn't play baseball or pitch overhand. Instead, we used a larger, softer ball (to cushion the impact on our weaker bodies and give us a larger target to hit), and pitched underhand—to spare our weaker elbows. In basketball, we were confined to half of the court and shorter periods because, they said, we weren't so good at sports as the boys—we might strain ourselves. As for running, girls just *didn't*. Of course, we all assumed that if running wasn't permitted, we must be totally incapable of it. We all admired Wilma Rudolph when she won her 3 gold medals in 1960—as a *runner*. But obviously, we thought, she must have been specially trained from the time she could walk. *Ordinary* girls couldn't run. In fact, they weren't much good at anything, except of course ballet—a nice, feminine activity. All the little girls of my generation took ballet. Nowadays, they can dream of being gymnasts, or tennis stars—Olga Korbut and Billie Jean King were the first great role models for these new activities. In my day, though, there were no sports options for women.

Imagine what happens, then, when a woman, who has

always been told she can't run, runs a mile—and she's over 30! She feels buoyed up—superhuman. If a mile is possible, anything may be possible. She feels herself a physical creature, perhaps for the first time since early childhood. She feels competent, in control of her life. If she becomes a marathoner, she no longer worries about being stranded 20 miles from her home with a flat tire—if worse comes to worst, she can always run home. If she's stranded in the mountains, she can hike out. She begins to suspect, if there's *anything* she's told she can't do because she's a woman, that she's being fed a line.

Psychologically, that first mile is a tremendous step toward self-confidence. It's the female equivalent of that "giant leap" for mankind, onto the moon. For most women, the self-knowledge that is gained by running is not merely an exploration into previously unknown areas, not merely a time to reflect, as it may be for men. Instead it involves a breaking down of previous assumptions about our capabilities. Small wonder that the personality evolution in such a woman can seem extreme! And it's equally unsurprising that a husband may not recognize, understand, or appreciate the new creature his wife is becoming.

Influence of Enhanced Self-Esteem and Self-Knowledge on Personality and Relationships.

Though I have discussed divorce in its most common pattern among runners—the traditionalist husband and the "liberated" wife—there are plenty of other situations in which similar elements come into play. The couple involved may not be married—I am sure that running has helped clarify the attitudes of as many "roomies" as spouses. The man may not always be the exploiter and the woman the victim who liberates herself—remember the suicide and the Boston Marathoner, who both ran to get away from their wives.

Of course, if the running spouse is a world-class runner,

putting in 100 to 180 miles weekly, that's a lot of time spent on the roads. And at that level of running, there's little energy left over when you get home. If you have a family, the quality of your time with them can suffer greatly. This—not age—is the main reason world-class runners tend to be younger (or unmarried, or childless). The partner of such a runner must realize that world-class running is like a job, not a hobby. Unfortunately, it doesn't pay so well as a job, and financial worries can further strain a marriage that already suffers from lack of time together. One former Olympian I know denied that running could have anything to do with his impending divorce—"after all," he maintained, "I told her before we got married that I planned to keep on running." "But that was twenty years ago," I pointed out. "She may have secretly hoped you'd get over your childish ways." This man was still training 120 miles/week, after years of world-class running. It's hard to warn a wife adequately about things like that. The runner knew himself extremely well after so many years and miles—but he never really figured out his wife.

I feel that the key factor determining whether running will have a benign or destructive effect on a couple is its effect on the power relationship between two people. The runner gains control over his or her life, along with physical prowess. If two people have been involved in a relationship where one is clearly dominant to the other, the dominant partner is more likely to feel threatened by increasing independence and self-assertion on the part of the formerly more compliant one. Though this pattern is traditionally that of husband/wife, the roles may be reversed. Sex is really irrelevant. I have been assured by a gay friend that lesbian relationships are just as susceptible to strain when one partner starts running and becomes more assertive.

Conversely, if the marriage or relationship involves two

people who are already independent and respect each other, running will not be a threat to their happiness. The few running couples who have endured and flourished together over the years are excellent examples of that elusive "relationship of equals." Usually, both run though one is often much more involved and serious about it than the other. They encourage and support each other, and rejoice in each other's triumphs. Athletic success in the woman is not regarded as a threat by a secure, mature man. My own long-time friend, a fireman, is a good example. When people ask him if he's going to start marathoning or try to keep up with me, he laughs, saying, "Would I play pool with Minnesota Fats?" My woman friends and I think that's a great answer. We're tired of watching our step in whatever we do (including running) for fear of crushing some man's ego. It's good to know there are men whose self-esteem does not depend on being able to run faster, throw farther or climb higher than a woman.

If you're fortunate enough to be already teamed up with such a person, you can stop worrying about divorce. Running will not strain a healthy marriage, just as it will not damage a healthy heart.

Chapter Five: Women of All Ages

Influence of Age on Performance. Many women over 20 in this youth-oriented society feel that their athletic life is past. They see young swimming champions and gymnasts "retiring" at age 16, they read of tennis and golf professionals who, at age 30, are called "grand old ladies" of sport. Even if a woman has been physically active throughout the high school and college years, she may be persuaded that growing "maturity" is incompatible with recreational sports. More commonly, non-athletic types—such as myself—may feel that they are "too old" to start something new and different.

Until the 70s, it was hard to find information to contradict these assumptions. Men, as well as women, hesitated to pursue athletic dreams after age 30. With the growth of running as a popular participant sport, however, the "Masters" movement for the over-40s started gaining momentum. No longer self-conscious standouts among crowds of "youngsters," no longer straggling along in the rear of high-speed races, Masters runners found support and challenge in growing numbers. Old myths about the effect of age were shattered—some men ran far better in their 40s and 50s than they had as college standouts. Women in their 30s and 40s consistently outran girls half their age, and in mother-daughter teams, it was frequently Mom who finished first.

It is hard to tell yourself you're "too old" if you see a grandmother jogging along in a race while you watch from the sidelines. It's doubly hard if you see your neighbor running—and you know that this neighbor is not only 5 years your senior, but was also 20 pounds overweight and a smoker until a few months ago. So, by example, many more women are taking their first jogging steps at age 40 and beyond. Thanks to the growing numbers of such runners, we are beginning to have a better idea of the relationship between vigorous activity and health—at all ages.

The underlying assumption has been that age inevitably leads to physical decline. Performance must drop off, endurance and strength are reduced, vision fails, along with hearing, sense of smell, etc., joints become arthritic—all this, merely because years are passing by.

Some medical authorities now are beginning to question these assumptions. They feel that "aging" may be caused by inactivity and lack of fitness, rather than the reverse. The obvious good health, energy, and agility of Masters runners—both male and female—are supportive evidence.

Women have traditionally feared the "menopausal years." The absence of fertility may be a godsend, but the accompanying symptoms—hot flashes, sweats, emotional disturbances and/or depression—are certainly not popular. Many women are routinely treated with estrogen replacements, to alleviate these symptoms and help prevent osteoporosis (thinning, fragile bones).

I am not about to announce—with trumpet fanfare—that "running prevents menopause." However, I do have my suspicions. Periods *may* stop, but several runners approaching 50 have asked me, a bit plaintively, if I have any idea when they'll finally be able to dispense with birth control measures. Continued fertility may be an unwanted side effect, but no one has yet complained about missing the hot flashes and other unpleasant accompaniments of "the change." My sample is still a bit limited, but of six menopausal runners I have questioned, five have had no symptoms at all, and the sixth one questions whether what she felt one time was a "hot flash," or just a fever—she woke up sweating and warm, with a cough.

There have been several reports in medical literature that physical activity helps prevent osteoporosis. Older women who should not or will not take estrogen are accordingly advised to go on long walks, bicycle rides or jogs. Perhaps the increased circulation and oxygenation of the bones—which are very active metabolically—help maintain adequate calcification. Similarly, patients with arthritis are now advised to keep active and *use* their joints as much as possible, to avoid loss of function.

If "aging" is indeed retarded by vigorous physical activity, as one may suspect from observation of Masters runners, what mechanism is involved? Most doctors say, in effect, "use it or lose it" (though their terminology is more complicated). It is well known that immobilizing a part of the body, as in a cast, causes the muscle to shrink ("atrophy") from disuse. Blood vessels and nerves supplying the muscle also regress. Any inactive part, from the heart to the skin, may do the same (even the brain, one suspects). Conversely, activity leads to increased blood flow, better oxygenation, and smoother function. This is the rationale behind Van Aaken's "active therapy" for injured athletes—bodies function better, and heal faster, when they are used, and oxygenated. Interestingly, some elderly bedridden patients are being treated with oxygen in an attempt to prevent senility—the extra O_2 breathed

69

for an hour daily appears to restore mental alertness and enhance recall. What's good for the body may be good for the brain as well.

But to return to our Masters runners—who are far from bedridden—their principal concern is how does age affect performance? Surely there must be *some* point at which physical limitations cause a decline. While this statement is true, theoretically, "age" limitations in practice have been set much too low. The reason most champion athletes in the past have been relative youngsters (under 20 in swimming, under 30 in running) is practical rather than physiological. To be a champion, or even to be very good at sports, demands a great deal of time and energy. Teenage swimmers and gymnasts devote 6 hours or more to practice, every day. Runners train to the edge of exhaustion, twice a day. When you are young, with all of your future ahead, a gold medal or a championship seems worth the investment. After age 20, other concerns tend to intrude— a spouse, children, work, social life. The willingness to spend long hours in training declines. So does performance level, of course. It's a matter of decreased training, not aging. Physically, one is not "over the hill" at age 20 or 30.

Athletes who have determined to train hard, despite their age and outside interests, can be outstanding in their 40s, 50s—even 60s. Jack Foster of New Zealand, who started at age 33, ran his best marathon (so far) in his 40s, and was on the Olympic marathon team in 1972 and 1976. His female counterpart, Miki Gorman, ran 2:39 at age 41— second best in the world that year—and her P.R. (Personal Record). "Sacramento Slim" Jim O'Neill, at 55, is running faster now than ever before. At age 20, he held the National Junior Collegiate 2-mile record, a mark he shattered at age 48, and has since surpassed many times. When does that "inevitable slowdown" start? We'll have to wait and see.

Older beginners—those who are just trying out their first jogging shoes at age 50 or better—do have certain limitations. The restraints are those of pace, though, not of potential. The older you are when you start, the more slowly and cautiously you should build up. More years of inactivity and "disuse atrophy" have to be overcome. A 10-year-old can jog 5 miles the first time out; a 20-year-old, if generally active, can easily do a mile. But older women, unless they have preserved good muscle tone and strong tendons with vigorous hiking, tennis, etc., should take their time. It's okay to start walking, it's even recommended. Dr. Cooper's program suggests 6 weeks of brisk walking, for the previously inactive, before you try jogging. Good shoes, of course, are essential—you shouldn't skimp on either cushioning or support.

Once you're out jogging, always aerobically (talking!), caution is still advisable in building up mileage. No one, in my opinion, should tackle a marathon within a year of starting. I simply think that distance is unphysiological, at any age. It takes *time* for the muscles and joints to return to the necessary strength and resilience for 26 miles of jogging. The longer you've been inactive, the longer it will take to rebuild your legs. If you insist on going that distance (in Honolulu, it's a fad), walk it.

Beyond the question of disuse atrophy, age does not seem to be much of a handicap. The limits are just where you want to set them. Training principles are the same, at whatever age. Build up endurance first, through mileage and long runs, then, if you wish, work on speed. Women over 40 show the same response to regular racing or interval workouts as young girls—they get faster, and more efficient biomechanically. And no matter how old you are when you start out, you can count on improving your speed and endurance over the years. Most runners who "burst on the scene" unheralded didn't just start running yesterday. They have been training steadily for about 10 years before they gain public attention. Women runners in their 60s and 70s, of course, still gain instant media attention because of their rarity. But if you follow their

71

future careers, you'll notice that they, too, will improve. The physiological advantage of continued practice more than offsets any gradual decline associated with advancing years.

Profiles from Each Age Group. In the following pages, you will find short profiles of representative women over 30, categorized according to the age at which they started running, illustrating some of the above points. There are so many outstanding and inspirational runners in each decade, that my worst problem was choosing the ones to profile. And many women have been running long enough to overlap two age groups. I finally decided to concentrate on those that we can all identify with—not the great natural talents, but the women down the street—the ordinary ones who have gone on to extraordinary achievements. If they could do it, so can you!

30s   SKIP SWANNACK   BORN: JUNE 1, 1941
             REDWOOD CITY, CA.

To me, Skip is the quintessential "Thirties" runner— resilient, persistent and tough, whipping girls half her age when she's in shape, always running along cheerfully when she's not. Skip has been around since the earliest days of running—she started in 1966—and has not been slowed down by increasing age and maturity. On the contrary—in 1979 she ran the 100-mile Western States Endurance Run through the High Sierra, and became the first woman ever to complete the rugged course in less than 24 hours—21:56, to be exact.

I first met Skip and her then-husband, Buck, in 1971—at a race. Buck was bald, fierce, tough and macho; Skip was small and quick, full of energy and enthusiasm. She also ran fast—against the feeble competition offered by us newcomers, she was virtually unbeatable. She and Buck sported matching, bright red track suits emblazoned with

"Portland Track Club," and were obviously experienced veterans. The rest of us, still clad in old cut-off jeans, Bermudas, or old gray "sweats," at best, were in awe of the Swannacks. They had done everything—climbed Mt. Fuji, Kilimanjaro and Popocatépetl, run the Pikes Peak Marathon, run over 60 races in one year. Impressive credentials. While Buck charged through races, demolishing opponents in the over-200-pounds category by brute force, Skip sped out in front of the women's field, light and tough. Obviously, I thought, a born athlete—trained from childhood, no doubt.

The truth, as usual, was different from what I imagined. Skip came from a highly athletic family, but she herself was a childhood klutz. Parents and brothers spent long hours on the tennis courts, winning tournaments, while Skip, wearing thick glasses, sat by, frustrated and embarrassed. She couldn't hit balls—and ball games were all that was offered in P.E. Skip hated P.E., but kept trying, especially in non-visual activities—trampoline, dancing, etc.

After marriage to Buck, an adventurous, outdoor type, Skip was propelled into a more active existence. But to her dismay, she couldn't even do a lap with him on the track. Her shape was good, but her condition was lousy. Then in 1966, the Swannacks moved to Oregon, where Bill Bowerman's book, *Jogging,* had started a statewide running boom. Well-fueled at a neighborhood party, their whole group of friends and neighbors resolved to meet the next morning and start jogging. If you weren't at the meeting place to jog, they'd come and get you. The group effort lasted only a few weeks, before shin splints and ruined "hairdos" took their toll. But Buck and Skip, together with one other hardy soul, continued the Bowerman program. For the next 3 years they did their daily jog, and even entered a couple of races.

When they moved to San Francisco in 1969, the Swannacks became instant stars. They joined the fledgling DSE

73

club, won its largest trophies, and edited the club newsletter. Encouraged by club president Walt Stack, Skip went on to longer distances. On the basis of 3-mile-a-day training, she entered a couple of marathons, finishing in 5:20 and 4:50. "We didn't know how to train," she now comments. Undaunted, Skip ran 7 more marathons in 1971—all of them slow. By dint of her racing alone, her mileage increased dramatically. The trophies for "first woman" began to accumulate at home.

After a few heady years of success, and more round-the-world adventures, Skip began to get bored. She had no special goals to work for, and let her running slacken off. Though her job as a P.E. instructor kept her reasonably fit, Skip put on some weight and slowed down.

Between 1971 and 1978, Skip went through several obvious up-and-down cycles, but never quite regained her preeminence of the pioneer running days—until 1979. Her most recent "up" in 1979 was a dazzler. After a previous marathon "best" of 3:10, set in 1978, Skip announced to club members at the annual awards gala, that she intended to break 3 hours in her next marathon. She did just that, running 2:56—and later, at Boston, 2:53. Racing cross-country for a local community college where she was taking courses, Skip was first on the team all season, and eleventh in the state. After "dabbling in ultradistance" since 1977, including a couple of "slow" 50-milers, Skip got serious about long runs. She ran 100 miles on a track in 26:11, then, confident and well trained, ran her record Western States Endurance Race. "I always *thought* I was tough!" she told reporters after that feat.

Analyzing the causes of her latest "super-peak," Skip can identify several factors. She and Buck were divorced in 1976, and for a while, Skip found her new independence troubling. Buck had always planned for both of them. Now that she was on her own, Skip's running fell off at first, but then she began to gain confidence, to make her own decisions, take responsibility for herself.

74

Skip used to run haphazardly, with no set pattern. Now she sits down, maps out training schedules, and keeps a detailed training log. Her mileage is generally low, about 40 to 50/week, though she did "push up to 80" before the 100-miler. She does intervals twice a week, and occasional long runs. Practicing for the Western States Race, she did a "quadruple Dipsea"—4 times over the toughest, hilliest cross-country trail in the area, a total of 28 miles, in 5 hours, on a hot day. She packed-in carbohydrates before the race, consuming over 4000 calories a day, but growing ever leaner. At 5 feet, 6 inches, she is a solid, fat-free 120 pounds.

Skip has an amazingly high energy level, which must be an important element in her success. Besides teaching physical education, she holds 3-hour aerobic dancing classes twice weekly. In both activities, she uses different muscles, so she doesn't feel too tired to run. Runs are squeezed in at lunchtime, early morning or on non-dance evenings. Skip finds that running gives her a "calmness of mind" which helps offset her hectic schedule.

Skip feels that her new emotional and mental independence is her greatest strength. Grueling challenges like the Western States Endurance Race can be fun, if you enjoy testing your physical limits, as she does. Such efforts are "testing grounds for inner strength—you have to be in touch with yourself to do them." Now that Skip has gotten "in touch," who knows what her next challenge may be?

30s   JUDY FOX   BORN: OCTOBER 22, 1940
            SUNNYVALE, CA.

Judy Fox came to running fairly late—at age 37. Most women of that age start out cautiously, feeling their way, gradually acquiring speed and experience. But not Judy— she arrived on the scene with a splash.

In January, 1978, a Bonne Bell 10-km. race for women

attracted about 800 entrants in San Francisco. Most had never raced before. One of the new faces popped up at my elbow as we milled about before the start—a thin, enthusiastic woman with long brown hair tied back in ponytails. "Are you Joan Ullyot?" she asked. When I nodded, she continued in great excitement; her name was Judy Fox, she had read my book, *Women's Running,* was just my age, and loved running. And now, she concluded, she was in a race with me and might even be able to beat me! She bubbled with excitement at the prospect. I smiled wanly, and wished her good luck, but secretly I thought to myself, "Fat chance, lady!" Even though I had just recovered from a bout of flu the previous week, I *was,* after all, an experienced and fast racer. No upstart first-timer was likely to outrun me—especially a 37-year-old. A noble ambition for Mrs. Judy Fox, I felt, but doomed to failure.

As sometimes happens, I was wrong. Judy Fox beat me by a wide margin, taking third place in the 30 to 39 age group. I didn't even place. I had a vague suspicion that even without the flu as an excuse, Judy Fox would have whipped me. Her time was darn good.

A few weeks later my teammate, Judy Gumbs-Leydig, was describing her recent victory in the AAU (Amateur Athletic Union) 15-km. championship. "It was tough," she confided. "This very thin woman I'd never *seen* before went out really fast and kept the lead as far as 10 km. I was getting worried. And, it turns out she's thirty-seven years old!"

"Don't say any more," I replied. "That's Judy Fox." It had to be.

The mystery runner who set such a fast pace was indeed Judy, and she wasn't an unknown any longer. She was our toughest competitor. Fortunately, she soon joined our track club and was running for our side, so we could all rejoice in her victories. In the 1979 Bonne Bell 10 km. on the anniversary of her first race, Judy finished third overall.

She was ninth in the National AAU 10-km. championship on the track, recording a 35:20. When lured into another "longer" (15-km.) race, she came within 1½ minutes of the world record. Judy's 52:57 was the third fastest time ever run by a woman. Not bad for a lady pushing 40!

Judy is obviously a "born" runner, but her records are still amazing when you consider her lack of background and training. At age 36, out of condition and wanting to jog with her family, Judy joined an exercise-jogging class at a nearby community college. She ran her first mile in 8 minutes, but was "completely out of breath." When the quarter-long course that met biweekly was over, she stopped running for months, only occasionally running a mile or two on the track with her husband.

A job at Stanford, starting in September 1977, gave her access to the Angell Field track, and Judy's running became more regular. She went out for a mile or two, 4 times a week. From this minuscule amount of training, she entered her first race—the Bonne Bell 10 km., in which she whipped about 800 other women and me.

"Serious" running didn't start until the summer of 1978, and even then it was primarily social, not competitive. Judy and her husband run with the "Angell Field Ancients," a group of (mostly) older men from the Stanford campus. Lunch breaks aren't very long, so the group usually runs a fast 5 to 7 miles, rarely longer than 40 minutes. On Wednesdays, they do an interval workout. Judy's motivation is to keep up and socialize with the group. At first, she found it hard to keep up with the "slowest" bunch in the workouts. Now, encouraged by the "Ancients" and in better condition, she runs with the lead group—as does her husband. "I have yet to beat him," says Judy wistfully. "Maybe one of these days . . ."

The total mileage most weeks is under 40, since Judy doesn't run weekends unless there is a race. She never "trains," and doesn't go on long runs—her longest ever was a 25-km. *race.* She has no intention of running a marathon—that would take too much training, too much time away from other things.

Recently, at the start of a crowded road race, Judy collided heavily with a photographer who refused to move out of the way of the runners. Judy sustained severe tears of the knee ligaments, and was laid up for the first time in her running career. Grounded for several months, she had time to reflect on goals and racing. After that last bad experience, she thinks she'll avoid the roads and explore the world of track racing instead. So far, with minimal practice, she has run a 5:04 mile, a 2:18 half-mile, a 63-second quarter. She hopes to get under 5, 2:10 and 60 respectively—but not if it means leaving the Angell Field Ancients. Judy runs purely for fun, and races for the social life. If she had to supplement noontime group runs with extra interval workouts, she's afraid she'd get bored, or lose the joy of running. Still, she hopes to participate in the International Masters Track Meets, as soon as she turns 40.

Obviously, Judy's running achievements are remarkable, and incomprehensible to the many women who have run more miles and more years, and have yet to break 7 minutes for a single mile. How much of Judy's excellence is due to genetic endowment, and how much within the reach of a hard trainer?

I feel that the division between native talent/acquired skill in Judy's case, is closer to 50-50 than in most cases. Judy's physique and weight, which have not changed since she began running, are ideal—she is 5 feet, 8 inches tall, weighs only 116, with under 10 percent fat. Though she has yet to be tested in a laboratory, I suspect that researchers may find a high vital capacity (lung volume) and maximal O_2 ($\dot{V}_{O_2}$ max) consumption. While $\dot{V}_{O_2}$ max may be dramatically increased by training, it doesn't hurt to start with a high baseline. Another factor that may be significant is that Judy, unlike some other top women runners, never smoked. If humans, like dogs, can develop permanent fibrosis (scar tissue) in the lungs after a mere 2 years of smoking, this could cause a permanent impairment of oxygen diffusion and uptake. In other words, top runners who once smoked may never achieve their true potential, giving the advantage to those, like Judy, who have "virgin" lungs.

Finally, Judy is a 3-times-over mother, and many sports doctors now believe that women who have borne children are better athletes than those who have not.

Judy herself attributes her rapid progress more to mental readiness. She runs with her male friends, who happen to be fast runners. They don't have time to dawdle or jog slowly. So, if Judy wants to keep up, she *has* to run briskly. She is encouraged not only by the Angell Field Ancients, but also by her husband, and even the kids— once they got over the shock of having Mom beat them. And Judy never felt that she might not be able to keep up the pace, simply because she was a woman. She figured she could do what any other runner could do. In effect, Judy escaped the mental blocks that hold some women back from hard efforts and/or a fast pace—the worry, the hesitation about whether something is *possible* for a woman. She just runs with the group. In this mental attitude, Judy Fox is truly a "liberated" woman runner.

40s	RUTH ANDERSON	BORN: July 27, 1929
	OAKLAND, CA.	

Ruth Anderson, now in her 50s, is widely known as both a star and organizer of Masters running for women. She has competed nationally and internationally, winning innumerable championships and age-group records in the process. While not as speedy as that paragon Miki Gorman (whose 2:39 marathon puts her in a class by herself), Ruth

79

competes more frequently and is easier for older women to identify with, having started her running in middle-age—43, to be precise.

Ruth is a tall, rail-thin woman, about 5 feet, 8 inches and 125 pounds—with short-cropped blond hair and a wide smile. She is envied for her absolute lack of fat. Underwater measurement has pegged her fat content at 8 percent, not even enough to keep Ruth warm on wintry runs, when she'll be bundled up in long-sleeved sweaters, cap, mittens and tights. Conversely, Ruth runs excellent times on warm days, when plumper types around her are dropping like flies.

Ruth wasn't always built for running. At age 43, she weighed a more "normal" 135 pounds, indicating that she probably also contained a more "normal," if less healthful, 30 percent fat. In those days, Ruth was a swimmer, getting her exercise by paddling around the pool during lunch breaks at the Lawrence Livermore Laboratory, where she works as a research assistant. Then, in 1972, the pool was closed for repairs. What was a compulsive noontime exerciser to do? Ruth's "buddies at work," two women who were jogging to keep in condition for their karate lessons, dragged her along on a "jog"—only ¾ of a mile, but at a rather fast clip—8-minutes/mile pace. After her 6-minute introductory jog, Ruth had to walk—"I thought I was going to die! Those two always started out too fast!" she comments. But she survived, to be dragged along again. She progressed rapidly to a 1½-mile run, stuck there for a while, then continued on to 2 miles, 3 miles, and 4 miles—within a few months. Competitive from the start, Ruth tackled her first race 3 weeks after her first steps. It was a 2-mile "novice" run, and thanks to "good luck and adrenaline," Ruth whizzed through it in 15 minutes—a time which would encourage any woman to new efforts.

Meanwhile, Ruth's weight dropped rapidly—apparently, the jogging was more taxing than swimming, and burned off 20 pounds within months. At 115, she felt a little *too* thin, and has since put back 10 pounds—of muscle, not fat. Her running distances increased, and within a year, Ruth owned the Masters—over 40—record for the marathon. It was the first of many records—none of which last very long in these days of the women's running boom. Championship medals and trophies, more durable, accumulate on shelves around the Anderson home. Ruth, who loves to compete, enters almost every local race, and usually wins her division. For years, thanks to her high racing mileage, she won the Walt Stack Trophy for DSE Woman-of-the-Year, the highest (and largest) award given by her running club. Eventually, Ruth stepped back to give other women a shot at the title.

In recent years, Ruth has set her sights beyond the marathon, leaving the shorter distances to younger Masters—those just turning 40. Ruth hates to do "speedwork," but has no qualms about going long distances—50 km., 100 km., 100 miles even. She turned to ultramarathoning shortly after breaking her foot in the rugged "Double Dipsea" race. Emerging from a cast some weeks later, Ruth found her speed reduced, but endurance unlimited, so she tackled a 100-km. race—and finished it, setting another Masters women's record. Her best ultramarathon to date is the 100-miler she raced in 1978—in an astounding time of 16:50:47, a women's (track) world record. She now has her eye on more challenges abroad—the 52-mile London-to-Brighton race, and perhaps the "Comrades' Marathon" in South Africa. Apart from races, Ruth "trains" only about 60 miles/week, low for an ultramarathoner. Oddly enough, she hates long training runs, and still does the bulk of her running at lunchtime.

One of Ruth's greatest strengths is behind the scenes— her family. She enjoys enthusiastic support and encouragement from husband John, a veterinarian, and teenage daughter Rachel, who has herself run the Pikes Peak Marathon. Ruth is actually encouraged to enter competitions worldwide. "I think Ruthie should run that," states

John firmly, when an important Masters meet is scheduled in Germany, or Sweden, and he often gives Ruth such trips as a birthday or Christmas present. With her mind thus relieved on the home front, Ruth is free to concentrate on her running and travels. Her record gives eloquent testimony to the value of such concentration.

40s   SISTER MARION IRVINE   BORN: OCTOBER 19, 1929
        SAN RAFAEL, CA.

Sister Marion is a tall, slender woman with short, curly gray hair and a pleasant, direct manner. I first met her at a dinner party before the Avenue of the Giants Marathon in 1979. Sister Marion, who said she ran, "but not marathons," paced her niece over the last few miles of the race, at about 9 minutes/mile. I had no idea that this unassuming nun was a "ringer" I might have to look out for in races. Neither did she—Sister Marion's competitive days were just beginning.

In September, 1979, we met again—in a 10-km. race. After covering the first 3 miles in 18:50, I scanned the backs ahead, in search of female rivals. There, unmistakably, was Sister Marion's lanky form, moving along faster than I would have believed possible. I felt a moment of consternation—the woman had to be at least in her 40s, so how could she run that fast? Pulling myself together, I surged past—but not very far. Sister Marion finished in 39:45, just a few seconds behind me—a pace of 6:24/mile. Not bad for a 49-year-old "non-athletic" woman, who had started running only 15 months earlier, and stopped smoking less than a year before the race. Very impressive, in fact. I determined to learn Sister Marion's "secrets" and communicate them to readers who may aspire to equal success.

As usual, there are no real "secrets," apart from a love of running and an "adventuresome" approach. Sister Marion

82

went for her first jog on May 31, 1978, driven by "cabin fever" and her niece's suggestion that she'd probably enjoy running. She jogged about 80 percent of a mile course (the shady parts), walking when she hit the sunny areas. It was sort of a game, and she enjoyed it. Future runs took her farther, till she finally did 2 miles, all jogging. It wasn't easy; she thinks she may have "overdone" things a bit that time. "I clung to the banister, dizzy, while the house moved up and down the street."

Fortunately, Sister Marion, while never an athlete (except for playing high school basketball), must have had a strong constitution, and strong legs. Not only did she survive occasional episodes of "overdoing," she also ran in "tennis shoes" the first few weeks, without any leg problems. Then she invested in a pair of running shoes, and got serious. By then she knew running was going to be an important part of her life, and was incompatible with smoking. So after having smoked one to one-and-a-half packs/day for over 10 years, Sister Marion decided to stop, "on September 13, 1978." She quit cold turkey, apparently without severe withdrawal difficulties. One gets the impression of a very determined character. Once Sister Marion decides to do something, she goes ahead and does it. No excuses, no retreats.

Sister Marion is tall and thin, with strong legs—"natural" runner's build. But it wasn't natural, after all. Until age 45, Sister Marion had a weight problem—198 pounds, to be exact—a bit much even for a 5-foot, 10-inch frame. "I've lost two hundred pounds," she informed—"the same fifty pounds, four times." After the fourth dieting regime, she changed her eating habits drastically, and kept the weight off. Since starting to run, she has put on 4 to 5 pounds, but looks thinner and healthier—and her clothes fit better.

Sister Marion belongs to the Dominican Sisters of San Rafael, an enlightened order that permits her to run around in shorts (less fortunate nuns have been compelled to jog in their long habits). She worked up to 20 to 40 miles weekly in her first year, and then increased to about 55 miles weekly. Times have "just come down by themselves," she feels. Perhaps her runs through the hills near San Rafael help. She despises track work, but loves races—the people, the excitement, the chance to excel. At age 50, her goals are to keep running, improve her 39:45 10-km. time, and "maybe someday," run a marathon.

Locally, she has already earned an inevitable nickname: "The Flying Nun."

40s   FRANCES SACKERMAN   BORN: JUNE 2, 1929
            BURLINGAME, CA.

Frances Sackerman is a small, lean woman who works as a lab technician in the Metabolic Unit of University of California Medical Center, San Francisco. This Medical Center, blessed with a gymnasium complex and located two blocks from beautiful Golden Gate Park, became a hot bed of runners during the 70s. In 1972, however, the idea of running had not occurred to Frances, who was then 42. She might never have started, except that she couldn't resist a bargain—co-worker Gail Gustafson urged Frances to buy a pair of Adidas that were too small for Gail—$18 shoes, good as new, offered for only $12. Frances hesitated—they were indeed a bargain, but a bit large. Come try them out in the park, suggested Gail. So off they went, to test the shoe fit. A mile should be sufficient, they thought.

"It just shows how little we knew in those days," comments Frances now, appalled (in retrospect). She actually jogged the whole mile, on determination rather than conditioning. Her ears were ringing, lights flashed before her eyes, she was utterly exhausted—but she made it to the finish. "Forty-two years old, can you imagine?" she says now. "I probably got my heart rate up to the highest it's ever been, maximal effort. No warm-up, no stretching or anything. I'll bet I was on the verge of a heart attack."

Nevertheless, the mile had been conquered, and Frances was exhilarated. She bought the shoes, even though they were too large. She informed husband Ralph of her achievement. Ralph scoffed. "No one can run a mile the first time out, and you're forty-two besides," he pointed out kindly. An attempted repeat performance on the track failed; Frances could only make 3 laps, and Ralph said, "See?" But after a few more practice sessions, Frances did another nonstop mile—a week after the first run. Ralph lapped her ("Now, of course, I lap *him* in a mile," she says, smugly). But Frances was hooked. Tuckered out after each run, she still felt that exhilaration, and hasn't stopped running since.

Competition came more slowly. She trained for the 1973 Bay to Breakers (7.6 miles), a year when there were "only" 3000 runners, and officials still made an attempt to run it as a race, not a happening. But aside from this one venture, Frances remained purely a weekday runner, using her lunch hour at work for exercise. By 1975, she was doing 5 miles each weekday, but she never ran on her "own" time—after work and weekends were for home, Ralph, other activities. Gail and I, and other competitive types who often ran with Frances at lunchtime, tried to persuade her to come along to weekend races, but Frances refused. "I'm basically not competitive," she stated firmly. "I'd rather do other things on weekends."

That attitude lasted until May, 1975, when Frances was lured into an all-Masters (over-40) race. Women were still a distinct minority, especially in the upper age groups, and Frances placed third—she thinks. More to the point, she ran 37:50 for 5 miles—even better than the 8-minute pace she had hoped for. She developed a gleam in her eye, and began to sound different on daily runs—"You know," she commented, "I'll bet I could train a little harder and break 35:00 next year."

She did, of course, and the increased mileage led to expanded ambitions. By 1976, planning to run a 20-mile workout in a local marathon, she went on and finished the whole distance in 4:08. A year later, running more deliberately, she improved to 3:33 and was admitted to the hallowed Boston Marathon. Ever improving, Frances had run 10 marathons by mid-1979, with a P.R. of 3:18. She trains about 60 miles a week (including a long run on weekends, these days) and has again upgraded her goals. She'd like to close in on a 3-hour marathon, and break 6 minutes for the mile. Her best mile so far is a 6:02, recorded before thousands of spectators in the annual Examiner Indoor Games, which features a Women's Masters Mile—a truly progressive event.

Frances, now 50, despairs of ever catching up with her illustrious local rival, Ruth Anderson, but she does collect "hardware" in many local events, and looks forward to more competition in the 50-and-over division. Her running style has not changed—she still takes short, quick steps— nor has her weight changed much. She *has* gone from 107 to 102 pounds, and from being somewhat "pear-shaped, with jiggling thighs" to lean, even wiry. The average 50-year-old woman has about 35 percent fat—Frances has been measured at 18 percent, and friends suspect that a laboratory error must have pegged that figure too high.

Recently, Frances decided to share her love of running, and its benefits, with other women. She now teaches a jogging class for a local recreation center. The class is limited to women over 40, since Frances feels that her own experience can be most helpful to older beginners—"After all, I didn't get started till I was 42, and I know their limitations and hesitations," she reasons. Frances is apparently a persuasive and successful teacher, and her class is popular. Many younger women have called the center in hopes of evading the age requirement. They complain of discrimination against younger women. But Frances figures the younger ones can do it on their own or join the regular jogging classes. She would rather inspire those her own age. "They often sit around and think they're too old, there's no chance for them to do something new. I'm hoping to show them that they *can* get in shape, and enjoy running, no matter when they start. It's not too late." And to help convince others, she'll continue to improve her marathon time, and break 6 minutes for the mile.

50s   MARCIE TRENT   BORN: DEC. 22, 1917
           ANCHORAGE, ALASKA

In the summer of 1974, my young sons and I were camping out at Barr Camp on the Pikes Peak Marathon trail—halfway up the trail, to be exact, at 10,000 feet. We had seen a number of hikers, and a few of the hardier runners, practicing for the marathon that weekend. Toward dusk, as we hiked down the trail heading for town, the runners had disappeared. No one was eager to tackle that 14-mile round-trip run to the halfway point so late in the day. But as we rounded a bend in the steep lower trail, there was one more runner headed up—a woman, small, tanned, blond and wiry. She stopped to chat and introduce herself as Marcie Trent from Alaska. She and husband, John, were staying in Manitou Springs, near the trail head, and she was jogging the trail every day to get used to it. Dusk didn't bother her, and she trotted on up the steep grade, steady and cheerful—already at 9000 feet.

As a contender in the race myself, I felt a tinge of uneasiness, which I quickly suppressed. I had heard of Marcie's tough Alaskan marathons, but after all, the woman was in her late 50s, and thus no threat. I was wrong. In the race that weekend, I made the turn at the 14,110-foot summit, and started back down, eyeing the (female) competition. Marcie was the third woman I saw, and surprisingly close. And I knew she wouldn't take the option of stopping at the summit. This was a tough Alaskan! Sure enough, while I finished the race as first woman, Marcie was uncomfortably close behind—5:23 to my 5:20. Her descent time was faster than mine. It was a sobering experience.

Marcie was gracious about finishing second (and first Master), but in her Alaskan marathons, she often wins first place among women. Age seems irrelevant to her. She is lightweight, a hard trainer (3450 miles in 1978), and enjoys running. She and John founded the Pulsators Club of Alaska, with the motto "Run and Rejoice!"

Marcie came to Alaska as a homesteader in 1946. Although she has always been a hard worker and an outdoor person, athletic endeavors are relatively new to her. With the vague goal in mind of *walking* the annual 26-mile Equinox Marathon in Fairbanks, Marcie began jogging 1 mile a day at age 51. Finding herself not far behind the last *runner* in that marathon, she ran 2 miles a day, every day, the following year. Then came some longer, steady runs, higher mileage, more races. Marcie was hooked. And she was accustomed to the rugged Alaskan runs, where a "marathon" over trails, rocks and mountains seems to take twice as long as the usual kind. In 1975, Marcie ran a "flat" marathon officially, and surprised herself, if not her fans. Her time in the Boston Marathon in 1975, at age 57, was 3:27:45—under 8 minutes/mile.

Now in her 60s, Marcie does not consider herself an athletic phenomenon, just an ordinary woman who enjoys running and racing. However, her story illustrates certain key points about training that deserve to be emphasized.

First, the older you are, the more important it becomes to start gradually. Marcie spent 2 years running consistently, 1 to 2 miles daily, before she tackled higher mileage. In recent years, she has equally consistently racked up 60 to 70 miles weekly, with predictable results—she has acquired more speed and endurance. Though she does not do "leg-speed" or "interval" training, Marcie runs a tough 10-mile mountain run each week, and takes frequent 2- to 3-hour "endurance" runs.

With such high mileage, Marcie carries no extra fat around. On an underwater weighing test, I'd guess she'd be under 10 percent fat. Like most runners, she appears healthy and wiry, but not undernourished. Her light weight undoubtedly adds to her running success.

Finally, Marcie serves as an important reminder that it takes years to reach your peak. Most top runners have been training consistently for 10 years or more when they finally achieve prominence. No matter what age you start at, you can bet on the 10-year peak. Yes, ladies, if you jog your first steps at 80, you will run your best races at 90.

Marcie Trent ran her first mile at age 51, and her best running year to date was at age 60, when she ran six marathons, plus many shorter races, in 8 months. Here's Marcie's marathon schedule for that year, 1978:

February:	Trail's End, Oregon	3:34:04	
May :	Avenue of the Giants, Ca.	3:26:16	(personal best)
May :	Glacier, Alaska	3:31:10	(one week after her P.R., and Women's course record)
June :	Mayor's, Alaska	3:36:10	
July :	Resurrection Pass, Alaska	3:58:24	
August :	Equinox, Alaska	4:04:41	(her best time)

This list is especially impressive when you realize that the last 3 marathons are those Alaskan "toughies" over trails.

Marcie enjoyed a brief lull from racing and celebrated her sixty-first birthday in December. In March, 1979, braving snow flurries and ice, she tackled her first 50-

miler, finishing in 8:22. Her eye is now firmly set on more ultramarathons, the wave of the future.

50s   MARY RODRIGUEZ   BORN: NOV. 2, 1921
             NEW YORK CITY

One of our local Masters runners, Flory Rodd, goes East "to Boston" every year. It's a tradition with him. Flory has an extensive and enthusiastic family support system on the East coast; sisters and brothers, nieces and nephews flock to help him celebrate both before and after the marathon. They provide hotel room and champagne, they take movies and slides of their family hero, they welcome and cheer all his running friends. Sometimes their cheers are a bit indiscriminate, extending warmheartedly to rivals. I ran past the family cheering section once in the New York City marathon. "Go, Joan," they shouted loudly when they recognized me, "Flory's just a little ways ahead." As I caught their fading relative, I mentioned that his family had egged me on—but Flory just laughed, undaunted.

Loudest among the cheering group, year after year, was Flory's sister Mary. Knowledgeable watcher that she was, Mary never considered running herself. One nut in the family seemed to be enough. It took the boom in women's running to change her mind—at age 54. Watching the Bonne Bell 10-km. race in New York one year, Mary noticed other "older" women running along with the thousands of youngsters. "Maybe I could do that myself," she thought—an ambition never inspired, somehow, by Flory. Mary happened to hear of a new running program, led by Bob Glover of the Central YMCA. Glover was building the nucleus of a fine women's running team (Greater New York AA) and encouraged people of all ages to try jogging.

Mary joined the group—and before long, she was the star

90

of a running film—the Bonne Bell film of their 1977 New York extravaganza. Mary plays herself—an older woman starting to run, awed but encouraged by the presence of world-class runners in the same race, dreaming of someday competing with veterans in her own age group, like Marian Epstein. At film's end, Mary has finished the race successfully, is enthused and plans to keep on running. Brother Flory was astounded to hear that his "Sis" had not only started to run, but appeared in a widely circulated film designed to inspire other women to join the fun.

Mary not only kept on running after her 10-km. debut, she got faster and more ambitious. In the fall of 1978, she entered the New York City Marathon—along with twelve thousand others. The family party that year was for two runners, both looking equally fit and happy. Mary had slimmed down considerably since the movie, and looked like a lean, strong contender. Despite the heat and air pollution (which obscured the famous view of Manhattan from the Verrazano–Narrows Bridge), her marathoning debut was a great success. At age 56, Mary ran 4:28, and collected a trophy for third place in the 50 to 59 age division. She is a testimonial to the value of good training and enthusiasm, at any age. In the middle of the family circle, Flory clapped louder than anyone.

60s   KAY ATKINSON   BORN: MAY 23, 1917
          SAN FRANCISCO, CA.

Kay Atkinson is a familiar figure in the San Francisco area; she enters almost every race, and if there's a 60-and-over division, she wins it. Sometimes, she says proudly, she even wins the 50-and-over division. Kay is now 63, but she started running at age 57. The start was not easy for her; in fact, an overzealous (non-running) doctor grounded her for a heart murmur detected during a preexercise checkup. He sent her off to an eminent but sedentary cardiologist, for more elaborate tests. Alarmed by all the fuss, Kay asked me what she should do. Her murmur didn't impress me very much, nor did it the cardiologist-runner who checked her out next. "Go on and run," we both suggested, so Kay did. She joined a supervised jogging group in Golden Gate Park, and was encouraged to build up endurance slowly, steadily, and at her own pace.

Kay was talked into jogging by her younger friend Annabel Marsh, a golfing companion. As Annabel explains it, she was tired of always finishing last in local races, where at 52 she was usually the oldest woman. She decided to lure Kay away from golf, into running, reasoning that since Kay was 5 years older, and inexperienced, she would finish behind Annabel. A good plan, but it didn't work out that way. As Kay grew fit, and dropped 10 pounds (she's now 108 pounds, at 5 feet, 2 inches), she began to overhaul Annabel. The friendship persisted, however, and the two women usually tackle new challenges together. According to Kay, Annabel is the more adventurous one, and has talked her into all sorts of wild escapades, from the Pikes Peak marathon to a 50-mile race.

Kay has flourished in this athletic milieu. She and Annabel both look wonderful—alert, bright-eyed, and energetic. Most people don't realize Kay's age, and even friends can be fooled. Once, in a 30-km. run of 6 laps, I spotted a slim figure ahead, some teenager I was about to lap. I wondered briefly who this new club member could be—from the slim hips and legs, the cute tan shorts and matching knee-socks, I figured she was about 16. As I passed, I realized that the "teenager" was Kay. She doesn't quite believe this story, but it's true.

Kay's speed and endurance have both improved in her 5 years of running. After only 1 year, she and Annabel tackled "the tough one," Pikes Peak, finishing the ascent arm-in-arm with a much younger San Francisco teammate, Margo St. James (better known as president of Coyote than as the long-time runner she is). Emboldened

92

by the Pikes Peak accomplishment, Kay went on to "flat" marathons, of which she has now run ten (fifteen including Pikes Peak). Her best time to date is 4:23, but she's aiming for 4:15. "I've got to increase my mileage, though," she acknowledges. Her usual weekly average has been 40 to 45. This year, in preparation for her first 50-miler (another of Annabel's brainstorms), they did some 20-mile training runs, but usually Kay limits herself to an hour daily.

Kay's habits have changed in the past few years. On weekend races through the golf course, we used to see her—out on the green with her clubs. "Weekends are for golf," she'd shout as she waved at us. Nowadays she races on weekends, and plays golf maybe twice a month, rather than twice a week. Consumption of alcohol and red meat are way, way down from prerunning levels, though Kay still will eat a hamburger on occasion, and has the typical runner's fondness for a glass of wine. Her clothes are a size smaller than when she was a teenager. And her recreation tends more toward the unusual. For Kay's sixtieth birthday, her running friends got together for a surprise party at the yacht harbor, and gave her a collective gift appropriate to an adventurous young 60-year-old—a ride in a hot-air balloon. On the balloon ride, Kay encountered more new experiences—the balloon soared high over Napa Valley and the encircling mountains, then was forced down unexpectedly in a distant canyon, from which Kay was rescued by mountain search parties. What new challenges await her in the next decade?

70s   MAVIS LINDGREN   BORN: APRIL 2, 1907

Perhaps it is inaccurate to classify Mavis under the heading of "Seventies," because she started running long distances when she was still 69—and had been jogging a daily mile for several years before that. However, Mavis's best marathon times, and public recognition, didn't come till age 71. Her picture and story have appeared nationally in *Time, Newsweek,* and other publications—as part of an ad campaign for Blue Cross/Blue Shield. Your friendly health insurers want you to stay healthy, just like Mavis, who is shown jogging along on her daily run.

Mavis doesn't just shuffle along. In 1979, at age 71, she averaged about 70 miles of running a week, the necessary amount, she figures, for a serious marathoner, which she is. She started marathoning at age 69, with a 5:04 clocking in her debut. At age 70, she lowered her P.R. to 4:45; at 71, she ran 4:24. If the 10-year rule holds true, watch out for Mavis at age 79, when she should be closing in on the 4-hour marathon!

Distance running may still seem an unusual recreation for a woman in her 70s, but to Mavis it came quite naturally. Always troubled by allergies and chronic lung problems, she began walking, then jogging, in her early 60s. Soon her health problems disappeared—in fact, Mavis claims she has only been sick once in 10 years—a 3-hour bout with the flu. Her vegetarian diet no doubt provides healthful fuel for running, but it was not sufficient, by itself, to maintain her in the excellent health she now enjoys.

I take a modest pride in thinking that I may have helped, unknowingly, in the transformation of Mavis Lindgren from jogger to marathoner. Mavis's son Kelley (a physician) and his wife were on a run/study holiday with me in 1976, and picked up a copy of my book *Women's Running,* to help them train for an upcoming "Pepsi-Twenty-mile" race in Sacramento. Warming up for that race, myself, a few months later, I spied Kelley and his wife at the sidelines—but in "civilian" (non-running) garb. "What's the matter, aren't you running?" I inquired. "No," sighed Kelley, "we both hurt our knees when we got back from the trip. But I passed your book on to my mother, and *she's* going to try this."

"Your mother?" I replied, stupefied, knowing that Kelley was about my own age. "How old is she?" "Oh, sixty-nine," admitted Kelley, "but she's in good shape." He pointed proudly to a small, trim lady with carefully coiffed gray hair. I was impressed. According to her son, Mavis had decided, after reading the book, that there was no reason she couldn't run farther than her accustomed 2 miles daily. So she increased the daily stint, and went even longer once a week, and now was going to tackle the 20-miler. As the first woman over 60 ever to run the "Pepsi-Twenty," she would automatically set the 60-and-over course record, just by finishing.

Finish she did, earning a trophy and commemorative jacket as well as the course record. Emboldened by success, she went on to the next available distance—the marathon. In her first attempt, at the Avenue of the Giants, she finished behind veteran marathoner Walter Stack, but won the trophy Walt had always walked off with before—for oldest finisher. Walt was as impressed as everyone else, and became one of Mavis's greatest fans. Ever since, he's been trying to get her to run Pikes Peak. But Mavis prefers flatter courses—a sign of good sense, one of the benefits of greater age and maturity. Always neatly dressed and impeccably groomed, she can be seen, running along and smiling, in many California races. The day before a race, she likes to have her hair done at the beauty parlor. After all, she once explained to Walt, she has to look her best for the photographers. Marathoners of Mavis's age and ability are still a rarity, and must be prepared for publicity.

80s   EULA WEAVER   BORN: 1888

I have never met Eula Weaver, but I feel as if I know her intimately. She is one of the "stars" of the running movie, *Coping with Life . . . on the Run*. Her cameo appearance is brief, but memorable. The camera focuses on a sweet-faced, frail, gray-haired little old lady, who sits in a chair knitting and rocking. The sound track plays her words: "You're *never* too old, if you care for yourself and your loved ones. I'm Eula Weaver, and I'm eighty-seven years old."

The audience gasps, impressed. Is this sweet old lady going to endorse running? Better than that. The camera switches to a scene of this sweet, frail great-grandmother jogging daintily but briskly down the road, clad in a brightly colored sweat suit. "I run a mile every day, bicycle sometimes as much as twenty miles a day, do all my own shopping . . ." As she jogs on, Eula explains that when she was once (at age 80 plus) bedridden with heart failure, she was given a choice—stay in bed, getting weaker, being spoon-fed and carried around like a baby—or get out and walk. Eula lay in bed and thought that one over for a while. "When that little doctor came back, I told him, I've got my mind made up, I'm getting up in the morning and going for a walk."

Eula has never regretted her decision, and thanks to a combined diet-and-exercise program, she has obviously regained much of the health she had lost. The film's final view of her starts with another head shot, as Eula concentrates on reading *Live Longer Now*. Then the camera pans away and we see that Eula is not idle while she reads—she is pedaling steadily and calmly on her Exercycle.

The story does not end there. Eula is now 91 years old and still active. Her new lease on life began with the now-famous Pritikin program, which combines a strict low-fat diet with hours of daily aerobic exercise. Once Eula was able to jog comfortably, rather than just walk, she was quickly lured into competition—the Los Angeles Masters Track Meet, to be specific. Eula won gold medals in all the events she ran—not bad for a former heart patient.

Since those early days, Eula appears to have lost weight—undoubtedly in the form of undesirable fat, the curse of the sedentary of all ages. She looks lean, healthy and sparkling. To all those who hesitate to become active because of their age, she is living proof that, indeed, "You're never too old!"

Women running in a Marathon race, San Francisco, 1978; © *Lorraine Rorke*

All sizes and shapes finishing five-kilometer race, Golden Gate Park, 1979; © *Lorraine Rorke*

Boy runner warming up; © *Lorraine Rorke*

Young cross-country runners; © *Lorraine Rorke*

Dr. Ernst Van Aaken with some U.S. runners in Waldniel, on the occasion of the Second Women's International Marathon Championship in 1976. Joan Ullyot is second from the right; © *Sven Simon.*

A Sampling of Late Bloomers

Skip Swannack at age 38 in training for her 100-mile race (the Western States Endurance Run) in 1979; *Joan Ullyot*

Mary Rodriguez started running
age 42. In 1978, at the age of 56, s
placed third in the 50-to-59 age di
sion in the New York City Marath
Jose Soto

Frances Sackerman, now over 50,
who started running at age 42, trains
about 60 miles a week, and by
mid-1979 had run in ten marathons.
She currently teaches a jogging class
for women who are over 40, at a local
recreation center; © *Lorraine Rorke.*

Rachel Anderson, daughter of Ruth, age 50; Ruth started running at age 43 and has competed nationally and internationally; © *Lorraine Rorke*.

Kay Atkinson (second from the right), running with a group of friends, is 63 years old. She started running at age 57 and enters almost every race in the San Francisco area. If there's a 60-and-over division, she wins it. Sometimes she even wins the 50-and-over division; © *Lorraine Rorke.*

II: RUNNING PEOPLE

Chapter Six: The Elite Runner

When you are running your heart out in a race, and some other woman whizzes past you, seemingly without effort, do you ever wonder what she has that you don't? Lately, I have found myself answering this question rather philosophically. Instead of running myself to exhaustion to keep my rival in sight, I think, "Well, she's trained harder, she deserves it." Later on, I sometimes learn that she hasn't trained harder. So I blame my lack of speed on overweight, or some similar, tangible difference. I always try to hang on to the idea that if I lost enough weight, trained correctly, put in the hours needed—I, too, could set world records.

But when a lot of women come together in a race—say

the Boston Marathon, or the International Championships—and all are equally lean, equally well trained—what determines who will win? Are there any measurable physiological differences which predict success, which distinguish the "elite" runner from the merely "good"?

Given the short history of competitive long-distance running for women (less than 10 years), no one has yet undertaken a detailed study of female champions. However, there are plenty of elite male runners around, reflecting the greater numbers of men at all levels of the sport. A couple of years ago, twenty of the best road and track runners in the United States were gathered together in Dallas, at the Aerobics Research Institute, in an attempt to discover what made them so different from ordinary people. For 3 to 4 days, these world-class guinea pigs submitted to extensive testing—cardiac and pulmonary function, body composition, blood-testing, biomechanical evaluation, psychological questionnaires—even (a true measure of their dedication) a muscle biopsy, a procedure from which I would recoil in horror, having seen the gleaming steel biopsy needle.

Characteristics of the Elite Runner.

Almost all the subjects in this study were Olympic or Pan-American Games competitors; all had won national championships. You can imagine that chief investigator Michael Pollock and his fellow scientists put in considerable effort to recruit such a galaxy of stars for their research. A persuasive letter from Olympic marathoner and writer *(Sports Illustrated)*, Kenny Moore, helped convince them—as did the promise that the runners would have immediate access to the results and their interpretation. Like almost all runners, the elite bunch were eager to demonstrate their superior physiology, and learn more about themselves in the process, so they agreed. Since most of the twenty subjects were being tested simultaneously, a healthy element of competition was introduced—culminating in a 6-mile race the final day.

Comparison Between Elite, Good, and Untrained Runners. The results of the testing were rather striking.

Put briefly, no one could identify any physiological characteristics which could reliably distinguish the Elite from the Good control group (members of a local university team). All the runners, of course, were lean and fit. They were matched against an equally lean collection of sedentary controls, and most of the physiological differences determined simply showed that all the runners were fit and all the non-runners were not. A few measurements indicated that the Elite were even fitter than the Good—the average resting pulse of the Elite was 47.1 versus 52.4 for the Good, and maximal oxygen consumption (V O_2 max.) was 76.9 versus 69.2. Hardly a very dramatic difference, except in comparison to the untrained controls. Below is a chart showing *mean* results for each group for all of the tests which showed any significant differences between groups. (The original results are shown in much greater detail in the papers collected by Milvy in *The Long-Distance Runner*—see Bibliography.) It's okay to skip this chart unless you're intrigued by such things.

Physiology	Elite	Good	Untrained Lean
Resting Heart Rate	47.1	52.4	65.0
Heart Volume	1028 cc.	998 cc.	—
Heart Vol/Weight	16.4	14.9	—
Treadmill Time (length of run)	7:30	5:30	—
$\dot{V}_{02}$ max. (oxygen processed at maximal effort)	76.9 mg./100 ml.	69.2 mg./100 ml.	54.2 mg./100 ml.
Pulm. Vent ($\dot{V}_E$) (amount of air moved through lungs)	168 mg./100 ml.	169 mg./100 ml.	132 mg./100 ml.
% Body Fat	4.7	6.1	8.2

BLOOD TESTS

Hematocrit (% of blood volume made up of red cells)			
SGOT enzyme	43.8	43.6	47.2
LDH enzyme	35.8	27.9	24.3
Bilirubin	230	204	169
Total Cholesterol*	1.075	1.175	.744
HDL Chol.*	175	185	189
LDL Chol.*	56	52	49
TG*	108	121	124
HDL/LDL*	74	73	92
	.56	.45	.39

*Blood fats—see pages 240-44

I have included the chart mainly for those who like and understand laboratory data, who can spend many happy hours speculating as to the subtle causes of the minute variations observed.

All those numbers, all that wonderful *quantification* and raw data, may look impressive. But in fact, it tells us nothing beyond what our eyes and common sense tell us. The best runners are the leanest, and have the highest oxygen consumption (a factor that varies inversely with fat content), and largest heart volume relative to weight. Most of the blood tests suggest, to the practiced eye, that Elite runners train harder than the merely Good, and both groups show changes associated with training, whereas the Untrained Lean do not. It helps to have concrete data to prove the obvious, but it doesn't leave us very enlightened about the factors involved in athletic excellence.

Some of the most valuable predictive information, in fact, came from questionnaires rather than the laboratory. The Elite group as a whole trained an average 85 miles/ week, with the marathoners favoring distance (100.7 miles/week, mainly aerobic) and the middle-distance runners emphasizing speed (75.4 miles/week, with more interval work). The Good runners only trained 60 miles/week, a handicap sufficient to explain the observed differences in fat percent, treadmill performance and O_2 consumption, between the running groups. The Untrained, by definition, didn't run at all, and were naturally found to be unfit (= untrained). Their resting pulses were up, $\dot{V}_{O2}$ max down, and they weren't even tested on the treadmill (for fear of straining them, perhaps?).

It is safe to conclude, then, that those runners who train harder will do better, unless they are handicapped by excessive weight. None of the studies indicate that champions are simply the beneficiaries of good genes. I'm sure many of the sedentary group have excellent, champion-caliber running genes, but the genes can do no good if you don't put in the miles of training.

Tests can, of course, distinguish the fit from the unfit, and even the Elite from the Good, in some respects—but within each group, comparing measurements doesn't help predict athletic success. the V_{O2} max., for instance, is considered the best *single* measurement of fitness, and the high value, 84.4, was found in Prefontaine, who held ten American distance records. But the *lowest* value in the group, 71.3, was measured in Olympic gold and silver medalist Frank Shorter, that year's outstanding athlete, who had beaten just about every one in the Elite group in races. The researchers postulate, a bit lamely, that Shorter can work at a higher percentage of his maximum for longer than most athletes. But we still don't know *why* Shorter can run marathons at 95 percent of maximal efforts, whereas most runners feel wasted at 85 to 90 percent. Is he a masochist? Doesn't he feel pain? The questions are still unanswered. Excellence remains a physiological mystery.

Physical and Psychological Toughness. My own conviction is that excellence is about 5 percent physical and 95 percent mental. That doesn't mean you can just sit around and think yourself into an AAU championship

(though some Tibetan monks are rumored to perform fabulous endurance runs while in a meditative trance). It means that what really divides the Elite from the rest of us clods is their drive, their will, and their attitude toward competition, rather than their physical endowment. Sure, a Frank Shorter is extraordinarily lean, while Joe Schmo is fat and gets palpitations whenever he walks to the refrigerator. But you can bet that they started out fairly even as babies or teenagers. Anyone who wins an Olympic Gold Medal, however, has spent years of hard work pursuing this ultimate dream. It takes considerable mental toughness and self-discipline to put in high mileage, it takes even more to do training that is physically painful, like high-intensity interval work. Once you toe the starting line, along with many others who are equally lean and fit, equally well-trained, it takes more competitive drive to outrun the lot of them. You have to have self-confidence and complete faith in your own running, your own abilities, and your own timing. This is why "the Psych" is so important. Athletes know all the little ploys that can be used to undermine self-confidence. An experienced competitor with faith in her training will be impervious to these darts, but newcomers can be easily rattled. Just shooting past someone with apparent ease, and perhaps a friendly, encouraging remark, can reduce a competitor to quivering jelly—if she is breathing hard, on the verge of exhaustion, and thinks that *you're* not suffering at all. The secret, of course, is to look and act better than you really feel, as you pass your rivals.

A classic example of the subtle "Psych" was given by bodybuilder Arnold Schwarzenegger in his film *Pumping Iron,* which I recommend to those pursuing excellence in any sport. Arnold, the consummate competitor, and an old hand at important international events, joins his younger and less experienced colleague, Lou Ferrigno, for a precompetition meal. Lou's father should have kicked Arnold out at once, but Arnold acts so friendly and encouraging, it's hard to resist his charm. "Gee, you're looking really good," he assures the young Lou, who has been working like a dog to get his body in perfect shape. "You'll be at your peak in another few weeks," continues Arnold. He'd hate to be matched against Lou *then,* he says. The audience already knows that Arnold's real concern is Lou's shape not a few weeks later, but in the competition that evening. He has just made his bid to throw off Lou's confidence in his timing. The ploy works, and Arnold wins again.

Knowing how to keep your competitors from realizing their own best performances is useful, if a bit underhanded. The true mental edge, however, comes from self-knowledge—the ability to tune and play your own body like a fine musical instrument. The Elite runners all have learned, through years of training and self-evaluation, just what stress load they can tolerate, and for how long. They know their own strengths and weaknesses, whether they run better by utilizing basic speed or a last-lap "kick." They don't panic at a fast pace, if they've accustomed themselves to that pace during hard workouts. Similarly, the runner who has trained in the heat is not likely to be lured into a too-fast pace on a hot day. Those who collapse in hot, humid weather, or run themselves into unconsciousness at high altitudes, are either unfamiliar with their own body's danger signals, or haven't paid attention.

Psychological tests done on the Elite group of runners tend to confirm the importance of mental set in competition. The Elite were found to be significantly different from the Good, in two main areas. First, the Elite showed greater awareness of the true work load, in that their subjective evaluation of discomfort and effort accurately reflected the actual stress applied. The Good runners tended to perceive the work load far less accurately. Dr. William Morgan, the psychologist who performed these studies, speaks of a "perceptostat" which drives the runner, analogous to the thermostat in a furnace. The more accurately the "perceptostat" functions, the more efficient the runner, since he can avoid "overshooting" in either direction, i.e., running too fast or too slow for the circumstances.

Morgan also determined that the Elite marathoners "associate" during competitive runs, while the lesser runners "dissociate." In lay terms, the best runners concentrate on the race and on their bodily perceptions—they monitor sensory input: pain, breathing, discomfort, relaxation, stiffness, effort, and adjust themselves accordingly. Their minds are totally focused on the run.

Less "gifted" (or less trained) marathoners are more inclined to let their minds wander. They try to ignore pains, think of something else, sing, hum, get through the distance without really noticing it. Some of Morgan's examples of "dissociative" strategy are remarkable. One marathoner reviewed his entire educational career during the race, from kindergarten through post-doctoral work. Another built a house mentally; one thought of himself as "The Little Engine That Could" when he encountered a hill.

Suffice it to say that the non-champions try to distract themselves from the race. And that is probably one good reason that they remain non-champions. Running a hard race requires one to push hard, to perform at the limit of one's physical ability, to "hurt" to some degree. It is impossible to achieve a near-maximal performance if your mind wanders to other matters. Your mind has to be on top of the current situation, evaluating, processing information, *pushing*. Concentration is the key, whether the event is a marathon, a downhill ski race or a swim. The body would generally prefer to relax and take it easy for a while; only when subject to the discipline of the mind (or will, if you prefer), does it perform physical wonders.

So the next time you look at a Boston Marathon winner,

such as Joan Benoit in 1979, you don't have to envy her trim figure, her ability to run fast, to train hard, and sigh "I wish I could do that!" The truth is that you *can* do that—if you want to. Unless you are truly physically handicapped—not just overweight, or a "klutz"—you can become a champion, if you have the mental drive to do so. You have to discipline yourself to slim down, go for the long runs, suffer through the requisite speedwork, and teach yourself to *concentrate*. When you emerge from your inwardly focused trance, you may find yourself wearing a laurel wreath.

Chapter Seven: Doctors *vs.* Runners

Whether they realize it or not, most runners have been strongly influenced by a handful of medical mavericks, the "Running Docs." Dr. George Sheehan's column in *Runner's World* was for years the only source of helpful information for broken-down runners, who usually received blank looks and suggestions of rest from their "own" physicians. Dr. Jack Scaff of Honolulu, who possesses a strong personality and frequently adamantine opinions, organized the first marathon clinic, a movement which has made Hawaii Number One in per capita joggers, and turned the annual Honolulu Marathon into a mass "happening" and luau. Millions, learning of Dr. Tom Bassler's guarantee of virtual immortality to marathoners, have taken to the roads in search of immunity from heart attacks. In Europe, the medical counterpart of these running advocates is Dr. Ernst Van Aaken, who also single-handedly organized the first international marathons for women. And the most widely known of the fitness physicians, Dr. Kenneth Cooper, likes to point to 1968, when American deaths from

106

heart disease began to decline, as (not entirely coinci-dently) the year that his first best-seller, *Aerobics*, was published.

Traditional Medicine vs. Sports Medicine. The American public, accustomed to looking to their doctors for guidance in health matters, naturally assumes that these leaders in the fitness movement must be equally influen-tial among their medical colleagues. Surprisingly, this is not the case. On the whole, conventional American medi-cine has taken a skeptical, sometimes hostile approach to the prescription of exercise in lieu of drugs or surgery. The attitude of many has been "Oh, yeah? Prove it!" when told about the benefits of jogging. Counterclaims have been published. A few years ago, an article entitled "Jogging Can Kill You," by a "Dr." Schmidt, appeared in *Playboy* and caused quite a furor. Readers assumed that if the author was a doctor, his words must be gospel—however ridiculous the anatomical catastrophes listed might sound. A better known physician, Dr. Meyer Friedman, co-author (with Ray Rosenmann) of *Type A Behavior and Your Heart,* insisted that exercise was a very dangerous undertaking (as it can be, for persons with severe heart disease who exercise without supervision).

The public remains somewhat confused by the conflicting views among "experts." They tend to believe whatever side supports their own bias. Thus, sedentary smokers quote Friedman and Schmidt, while runners cite Sheehan and Bassler, verse for verse. To achieve a more objective view, it is important to understand the background and training of American doctors.

Physicians are not, as they are often called, "health professionals." A better designation would be "disease experts." In 4 years of medical school and up to 8 years of post-doctoral specialty training, they learn how to diag-nose, treat and, occasionally, how to cure illnesses. Their patients are not healthy people; in fact, by the time most people feel sick enough to consult an M.D., they have deteriorated considerably even from the American "norm" of "not sick." And this "norm" itself, to which the patient will, with luck and good treatment, be restored, is not the same as optimum health. It is merely a state in which we cannot, with our present technological tools, detect any disease.

My own progression from a conventional medical education to the new concept of "wellness" may be illustrative. At Harvard Medical School, where I earned my M.D., the first "preclinical" year was devoted largely to the study of "normal" human anatomy, biochemistry and physiology. Like my classmates, I was much more interested in learning about the abnormal, diseased states—in second year—so I could go about the business of being a proper doctor: diagnosing, treating and curing disease. The two "clinical" years were spent learning to apply the theoretical concepts to actual patients. This was a sobering, often heartrending and very educational process. We budding doctors learned much about human weaknesses, fortitude and suffering, and we became, I hope, better and more sympathetic human beings as a result. But while we concentrated all the power of our minds and all our physical resources, often to the point of exhaustion, on a sick hospital population, the wide world of good health escaped our attention. Healthy people did not have diseases to be studied and cured; hence, they were considered "uninteresting." Most students and doctors avoided work in the "well-baby" pediatric clinics. Our focus was elsewhere, on healing. Our life was spent, night and day, in the hospital—white beds, sick patients, endless corridors, emergencies, lab tests, poking and probing, catching a few winks now and then. Our nostrils were filled with the normal smells of that environment—disinfectant, blood, medicines, urine, alcohol. Fresh air smelled peculiar, when we stepped outside for brief moments.

After graduation, I specialized in pathology, doing an

internship and 4 years of post-doctoral research. The internship year was devoted not to diseased persons, but to diseased tissues, organs and bodies—analyzed in biopsies, surgical specimens and autopsies. The aim was to diagnose the disease accurately, advise the clinical doctors about its natural behavior and susceptibility to various treatments, and to chart and record its ravages within the body. A very depressing interlude, only relieved by the thought that once we know the enemy—the disease—well, we can fight it better.

This preoccupation with first causes continued during my training as a cellular pathologist. Having already dispensed with living patients, I now looked beyond the body, the organ, or even the tissue involved with disease, and used an electron microscope to peer within the aberrant cells themselves, in hopes of finding clues to their disordered behavior. I was a thoroughly conventional doctor, following the research path for which I had been prepared at Harvard. So deeply engrained was this traditional view of medicine that now, 8 years into a new health career, I still feel twinges of guilt, that I may have betrayed my medical background in some way.

It was not medicine that oriented me back toward the world of non-patients, otherwise known as the healthy population outside the hospital. It was sheer curiosity about the strange things that were happening to my body after I had taken up jogging. Nothing I had learned as a doctor could explain what was going on.

In my field of pathology, electron microscopy, we do a great deal of darkroom work. The electron beam passing through the specimen is focused onto a fluorescent screen, where the image can be studied only briefly before it "burns up" in the beam. If the image is worth preserving, it is recorded on a photographic plate, exposed by raising the screen briefly. Learning just how dim the beam must be, and how long the screen must be raised for a perfect exposure, not to mention how to focus accurately, is a real art, and the best electron microscopists are true artists, working in the field of science. Later, the best plates are selected and printed to give the final picture of what is going on within the cells.

I was not yet an artist, but in 2 years of research, I had become competent and could take decently focused and exposed photographs for my project. I was not the most efficient of workers, however. The electron microscope is large, taller than a person. The chair used for viewing was comfortable, the room darkened to allow for better visualization of the fluorescent images. Etiquette forbids disturbing the researcher during use of the microscope (usually hours at a time) and most afternoons I would find myself sluggishly drifting off to sleep, with my head resting against the scope. I always was careful to turn off the beam and save the specimen if I felt a catnap coming on.

Enlightenment. After I took up jogging, for reasons detailed afterwards, I noticed I became more productive, since I felt quite energetic following my noontime jogs. But the increased number of plates and photographs I was turning out caused me some concern, because they were uniformly overexposed. I tried turning down the beam, shortening the exposure, but this involved a whole relearning process, for something which had been automatic.

One day a lightbulb lit up over my head: I realized I always timed exposures by checking my pulse, which had been a steady, "normal" 72/minute for at least 10 years—since I stopped smoking, before which it had been 80/minute, equally steady. Perhaps, I thought, since I was older and presumably more decrepit, my pulse, which was my timing instrument, had changed again, leading to incorrect exposures.

Indeed, it had. To my shock, I had a resting pulse of 54—down 18 beats per minute. This was quite a massive jolt, and a bit disturbing, too, since I knew from my medical training that the "normal" pulse is between 70 and 90. I checked every medical textbook I had; sure enough, "normal" is 70 to 90. Below 70 is "bradycardia," (slow heart), above 90 is "tachycardia" (fast heart). A pulse under 60, like mine is called "pathological bradycardia," the "pathological" meaning that it is abnormal and presumed dangerous. But I didn't feel sick, I felt good—better, physically, than I had in years. Could the books be wrong?

I checked two other women in the lab, who had been jogging daily with me, though I didn't think of that at the time, they were just conveniently located for pulse checking. They, too, turned out to have "pathological bradycardia." Something, obviously, was screwy here, and I began to suspect it was the books.

Any runner today will be amazed at my ignorance. Everyone *knows* now that the resting pulse falls with aerobic conditioning, that this decrease in rate reflects a stronger, more vigorous heartbeat and more efficient heart action, that this is one of the first and more dramatic changes found in those who take up jogging. How could I, a doctor, be so *dumb*? Or, at least, maddeningly slow at catching on?

Beware of Most Physicians. I tell this story precisely to show how totally ignorant of good health the conventionally trained doctor can be. Our education is entirely about disease. In 1971, when I had this great and original insight, I was almost alone among doctors. I had not yet read Cooper's *Aerobics*, which explains the falling pulse phenomenon as part of the "training effect." I had not yet heard of Cooper, though his first book appeared in 1968. After 3 years, *Aerobics*, written by a doctor for the layman, had not yet penetrated the medical profession. Those doctors who were aware of Cooper's studies tended to dismiss them as "unscientific" or "unproven." A few months later, having educated myself rapidly about cardiovascular responses to exercise training, I was arguing about pulses with a non-medical, sedentary acquaintance.

Since I, a woman, had a pulse of 54, and he, a man, confessed to 70, I claimed I was fitter than he. Indignant, he informed me that "any doctor" would disagree, and call a pulse as low as mine a sign of disease. We checked by calling around to several hospitals and speaking to the doctor—usually a young resident—in charge of the Coronary Care Unit. The first few expressed extreme concern for our hypothetical "healthy" woman whose only complaint was a slow pulse. The general recommendation was for further diagnostic studying, with an eye to a possible pacemaker implant. The last doctor we spoke to, when asked specifically if a slow pulse could be "normal," admitted as an afterthought that an athlete could show this phenomenon. However, he doubted that our "patient," being female, would fall into this category.

This was in 1971, and times have changed, bringing new awareness even into the medical ranks. In 1980, it is unlikely that any marathoner could be hit over the head, knocked unconscious, and wake up with a pacemaker installed. However, this would have been a true hazard for much of the 70s. More routine mismanagement of athletes is still common. One college cross-country runner I trained with fainted, not surprisingly, following a hard workout.

He had foolishly dragged himself out of bed, with a 103-degree fever, so as not to let the team down. Taken to the infirmary, he was checked and found to have a heart murmur and an "enlarged heart"—both normal for a lean young athlete (see Chapter Fourteen). But the student health doctor, worried, referred him to a cardiologist, who took several electrocardiograms and an echocardiogram to analyze the heart valves. Finding nothing abnormal on these tests, except for a large, strong left ventricle (the chamber which pumps blood to the body), the specialist recommended catheterization, a somewhat risky and expensive procedure, to "try to find out what was wrong." Fortunately, the worried young runner consulted me before submitting to further attempts to diagnose his sus-

112

pected heart ailment. I was able to reassure him that his heart was undoubtedly much healthier than the specialist's.

Another true story illustrates the tendency of conventional doctors to regard the unusual as pathological (bad for you). A female cross-country runner wrote me that she felt great, was training 80 miles/week, and was full of energy. Only one problem—she had not had a menstrual period for several months. Not knowing that this "amenorrhea" is common among outstanding women runners and apparently a temporary and harmless condition, she consulted a gynecologist to make sure nothing was wrong. The doctor declared her completely normal on physical exam, then gave her hormones similar to the "Pill," to induce withdrawal bleeding. The pills worked, but in the months thereafter, without the hormone treatment, the young woman continued to have amenorrhea. Her doctor next proposed that she undergo exploratory surgery to hunt for some condition that could cause amenorrhea, or alternatively, continue on the hormone pills so as to ensure monthly bleeding, with all its attendant inconvenience. I told this runner not to worry—if she felt healthy and fit, and was running well, she shouldn't waste her money trying to conform to the gynecologist's idea of normality.

Health-Watch and the Health-Oriented Physician. One can't really blame the doctors for their misguided concern. After all, their training has been to diagnose problems, and the more subtle and esoteric the diagnosis, the greater the doctor's cleverness and self-esteem. Moreover, medical textbooks still perpetuate the concept that "non-sick" values are normal. Thus, a young woman with a cholesterol level of 230, triglycerides 120,* who is 20 pounds overweight, smokes, and has a sedentary

*See Chapter Fourteen, page 242. I would consider a cholesterol level over 180 and triglycerides over 80 uncomfortably high.

job, could be called normal and healthy on a routine medical checkup. Actually, she is headed for disaster—a physiological basket-case.

For 6 years, after I became a runner and an ex-pathologist, I worked as a physician and did research at San Francisco's unique Institute of Health Research. Our 2000 healthy volunteers, who were called "participants" rather than "patients," paid annual visits to our facilities for multiple blood tests and physiological measurements. In return, they received not a casual "everything's normal," but a detailed analysis of where they stood on a scale of healthy people, and how they matched up with their own previous measurements. This program, called "Health-Watch," has helped to establish optimal biological values for each individual and to develop positive means to maintain optimal health. Not surprisingly, simple life-style changes have the greatest influence on health. Better diet (less salt and animal fat), cessation of smoking, and regular aerobic exercise are the most important means of staying healthy, and the impact of change in life-style can be quickly assessed by the chemical and physiological data gathered each year. If our "normal and healthy" young woman with the cholesterol of 230 stops smoking, starts jogging, loses 20 pounds and becomes a vegetarian, she should find out at her "update" that her cholesterol is now 175, triglycerides 60, and pulse 50—a remarkable change and one that coincides with her increased energy and self-esteem. But in the ordinary American health-maintenance system, she would be unaware that there had been any measurable changes in her health. All her values were "normal" to start with (most doctors don't give their patients the actual figures, just an interpretation—sick or normal) and they are still "normal"—only the actual, accurate figures show the change. In our experience at the Institute of Health Research, this ability to demonstrate significant changes in laboratory measurements is the greatest single motivator for adopting healthful habits.

Significantly, the founder of this Institute, Dr. George Z. Williams, was raised in Korea, as the son of missionaries, where he learned the traditional Chinese pattern of medical care, in which the doctor is only paid so long as the people he is responsible for remain healthy. He is considered to have failed in his job if his patients fall ill. Indeed, the Emperor's physicians, in ancient times, were executed if their patient died.

After several years of working in this rarefied atmosphere of good health—no one even smoked anywhere on the premises—I was invited to be a visiting lecturer at a midwestern medical school. I spent several days on the wards of the big city hospital, which was used as the principal training arena for the medical students. This experience brought back vivid memories of my own days in medical school, but I now saw the entire scene through new eyes, eyes that were tuned toward healthful practices. I was appalled. All of these budding "health professionals," as well as their learned clinical teachers, seemed to have blinders on. As we traveled from bed to bed, discussing each patient's illness, laboratory tests, prognosis, and "disposition" to family, or nursing home, or even back to prison, I thought of the tremendous waste of intelligence, energy and medical knowledge in this setting. The concern was almost entirely with patching-up the sick bodies, holding them together a little longer. How much more meaningful it would be, I thought, to devote a fraction of the same energy to keeping people in good health, *away* from this end-stage hospital ward.

I also realized, more clearly than ever, that 95 percent of the sad, sick patients we visited were victims of entirely preventable and self-induced diseases. They, like much of our society, suffered the ravages of overeating, drinking, smoking, and inactivity. One elderly lady was so obese that she was unable to get out of her chair without assistance. Her obesity and inactivity led to chronic constipation and diverticulitis. Surgery for the diverticulitis was complicated by infection, a special hazard in the obese, and by pneumonia—her lungs hadn't been exercised properly for years. Other patients were dying of lung cancer, cirrhosis of the liver, infection in poorly circulated limbs—*all preventable diseases.*

Shocked, I later gave the students a lecture on my own kind of medicine, which emphasized true health maintenance rather than disease treatment. Unfortunately, the government-sponsored and -financed HMOs, or "health maintenance organizations" are almost entirely disease-oriented, as are the doctors who staff them.

Sportsmedicine. It must be obvious by now that the concept of a health-oriented physician is almost a contradiction in terms. They do exist, but they are almost universally self-educated, as I was. That is, their concepts of optimum health and how to achieve it have been developed apart from the traditional medical mainstream, and sometimes in defiance of it. When I found that my body was undergoing unexpected changes, as I became truly fit for the first time in my life (at age 30), I found no discussion of these changes in my medical texts. Instead, I read Dr. Kenneth Cooper's *Aerobics,* written for the "lay" population, from cover to cover. When I was injured, with a sore knee, ankle or leg, no physician friends could help me. I turned to Dr. George Sheehan's monthly column in *Runner's World,* searching for cases which resembled mine, and trying out the suggested treatments.

Like Sheehan, I suffered from almost every ailment which can plague the beginning runner. Being female, I acquired knowledge of several other interesting disorders which Sheehan had escaped. Now, when people ask me my medical specialty, I smile and answer, "Sportsmedicine." They look blank. As well they should, for although Sheehan and others, as well as myself, are truly specialists in sportsmedicine, there is no such specialty . . . officially.

116

That is, if an enthusiastic young physician/athlete wishes to combine her interests and seeks post-doctoral training in the field of sportsmedicine, there is no place to go. European physicians can train at special physiological and sports institutes, but in America we have yet to bring generalized medical interest to bear on the problems of athletes. Team and school athletes, for years, have been supervised by specialists of another kind—orthopedic surgeons. Orthopedists, however, have been trained on the average, sedentary, American population, and take a conservative approach to athletes—especially middle-aged joggers. They tend to set obvious fractures, operate on football/ski knees, and advise rest for all other conditions. Many are not even aware that aerobically conditioned persons of any age heal almost twice as fast as their sedentary counterparts. Orthopedists have an appalling tendency to inject cortisone for bursitis, tendinitis—almost any "-itis." Like all surgeons, they tend to be "doers," somewhat impatient, anxious to intervene and treat disorders, and frustrated when they cannot.

Having by now antagonized all my orthopedist friends, let me add that in all the above, I am talking about traditional stereotypes, and fortunately, there are exceptions. The best orthopedist for a runner to consult is one who is a fellow runner; rugby players should try to find similarly inclined orthopedists for their afflictions, etc.

Many of the letters I receive are from medical students who are interested in sports and want to know what kind of training to look for. Most do not want to become orthopedic surgeons and care for professional football teams; they are more oriented toward participant sports, which grew in popularity so astoundingly during the 70s. It's hard to advise them how to become sports physicians within the framework of traditional medical training. I usually suggest a year of internal medicine with emphasis on cardiology, so they'll be able to analyze electrocardiograms and other data. Much of clinical cardiology deals with coronary artery disease, a condition which exercise is widely believed to prevent or alleviate, so it helps to recognize the enemy. Ideally, a year of apprenticeship with a college physician and athletic trainer should follow. If this college also retains a sports-oriented podiatrist as part of the medical team, the training would be invaluable. Finally, a year of graduate work in physiology, preferably in a university lab, would round-off the education of the ideal sports physician. At present, no such ideally trained doctor exists, and the afflicted runner must compromise. Often the best solution is self-treatment, using one of the several excellent manuals available, written by running doctors of various persuasions.

When looking for medical advice, don't be put off by lack of authentic "sportsmedicine" credentials, which are, as indicated above, impossible to obtain. You will find no certificate of "Board Certification" for the treatment of runners. Look instead for satisfied patients, sensible advice geared to keeping you as active as possible, and preferably a team approach to each patient. If the podiatrist you consult refers you to an orthopedist for your sore knee, or conversely, if an orthopedist sends you to a podiatrist to treat an "overuse" injury of the knee, you can trust them. If the "team" includes a trainer, a physical therapist, and a general practitioner, you've found a good sports clinic, even if the head M.D. was originally trained as a pathologist, gynecologist or dermatologist!

Conversely, if any of the personnel smoke, are overweight, won't tell you your own blood pressure and/or cholesterol level, leave at once. Chances are that they don't run either, and can't understand your aberration. They might even, after charging you $35, recommend that you take up a "less damaging" sport, such as swimming, or tiddlywinks.

Chapter Eight: The Medical Iconoclasts: Cooper, Sheehan, Bassler and Van Aaken

When I was a neophyte runner, just beginning to read about my new hobby, the names of these now-famous doctors were unfamiliar to me. Like millions of other runners, I first turned to their books when I was injured, or sick, or in need of reassurance and encouragement. Unlike many others in the medical profession, these doctors gave helpful, if unorthodox, advice, and kept me running. I give them full credit for my continued activity, and for many ideas which I absorbed from their writings.

In later years, as I began to travel and give lectures, I came to know "the Running Doctors" as colleagues and friends. My college German major proved unexpectedly useful when I traveled to Waldniel in 1974 and met Van Aaken, who does not speak English. After a few days of intensive vocabulary expansion—since German majors do not include many athletic or physiological expressions—I was able to understand and discuss Van Aaken's often startling theories.

This direct contact and friendship with the vital and warm individuals behind the "famous" names has been a highlight of my own running career. Many other runners, in the past few years, have had the opportunity to meet and talk with doctors Cooper, Sheehan, Bassler, and Van Aaken. I hope that the following profiles will provide a similar sense of personal acquaintance to those who have not yet had such a chance.

Dr. Kenneth Cooper. In 1968, America's soaring incidence of coronary artery disease (resulting in angina, heart attacks or sudden death) began to level off, then decline. Dr. Cooper likes to point to this significant date as the year that his book *Aerobics* was published. The remark is made in jest, but behind it lies the fervent hope and belief that the simple principles discussed in *Aerobics* will, indeed, salvage the national health. Cooper's later books, his years of research in the Air Force, and his formidable research complex/health club/clinic in Dallas all center around the health aspects of exercise. And not just *any* exercise. Bowling and golf won't help your heart. Cooper is the great quantifier, who measures the health benefit of various types of exercise, and expresses them in units. Aerobic units. He coined the word, at least as used in the exercise context. It means, "with oxygen," and the exercise Cooper advocates is the kind that causes you to process, to utilize, large amounts of oxygen.

Before Cooper's "Aerobics" program, doctors weren't very good at prescribing exercise, except to say that they thought the patient would benefit. Everything from gardening to golf was prescribed, with little justification, as it turns out. Cooper found a way to measure what kind of shape you were in, and then prescribe the aerobic units (or points) you needed to get fit. The points reflected an elaborate combination of intensity and duration, for a variety of sports. Looked at from the viewpoint of the weekend golfer, the 30 points/week goal seemed formidable. For a jogger, this goal was easily achievable, for a very small investment of time. So jogging boomed, as people rushed to get "fit" according to the charts. If any one man in this country deserves to be called "the Father of Jogging," that man is Dr. Cooper. Others, like Oregon's famous coach Bill Bowerman, had advocated jogging, but Cooper was a doctor, and wrote a best-seller. You can blame him the next time your car is halted by hordes of marathoners monopolizing the street.

I tried Cooper's program myself. The first attempt was in 1969, when I saw a summary in *The Reader's Digest.* "Test your fitness," it suggested. "Simply run around a track for 12 minutes." That sounded simple enough, so I put on my sneakers and drove off to the track with my husband. He, a former 440-runner, clicked the stopwatch and charged off around the track, while I tried to keep up. Two hundred yards later, I stopped, panting and exhausted after my sprint. I walked most of the 11 minutes remaining. My score was not very high—somewhere between "poor" and "fair." My throat hurt for hours afterwards. Enough of this "aerobics" stuff, I decided. Of course, the chart I had used was for *men* under 30 (later charts were modified by age and sex), but I was still miffed at barely making "fair."

Two years later, as described elsewhere, I started jogging. After some weeks, as I strode into the cafeteria, flushed and fit, for my daily yogurt, a friend looked at me admiringly. "I can see you're a fan of *Aerobics,*" he stated confidently. "What's that?" I replied, having repressed the name of that painful 12-minute session in the track. He explained, and I, eager to learn about the changes my body was undergoing, bought the book. I was fascinated and enlightened. Even now, years of running (and reading) later, I find Cooper's explanation of "the training effect" a model of clarity and sound information. We hadn't learned anything about such physiological *changes* in medical school. I began to grasp the notion that the human body has an immense, untapped potential. Cooper's later books, including the one co-authored by his wife, Millie, extended this potential to subgroups—those who were older, and/or female. By this time, I had gone beyond the "excellent" level for men under 30, and was beginning to look down on 30-point weeks as only suitable for armchair athletes. Cooper's plan suggested women could make do with only 24 points. To me, this seemed a patronizing attitude relegating us to second-class status in the aerobics world. I fought back with 200-point weeks, then dropped the system in favor of a mileage record. But Cooper's *Aerobics* had been fun, especially in the excitement of progressing from one level of fitness to the next, and then on to the chart for the "superfit." I know at least one 61-year-old woman who is at the "excellent" level for men under 30. That must be a heady sensation.

Several years after progressing from *Aerobics* to *Runner's World* in my reading, I met Dr. Cooper himself, at a *Runner's World* shindig. He was the keynote speaker in a week of running festivities. Cooper looked just like his pictures—tall, lean, ramrod straight, with short hair. Having retired from the Air Force, he still looked as if he'd feel more comfortable in uniform. Your typical tight-lipped military man, I thought.

Then Cooper began to talk, and I was shocked. He grabbed the mike like a rock singer, and strode back and forth on the podium, preaching about aerobics. His voice rolled over us, exhorting, convincing. It was hypnotizing. He sounded like Billy Graham. So it came as no surprise when Cooper showed a slide of himself at a Billy Graham rally, where he was invited to speak. The military man had turned into a Bible-Belt evangelist of exercise. It was an amazing transformation.

Cooper can indeed appear to be three different persons in his various roles of runner, doctor and evangelist. His career has been a lifelong attempt to combine the three, and to earn for his system of "health through exercise" the cachet of respectability conferred by scientific backing and medical approbation. Cooper's Aerobics Institute in Dallas performs stringent tests and analyses on thousands of healthy people who participate in aerobic sports. By the mid-1970s, Cooper had gathered data that demonstrated that physical fitness had a protective effect against heart disease—an effect *separate* from the associated beneficial effects of weight loss, not smoking, lower blood pressure, etc. The skeptics in the medical profession were gradually being won over. Cooper, in fact, is now regarded as old-fashioned and conservative by the more avant-garde running doctors.

In later years, I came to know Dr. Cooper better. Our most memorable encounter was in 1976, at a sports-medicine conference in Tahiti. Cooper, his wife, Millie, and I were staff members, as was Dr. "Black Jack" Scaff, Jr., of Honolulu. Scaff rehabilitates heart attack victims by training them to run. Many run the marathon, ultimately. Scaff believes in long, *slow* runs—an hour or longer. Cooper, like his point system, tends to encourage speed rather than distance. If you can't go fast enough to earn high points, you can always go a bit longer, he concedes. But the lines were drawn. I was somewhere in the middle of the controversy; but added the element of female potential. All of us—thirty doctors and four staff—had a most interesting week in the tropics.

There were two daily runs. The Scaff group, running 1 hour or more, gathered at 6 A.M., jogged along the dusty road for 30 minutes, turned and came back. The faster ones, ideally, would catch the stragglers back at the gates, *if* we'd all run an even pace out-and-back. We told jokes and dirty limericks the whole way, and got back in time to shower before breakfast. We also avoided the tropical heat by running at dawn.

Cooper's group, which I also joined—in quest of higher mileage as well as in a spirit of fairness—met at 4 P.M., when more torpid souls were indulging themselves in a siesta. Ten minutes of brisk calisthenics were followed by a pulse check, then a 30-minute run. This was no jog. We were all working hard, pushing those pulses up to near-maximal levels, breathing audibly. The atmosphere had a distinctly competitive tinge, and conversation lagged. My impression was that the younger, athletically inclined jock types preferred Cooper's runs, while recreational runners and women definitely gravitated to Scaff's morning jogs.

Cooper's lectures were fascinating. He talks extremely fast, a phenomenon we jokingly referred to in medical school as "mandibular fibrillation" (fast jaw movement). Every sentence is loaded with facts, statistics, solid evidence. He *has* to talk fast, to cover a fraction of the material he has mastered in years of research. My notebooks were filled with data.

I had, on a more theoretical level, a continuing disagreement with Cooper about women's abilities. His approach was to encourage them by coddling. Feeling that any participation was commendable, Cooper hesitated to demand much. I objected that women have always been led to believe they can't do as well as men, so they don't try. Lower expectations lead directly to lesser performance, and many women never realize their true potential as athletes. During Cooper's lectures, I challenged him on this subject several times, so he ultimately seemed slightly paranoid and avoided the subject of women entirely.

Trying to make my point, I almost wrecked my body. During the prerun calisthenics one day, Cooper had us all do 10 push-ups. "Women should just do knee push-ups, of course," he added as an afterthought, glancing uneasily in my direction. In this case, he was quite right. Women generally neglect their upper body strength and cannot do regular push-ups without practicing and developing the necessary strength. I had been using weights and doing push-ups for a couple of months and had gradually built up from 0 to 5 repeats. But *10!* Forget it; that was double my maximum ability. However, I *couldn't* let Cooper get away with that casual, sexist remark. Calling upon the spirit of Babe Didrickson, I did 10 regular push-ups—for the first and only time in my life. Cooper wasn't even noticing—but I felt vindicated. Also exhausted, but I refused to show it. Off we trotted on our run, during which I recovered slightly, though my shoulders ached for days.

I got a little revenge on another one of our runs, since I was in good shape, training for a marathon. One young jock, who had run with us (breathing hard) to the turn-around, decided to show off on the way home. Eschewing all conversation, he sprinted 100 yards ahead and stayed there. "Are we going to let him do that?" I asked Cooper. Competitive instincts temporarily drained by the Tahitian sun, Cooper wouldn't be baited by the youngster. "You go ahead if you like," he said. So I spurted ahead to overtake young Dr. Stud, who was breathing *very* hard. "Lovely sunset, isn't it," I remarked. No answer. "Listen to the parrots in the trees," I persisted. Heavy breathing, *still* no comment. Then I heard footsteps behind us and turned to discover Dr. Cooper, who had obviously changed his mind about letting a callow youth and a woman finish the run ahead of him. The pace picked up noticeably—we ran 2 minutes faster on the way back than going out. Listening to the breathing, I thought it ironic that the father of aerobics should prefer to run at a nearly *an*aerobic pace.

But Cooper has willpower, and tremendous drive, and doesn't mind hurting—he probably regards the pain as character-building, a form of self-discipline. His point system appeals especially to those who are themselves hard-driving and tough-minded. In fact, "Type A" runners who are time-oriented and compulsive especially appreciate being able to do their daily stint in a fast 10 to 15 minutes. For them, aerobics is a fine program and one they will stick with—if they can avoid a heart attack, the fate that awaits most Type A individuals, according to Dr. Meyer Friedman. Cooper himself is the quintessential Type A, and scorns the suggestion that his running might be harmful.

Many other runners, though, have started with aerobics and progressed, in my view, beyond it—to recreational running, running for enjoyment. Hedonistic running, if you like. They get into shape with Cooper's system, then find new realms to explore. Cooper himself, the pioneer, would be delighted if 75 percent of U.S. Army recruits could attain his "good" fitness level or beyond. His concern is with the health of the enormous unfit population. But the runners who progress past mere fitness, who attain levels beyond Cooper's charts, aren't interested in health so much as self-fulfillment. Running doctors used to such super-fit persons regard anyone who *can't* reach Cooper's "good" levels as a physiological basket-case—the standards seem so minimal, eventually.

Cooper continues his valuable research, seeking to prove to traditional medicine that exercise is good for your health. But while he goes over the territory he helped to explore, patiently backing and filling, the newer medical gurus of running go on to other fields, philosophizing and speculating. Cooper, the original iconoclast, has ended up as the most traditional of the famous "running docs."

Dr. George Sheehan. Like many runners, I was injured rather frequently in my first running years. This was not surprising, in retrospect, since I was doing everything wrong—from lousy shoes to a misplaced emphasis on speed. When rest and/or home cures didn't work, I limped off to the local orthopedist. Again, like many runners, about all I got was a head shake and a gloomy suggestion that I try some other, presumably less arduous, sport—like swimming. "But I'm a RUNNER!" I wailed, practically in tears. "Well, if you keep on running, you'll just fracture something else," was the lugubrious reply.

Then I found Dr. Sheehan, and was saved. Some friend introduced me to *Runner's World* magazine, and I devoured the "Medical Advice" column, month after month. It was the first thing I turned to, in each issue. This Dr. Sheehan had answers to all sorts of plaintive questions addressed to him by grounded runners. Victims of palpitations, diabetes, runner's knee, Morton's toe, stress tests, heart murmurs, sciatica . . . Dr. Sheehan reassured them all. A man of allegedly poor protoplasm, he confessed to having suffered most of the common ailments himself. He had gained a certain perspective about injuries, as well as the limitations of the medical profession. Don't listen to non-running doctors, was his admonition. They have never studied the stresses and strains of the athletic body, nor are they aware of its healthy peculiarities. Listen to your body, use common sense, put inserts in your shoes, and keep on running.

Such advice reinforced my own inclinations, and gave me the courage to explore remedies on my own. Injuries rarely occurred, and only when I had done something excessively stupid. I had learned to carry on the proper dialogue with my body. Thanks to Sheehan's column, my running career prospered. He became my guru, the only doctor who *understood*.

Several years passed before I actually met my guru. His best-selling books, with his portrait on their covers, had not yet appeared, and I had no idea what Sheehan looked like. I suppose I pictured him as a large, bluff (if lean) Irishman of the Boston mold—red of face and hearty of manner. At a podiatric sportsmedicine conference he was to speak at, I craned my neck for a view of the podium. I couldn't pick out the famous Dr. Sheehan. Finally, a small, diffident man with thinning gray hair was introduced as the renowned M.D. It's hard for me to recall my instant of shock, because I now know that Sheehan looks just the way he *should* look. After all, he now writes about his own appearance and body build, not just medical problems. "I am the fox," he says referring to a system of Sheldon body-typing* But for one expecting the lion, the fox can come as a surprise initially.

Sheehan's speech to the podiatrists was primarily concerned with the rather basic role of the *foot* in running, and the then-novel concept that you could treat knee, hip and back pains by correcting foot plant. This focus on the biomechanical causes of pain, rather than the affected joints higher up, was revolutionary in those days. Some podiatrists had been claiming success with the approach, but since their focus is *always* on the foot, they were suspected of bias. But Sheehan was a respectable M.D., and made other M.D.s listen.

Any faithful reader of Sheehan's column was familiar with the foot theme, but I had been unaware of the doctor's gifts as a speaker. He had the audience laughing uproariously. "The guy's a stand-up comic," gasped my neighbor, wiping tears from his eyes. Like all hams, Sheehan requires an audience for his best performances. His writing is often humorous, but with a dry, slightly biting tone. In person, Sheehan adds flavor with his expressive voice and slightly apologetic look. To hear him speak is a delight, even if you've heard him many times before. The quotes—from William James, Emerson, Santayana, Thoreau—recently, from Unamuno—may be familiar from previous talks, but the tapestry of speculation woven around them is different every time.

Sheehan never speaks from slides, or notes. He prepares for a lecture by going for an hour's solitary run. During the run, he gets his thoughts together and decides on the theme for his talk. But once on-stage, communicating with the audience, he is freewheeling. He pulls quotes out of his enormous repertoire and uses them as pegs on which to hang an hour of entertaining philosophy. It's an admirable

---

*For a discussion of body types, see Chapter Fifteen.

performance. Small wonder that Sheehan was a hit on the talk shows that accompanied publication of *Running and Being,* his best-seller. The verbal Irish tradition seems even better suited to him than the written word. Before an audience, Sheehan is truly in his element. He wanders the stage, occasionally tripping over the mike cord (if he hasn't discarded the mike), "just rambling on" about matters that concern runners. Sometimes after some long digression, he rubs his head briefly, glances at the ceiling, and asks, "Now where was I?" But the audience couldn't care less. Whenever Sheehan rambles and digresses, he dispenses wisdom with entertainment.

Despite the despairing glances upward, and the puzzled rubbing of the head, Sheehan is not lost. His talks are remarkably coherent, and manage to convey the message that running is a good thing not only for the health, but for the self and the soul. "Find your play," he urges listeners. "Become an animal, a child, an artist and a saint. Take yourself up to Boston some spring day, run the marathon, and find out who you are." It's heady stuff for the audience.

Sheehan's unassuming, diffident manner seems a bit at odds with his demonstrated ability to move an audience. He is not a theatrical person. Flashy clothes are foreign to him, as is the Werner Erhard look (open-collared shirt, and well-tailored slacks and jacket) favored by most holistic health advocates. Sheehan prefers the nondescript look— comfortable running shoes, faded jeans, an old sweater, usually blue or gray. Sheehan may consider himself a fox by body-typing, but it is not the flamboyant, aggressive red fox he resembles so much as the wily, gray fox of *Aesop's Fables*—the one who leads "a furtive, secretive way of life"—but is also characterized by "resourcefulness and endurance."*

Sheehan's casual outfit makes it easier for him to sit

Running and Being, page 28

down on-stage, take off his shoes and socks, and start instructing the audience. When enough philosophy has been thrown out for consideration, Sheehan reverts to the practical doctor role. He shows his own problem feet, demonstrates "The Magic Six" stretching exercises, examines knees, advises on hearts. Many runners who wouldn't bother writing a letter can't resist a chance to query the doctor, personally, about their *own* knee, or indigestion, or stress test. Sheehan responds patiently and sensibly. During breaks between talks, he is easy to locate—right in the middle of the largest clump of people, almost hidden, sitting down on a step and dispensing advice. If he emerges from the crowd at last, heading out on a run, he is usually again the center of a group—those who want to get to know him on the run. Sheehan never seems to mind; he enjoys talking. He has a large family, and crowds seem familiar, even homey. Asked once if the hectic lecture schedule bothered him, if he didn't get tired of talking to runners, Sheehan just smiled, "I love it," he said. "I'm a ham."

Sheehan recently turned 60. "Now I'm officially 'elderly,'" he stated with satisfaction, gearing up for a fast half-marathon race. To comments that the word hardly seemed appropriate, he countered, "At seventy, you're considered 'aged.'" Then he went out to put the lie to such stereotypes.

Sheehan is in fact an excellent runner. After some collegiate experience in track and field, he hung up his shoes till age 40 when he was "born again" as an athlete. Since then he has run consistently, and often fast, racking up victories in Master's competition and even running a remarkable sub-5-minute mile after age 50. His various responsibilities—as a doctor, father, husband, columnist, author and lecturer—often curtail his running schedule—he has subsisted, at times, on 3 runs a week. But he always persists, and can imagine no better demise than to succumb, at some advanced age, out on the run. "That's the best way to determine what sport or play is right for you," he claims, "whether you're willing to do it on the day you die. I really wouldn't mind dropping dead while running."

Because of this feeling, Sheehan refuses to get involved in the controversies about whether running prolongs your life, helps prevent heart attacks, or lowers blood pressure. Such matters aren't really important, he feels. Only the play, the activity, the joy are important. Lesser doctors, or lesser runners, may shudder. What about the marathoner with a highly abnormal EKG? they ask. "*Learn* from him," replies Sheehan grandly and simply. Certainly don't ground him just because that kind of EKG is abnormal for *non*-runners. Perhaps it's normal for champions. Doctors don't know much about champions, as yet. Who are we to determine what they should do?

These opinions naturally endear Sheehan to runners, who universally hate to be grounded for peculiarities in their laboratory tests. The medical establishment looks rather coldly upon Sheehan's summary dismissal of their expertise. A few years ago, the New Jersey Physician's Board, perhaps piqued by Sheehan's non-medical fame, admonished him for failing to notify them of his efforts at "Continuing Medical Education." Sheehan had to make some hasty phone calls pointing out that he had been speaker/faculty member at more than enough post-graduate medical courses. Bureaucracy was eventually satisfied and Sheehan retained his license.

He is still a practicing cardiologist, with private patients and a hospital position interpreting electrocardiograms. Sheehan could probably get by, in these days of relative fame, on lecture fees and writing income alone. However, he refuses to raise fees to unreasonable heights or otherwise exploit the running community that flocks to hear his words. Claiming that runners as a group are notoriously frugal, if not downright cheap, he continues to live simply.

Sheehan appears to take public recognition philosophically as an interesting, but transient phenomenon. He runs, as he writes, not for fame and recognition, but for himself. Though he claims to be undertrained and in a non-competitive phase, there is a certain gleam in his eye as he discusses his move into the 60-and-over age group. Once the hectic waves of publicity recede, I suspect he will establish new running goals and pursue them contentedly. The sub-3-hour marathon still beckons, and "the flesh is willing."

Tom Bassler, M.D. If George Sheehan's appearance and demeanor remind one of a quiet, friendly and philosophically inclined fox, Dr. Bassler comes across as a rather high-strung eagle. In the same room where Sheehan, hidden in a dense circle of eager admirers, is discoursing on Being, Bassler stands apart, aloof, with bald head and piercing eye, surveying the scene. One waits nervously for him to spy his prey, and pounce.

Beneath his imposing appearance, Bassler is a gentle and humorous man. But opinionated he is, and definitely wild-eyed, possibly even crazed, from the viewpoint of the traditional doctor. A pathologist by profession, Dr. Bassler is the biggest gadfly in the swarm of running doctors. His views on diet, exercise, and lifestyle are so unyielding, outrageous and generally unprovable that he renders traditionalists speechless and indignant. Among Bassler's views: Completing a full-length marathon renders one immune to a fatal coronary thrombosis for at least 6 years; Vitamin C and sunflower seeds (for silicon) will preserve the health of your Achilles tendon *and* your coronary arteries. Slow is better than fast. Eat roughage for longevity. And, the best beverage to consume before, after and during long runs is beer. Take another gram of Vitamin C for each six-pack.

None of these assertions is yet provable, and the medical profession loves proof, and controlled studies. Bassler's flagrant disregard for "proper" studies and analyses, his wild leaps of imagination, his dazzling displays of wishful thinking as he describes the virtues of "natural" peanut butter, yeast and wheat germ, tend to infuriate many other doctors. I believe that Bassler has performed a great service to the American public by his sweeping generalizations about the value of running. Much important research is being undertaken just to prove Bassler wrong. It used to be that any person who died while out jogging was presumed dead of a heart attack. Heads were shaken, sedentary passers-by renewed their vows not to exercise, and the body was trundled off to the mortuary, unexamined.

Now, however, Bassler has declared that a marathoner categorically *cannot* have a fatal heart attack. So now, any such unfortunate has his body minutely examined and autopsied, with slides made available to the medical profession—all in hopes of disproving the Bassler hypothesis. I doubt that any evidence of infarction would shake Bassler's belief in his own dogma. The rare fatal attacks in marathoners, he maintains, must be due to arrhythmias—disturbances in the heart rhythm—resulting from a metabolic imbalance, probably potassium. In Bassler's system, marathoners do not *get* fatal atherosclerotic heart disease. Mere 20-milers, yes, but not true marathoners. Maybe they ran the marathon too fast. They ran 2:40, say, but couldn't have lasted a full 3 hours.

I exaggerate Bassler's stubbornness, perhaps, but he himself is a figure of exaggeration, a bit more than life-size. His reputation as a wild man precedes him. My own first encounter with him was at the 1975 Boston Banquet of the American Medical Joggers Association (AMJA), of which he is an official. I found myself seated next to a fierce-looking, lean, bald man. When his gaze fixed upon me, there were no pleasantries or smiles. "You're Joan Ullyot," said the eagle. "Yes," I replied. "How much Vitamin C do you take?" was Bassler's next question. When I answered, "500 mg." in a small voice, knowing that to be a totally inadequate amount in his view, Bassler stared at me briefly, made a fierce noise, and returned to the conversation on his other side. I had flunked his test.

At later meetings with Bassler, I came to know him better and to appreciate the fine sense of humor that hides beneath his awesome façade. If you encounter Tom during a long run, he is apt to be well into his second six-pack of beer and at his mellowest, singing happily and stopping to photograph whatever scenes catch his eye. Believing that slow, sustained aerobic activity is more healthful than speed and pressure, Bassler has "improved" his marathons from an average of 4:30 to 6 or 8 hours, over the years. He tries to see how long he can make them last, and would rather undertake a 50-miler than a mere 26-miler. Tom complained that he was forced to run a "fast" 6-hour pace in the huge 1978 New York Marathon, because the official ambulance following the race kept bugging him to either speed up or climb onboard. He is in his element in the annual Honolulu Marathon, where the "slow" record is 8:28 and there are lots of 6 to 7 hour marathoners to keep him company.

Bassler is much in demand as a lecturer, since no one else can be quite so eloquent and authoritative in support of running. All health benefits, physical, mental and spiritual, flow from marathoning, he assures the audience. The lectures tend to be rambling discourses on pleasure running, nutrition, vitamins and minerals, woven around an equally rambling but fascinating slide show. Tom will cut from a view of the mountainous Tarahumara Indian homeland, to a close-up of recommended foods (lots of yeast), or a vegetable stand, to candids of lean, elderly former heart patients who have just finished a marathon. Or he will show a Marine in running jersey, cigarette dangling from his lips, and assure listeners that this *pseudo*-runner may have run a 15-miler but there's no *way* he could be a marathoner and smoke. Physiologically impossible.

I am personally grateful for Bassler for supplying me

with the greatest excuse I ever heard for asking people not to smoke in my presence. I used to meet with hostility or blank looks from smokers if I mentioned apologetically that I was allergic or sensitive to their cigarette smoke. Now I say politely, "I'll have to ask you not to smoke, because I'm a marathoner, and the oxidizing agents in your cigarette smoke form toxic oxides with the thirty percent polyunsaturated fat in my body." Smokers are overwhelmed by this elaborate explanation and quickly stub out their cigarettes before I explode.

As Bassler explains in his lectures, in order to finish a marathon, one must train long and eat right so that up to 30 percent of the body fat is unsaturated, versus the average 5 percent. Once you are polyunsaturated, you cannot tolerate cigarettes. If cigarettes don't make you ill, you can't be a marathoner. It's a simple test that could save would-be marathoners the pain of trying and failing.

Bassler is always moving on to new frontiers of health, never content within the limits of old ideas. When I heard him speak recently, he was describing a new diet—for losing weight, that is. "It's simple," he said. "You're allowed a hundred calories for every mile you run." As the audience murmured and calculated hastily that they'd be running 10 miles a day and ingesting only 1000 calories of nourishment—a spartan prospect, but bearable—Bassler continued, deadpan. "Of course, you can't count the first ten miles. You get 100 calories/mile starting *after* the first ten." Shudders and giggles ran through the audience, while Bassler elaborated. "When you're used to eating the way I do, you have to get in thirty miles per day. At the pace I run, I'm out running ten hours a day. People wonder where you are all the time."

Hearing Bassler, they may also wonder at what point practical advice crosses the border into fantasy.

If you wish to hear more of Dr. Bassler's radical ideas, authoritatively stated, you can subscribe to the AMJA

135

newsletter, P.O. Box 4704, North Hollywood, California 91607. He's the editor, and writes or approves all articles personally.

Ernst Van Aaken, M.D. American "running docs" tend to be specialists. They either theorize *or* treat injuries, write books *or* coach. But in Europe, a single man does it all. He is a famous coach/guru/lecturer/author/sports physician/G.P., and women's running advocate, all in one handy package. "He" is the eminent Ernst Van Aaken, now close to 70 years old, who resides and practices medicine in the small West German town of Waldniel. Coincidentally, Waldniel, with a population of only a few thousand, has earned over twenty European and German running records since Van Aaken's arrival in the grim days after World War II. He was recruited to be the town doctor, not a coach, but it's hard to keep an enthusiastic sportsman from preaching. Van Aaken's training ideas, based on physiological and biochemical principles, were quite unorthodox, but his results were excellent. Over the past three decades, his advocacy of high mileage training, always at an aerobic pace, has gained favor. The opposing system—high speed, high intensity, anaerobic interval training—so popular in the 50s, is now in disrepute. For perhaps the first time in his long career, Van Aaken finds himself in the mainstream of athletic thought. But this eternal rebel, not content to sit back and say, "I told you so," has moved on to other battles that wait to be fought. He campaigns for women distance runners, helping them batter away at the doors of the IAAF (International Amateur Athletic Federation, governing body for track and field), and the IOC (International Olympic Committee), who claim to control the sport. And he writes an endless stream of books and articles all aimed at the conventional medical establishment, which still takes a dim view of Van Aaken's favorite "oxygen and exercise" prescription.

Always unconventional, Van Aaken ran off to join a circus when he was a boy. Brought home, frustrated in his dream of being a trapeze artist, he took up pole vaulting as a substitute. He was serious about the sport, even taking his pole along when as a young doctor he was sent to the Crimea during World War II. Van Aaken retained his upper body strength through the years when he struggled to become an endurance runner. Handicapped by a muscular physique, he tried eight marathons before he managed to finish one. Today his arm and shoulder strength are again useful, for Van Aaken lost his legs in an accident, at age 60. Jogging home from work on a rainy night, he was run over by a speeding truck. Sheer grit and determination helped him survive; now, his powerful arms propel him from wheelchair to chair, from bed to bath, and (yes!) from trapeze bar to Exercycle. His energy gives him tremendous compensation for the loss of limbs. After our first meeting, I wrote that Van Aaken "dashed into the piano room to play us a march." "How can he *dash,*" asked a friend, "if he can't walk?" "I don't know," I replied, "but he certainly dashes everywhere, no doubt about it."

I had read about Van Aaken before our first meeting. En route to Waldniel for the first International Women's Marathon in 1974, I telephoned from neighboring Holland. Van Aaken was courtly over the telephone, but I was so nervous to be talking to the famous man, himself, that I almost forgot my German. The next day, the celebrity met U.S. Champion Judy Ikenberry and me in Düsseldorf. A proud man, he insisted on walking to greet us, on artificial limbs which pain him more than he will admit. Instead of the stern-faced Teutonic drill sergeant we had expected, we met a smiling, pink-cheeked and jolly host. Van Aaken was wearing his "formal" outfit, a conservative suit and a shirt carefully buttoned up to the neck—but without a tie. At home that evening, he switched to his more comfortable attire—prosthetic limbs removed, he wore a sweat suit and T-shirt and wheeled himself around his house and library.

Huge tables in the office hold correspondence and books in progress, all in neat but deep piles. The living room table can be quickly cleared of paper and loaded with refreshments for the press conferences and nightly parties that precede the marathon itself. The laboratory is in an adjacent room. Books fill all the available wall space and crowd the well-worn piano. While the rest of the world sleeps, Van Aaken reads. He prides himself on getting by on 2 to 3 hours' rest each night. Like Napoleon, Van Aaken catnaps at quiet intervals during the day—brief 1- to 2-minute naps, from which he emerges alert and oriented.

At this first meeting of European and American marathoners in 1974, Von Aaken seemed as moved to meet all of us as we were awed by him. Besides National AAU (American Athletic Union) champion Ikenberry, Nina Kuscsik and other outstanding running "pioneers" were there. Van Aaken, who reads—and memorizes—race results from around the world, knew everyone's PR (personal record), where and when it was run, and other statistics. We all spent hours telling about distance running in America, while Van Aaken plied us with beer, sandwiches, and training advice. His general advice to "eat little," so that we would be lighter and run better, conflicted at moments with his impulses as host. Judy Ikenberry helped once to hang out some laundry in Van Aaken's garden, while he sat bemused. "Just think, for months—years—I have read about these famous women runners—and now they are actually here at my table and even hanging up laundry, in Waldniel!"

It was entirely appropriate that the world's leading women marathoners should first meet in Waldniel (and later, in 1976 and 1979), in view of Van Aaken's long-standing advocacy of distance running for women. He is convinced, from observation and research, that women have a natural endurance that is hard for men to match. In part, he believes, their superior endurance is related to a higher "active" fat content and a postulated natural ability to burn fat more readily as fuel. Men, Van Aaken speculates, must train over long distances to acquire this ability, which depends on enzymatic adaptations within muscles. Women *may* already possess the enzymatic apparatus and hence do not need the long training runs considered essential for male marathoners.

During the 40 years (1928–1968) that women runners were forbidden to run farther than 400 meters in the Olympics (and not much farther than that in *any* competition), Van Aaken fought against this ban, which was based on the misconception that sprints are less "strenuous" than longer runs. It was thanks to his continued pressure on the European track powers, and to the example of his Waldniel-trained women champions, that the 800-meter and longer distances were finally reintroduced. This first Women's International Marathon Championship was to be a similar demonstration to the world that women are natural distance runners. Although barely tolerated by the IAAF, and not "official," the marathon received enthusiastic support from American "Road Runners" and European "Spiridon" clubs. Germany's own Athletic Federation sent official observers, who were to report back on how (and if) we all survived the "ordeal."

I was team manager/doctor/interpreter as well as the sixth runner for the U.S. As interpreter, I had much to learn, and spent hours closeted with Van Aaken those first few days. My college study of Thomas Mann, Goethe and Nietzsche had not prepared me to discuss physiology, nutrition and training methods in German. And in 1974, my knowledge of track records and times was as minuscule as Van Aaken's is encyclopedic. I had to learn quickly, because Van Aaken likes to toss out numbers: Paavo Nurmi's records in the 1920 (5,000-meter silver medal; 10,000-meter gold) and 1924 (1,500-meter gold; 5,000-

meter gold) Olympics; Emil Zatopek's performances over 20 years later (1948: 5,000-meter silver medal; 10,000-meter gold; 1952: 5,000-meter gold; 10,000-meter gold; marathon gold). The doctor has been to all the Olympic games since 1924, and appears to have memorized all the results—heat times as well as finals. Once I interpreted when Van Aaken was introduced to New Zealand running great Peter Snell (gold, 1960; 1964 [800 meter]; gold 1,500-meter, 1964). Van Aaken expressed his admiration for the triple gold medalist and added, "I knew you would win the 800 when I saw you run 1:46.6 in the first heat in 1960. You were still fresh." "Uh, thank you," replied Snell, "but I believe it was 1:47.2." "No, that was the final," said Van Aaken, firmly. "You see, I know it better than you yourself." He was delighted and Snell was impressed. I was happy just to get the numbers straight.

While being instructed in the necessary vocabulary, from "enzymes" and "carbohydrates" through "heats" and "race courses," I had the opportunity to learn more about the controversial "Van Aaken Method," which has been somewhat misunderstood in this country.

Van Aaken's training theories are remarkably similar to those formulated by ultramarathoner Tom Osler in his classic (1968) booklet, "The Conditioning of Distance Runners." Both advocate long, aerobic runs as a conditioning base, with mixture of fast runs (800 m. or longer) and short sprints (50 to 100 m.) for sharpening. Van Aaken's ideas having been imported to this country with emphasis on the endurance "base," he is often considered the "Father of LSD," which in runners' jargon stands for Long, Slow Distance. In practice, however, Van Aaken gives almost equal attention to the pace-work and speed-work done by his protégés. His training schedules, then, do not diverge in most respects from the better known (in the U.S.) methods of Arthur Lydiard and Bill Bowerman—except that Van Aaken scorns "hill-work."

140

On his first visit to America, in 1975, Van Aaken was delighted to see the influence of "his" theories in some very unlikely places. Visiting a Tuesday afternoon interval-training session conducted by Laszlo Tabori for his San Fernando Valley Track Club, Van Aaken saw more similarities than differences between his own approach and Tabori's. Tabori, formerly an outstanding Hungarian miler and now an outstanding coach, professes to adhere to the "hard" interval methods of his own mentor, Mihaly Igloi—lots of anaerobic work, many repeats, grueling hours on the track. But Van Aaken, impressed, watched Tabori's star runners (including Jacqueline Hansen and Miki Gorman), and explained to me the similarities in their systems. "You see, Joan, there is an emphasis on short sprints for leg speed, and longer distances for fast pace-work and endurance, with ample recovery time. Just what *I* advocate." He politely overlooked the crucial difference—in Van Aaken's system, fast running makes up only about 10 percent of the total mileage—Igloi used speed almost exclusively.

We had feared, initially, that Van Aaken and Tabori would spend the evening arguing over the relative superiority of endurance versus interval training. Instead, they were the best of friends, on a first-name basis, by the time we sat down to a late snack. I, the interpreter, was wedged between them, as affection flowed across the table. "Joan," Tabori would begin, his heavy Hungarian accent draping my name till it came out as "Chone"—"tell Ernst . . ." and he would lean heavily on my right shoulder with a new communiqué. Van Aaken, meanwhile would be tapping my left shoulder for attention: "Joan ("Zhone" in German), tell Laszlo . . ." The evening was quite a success, though the two coaches seldom stopped talking long enough for the poor interpreter (me) to eat.

Van Aaken was not sympathetic toward my lack of supper. He believes in frequent fasting, especially if one is overweight. It's important to remember, however, that this type of diet should be undertaken only under a doctor's supervision or sanction. At 5 feet, 9½ inches and 135 pounds, I definitely qualified as overweight, in his eyes. My weight is merely "normal." Van Aaken recommends a weight 10 percent *under* the "normal" level, 15 percent if you're a serious runner. The best way to lose weight quickly is to starve for a week. That way, you're *sure* that your caloric intake doesn't exceed your needs. For less drastic weight loss, he has developed a rather spartan 14-day system. A sample should suffice: 5 hard-boiled eggs, one every 2 hours (Day 1). One slice of Gouda cheese, 1 slice of whole-grain bread, 1 leaf of lettuce (Day 2). As the above suggests, Van Aaken doesn't worry about cholesterol or fat percentage. Eat whatever you like, he suggests, as long as you don't eat very much of it. And always, you must run a minimum of 10 km. per day, an hour or longer.

The only dietetic "secret," according to Van Aaken, is to keep your weight down. He scorns fads and supplements. Near the end of his American tour of 1978, Van Aaken was talking to the Washington, D.C., Road Runners Club. One of the last questions of the long evening involved diet. "What does the doctor think about bee pollen?" asked an earnest man in the audience. As Van Aaken doesn't speak English, I was again translating: "What do you think about bee pollen," I asked him. "What?" replied the doctor incredulously, *"Bee pollen?"* "Yes," I explained, "some people here take it for special energy." Van Aaken was astounded, but not at a loss. "Tell him," he replied, "that he can eat bee pollen, or rain worms, or SHIT, if he likes. It won't help his performance." Having made this statement in German, he smiled broadly at the audience and sat back, looking like a mischievous cherub. "Do you really want me to translate that?" I hissed at him. "Go ahead," Van Aaken replied sweetly. So I translated, literally. The audience roared with laughter. This famous German doctor wasn't the stern, humorless man they had envisioned.

Later, I learned that I had won a bet for one member of the audience, who spoke German. On hearing Van Aaken's reply, this man turned to his friend, also German, and whispered, "I wonder if she'll translate *that*." The friend bet $10 that I wouldn't, and lost his stake a moment later. Of course, I didn't dare *not* translate literally. Van Aaken is astute enough, and reads his crowds well enough, to expect laughter at the proper places in his talk—regardless of language differences.

Van Aaken may be as famous for his treatment of sports injuries as his training methods. Athletes from many countries visit him, after local doctors have shaken their heads and advised them to take up a less strenuous sport. Van Aaken feels he can restore any athlete to his sport, often within days—provided the patient follows strict instructions. Patients are not coddled. All of Van Aaken's therapies include movement, activity. Whether you have heart disease, cancer, or Achilles tendinitis, you will soon be out jogging . . . "*slowly,* of course," adds Van Aaken. The doctor has written several books detailing his approach to a host of illnesses and injuries. He sought help from journalist/runner Tom Sturak and me translating the title of one, *"Die Schonungslose Therapie."* We puzzled quite a while over that one. "Aggressive Therapy?" "Healing without Coddling?" "Active Treatment?" None of these conveyed quite the fierce approach of Van Aaken's book. We finally suggested "Merciless Therapy" as the most accurate and appropriate. Worried about the reader reaction, however, Van preferred the duller, but more conventional, "Non-Sparing Therapy!"

Many runners can testify to the value of such therapy. Van Aaken likes to recall the visit of American 100-mile runner Natalie Cullimore, unable to run because of a bad knee. Several orthopedists had examined the knee, at considerable cost, and recommended that Natalie return to cycling, her first sport. Undaunted, Natalie flew to Frankfurt, marched up to the airport information counter, and asked where she could reach Dr. Van Aaken. Van Aaken lives in a small town near Düsseldorf, some distance from Frankfurt, and is relatively unknown outside athletic circles. Natalie was in luck, however: the airline information agent was himself a runner. Not long thereafter, Natalie's knee was being checked out by the great man himself. "Merciless Therapy" in this case involved a potent shot ("Tübinger Bombe"), local heat therapy, and, of course—jogging, alternated with walking. Natalie jogged/walked 3 miles the same day. A week later, as a salute to Dr. Van Aaken, she ran the Black Forest Marathon.

I, and many other sports physicians, have learned much from the Van Aaken method. He was the first to insist, forcefully and in the teeth of conventional therapy, that our bodies are constructed for movement and use, and that *in*activity is the cause of most illnesses as well as injuries (when we overtrain parts that have atrophied from disuse). Movement promotes circulation and therefore speeds healing. Except in extreme cases, like certain fractures, casts and immobilization are frowned upon. Total body oxygenation, through jogging, is Van Aaken's favorite treatment for everything from diabetes to cancer. He tells about one man with advanced lung disease, for whom other doctors advised bed rest and an invalid existence. "If you're going to die anyway, better to die on the track—with your boots on, so to speak," was Van Aaken's contention. The patient agreed that he preferred a more active life and/or demise, and took to the local track, walking around it for an hour daily, at first. Years later, he is still out jogging, but has progressed to runs in the woods, even marathons.

In over 30 years, only two of Dr. Van Aaken's numerous patients with heart disease have died "on the run"—and both, he says, were ignoring his Number One rule, "Run slowly!" One decided to test his sprinting abilities, uncultivated since early schoolday successes. The other, against Van Aaken's advice, got heavily involved in Masters track racing, a definitely anaerobic activity. Van Aaken believes that anaerobic running, which entails building up an oxygen debt, is just as harmful—even to initially healthy individuals—as aerobic jogging is beneficial. The oxygen supply is what counts, not the activity. He scorns the belief that slow walking, or gardening, will provide "enough" exercise for anyone. "Each of you consumes one-quarter liter of oxygen each minute as you sit here listening to me," he likes to tell his audiences. "If you get up and go for a walk, or do some gardening, of course you'll increase that— to a half liter a minute. But if you go *jogging*—slowly— you'll consume two liters of oxygen every minute—an *eightfold* increase from your resting level. Do that for an hour a day, covering perhaps ten km. (six and two-tenths miles), and you'll be healthy. You'll make up for the lack of oxygen the other twenty-three hours of the day."

Surprisingly, Van Aaken's 10-km./day prescription matches the 6-mile/day minimum advocated by Bassler, America's own high priest of Long, Slow Distance. It even restores one's confidence in the medical profession to find two doctors who agree.

III: RUNNING ADVICE AND FACTS

Chapter Nine: Family Running

Priorities: Fitting running into your daily life has, in fact, more to do with your priorities than your actual schedule. If it's important enough to you, you make the time—even if you're a busy executive. Conversely, you can lie around on the beach all day, sunning, read all the books you like, and still complain that you don't have time to run. I've heard such complaints—or rather excuses. It's better to recognize them for what they are—a simple reluctance to run. Some people find it "boring," or simply not worth the energy. Don't waste your time trying to convert such non-runners. Smile, send them a copy of *The Non-Runner's Book* for Christmas, and save your energy for your own running.

Lots of busy people run. Dr. John Hutchinson, a cardiologist at University of California Medical Center, was one of my earliest running companions. In fact, he lured me into doing my first 3-miler. "How about doing two miles with us?" he said after I'd been doing a mile for about 6 weeks. Halfway into the run he admitted, "Actually, it's two point nine miles." Hutchinson himself had been a runner for about 5 years at that point, and managed to squeeze in runs after work, between cases in the operating room, or in place of lunch. Once, when we were riding down seven flights in the elevator on the way to the nearby park, we were joined by a young resident clad in green surgical shirt, shorts and running shoes. Since, in those days, anyone wearing running shoes was going out for a run, we asked him to join us on our 7-mile run to the beach. "I only have time for three," sighed the resident. He looked at us enviously. "How do you find time for your runs?" he asked. Hutchinson looked at the resident with amusement, "That's the wrong question," he twinkled. "The real question is, how do we find time for everything else in our lives?"

I made a similar answer once when I was being interviewed in Boston. The year was 1974, when women were still a novelty in the marathon, and a female physician who was going to run "Boston" was definitely newsworthy. Reporters were everywhere. One stuck a mike in my face and asked how I managed to train for such a grueling event (they always call it grueling), work full-time as a doctor, and care for two children and a husband (and, she might have added, a large dog). "It's simple," I answered blithely. "I just put running first and fit work and family in around it." I was unaware that these indiscreet remarks were being televised, or I wouldn't have answered quite so facetiously. What would the people at work think, not to mention my family? But I had to admit, later, that there was more truth than jest in my statement.

This attitude—putting the run ahead of the demands of work and family—may seem extremely selfish. However, almost all serious runners share it. Not just those who train long hours for the Olympics, or in search of records—even the young mothers who get up before their kids and run 2 to 4 miles. This is true dedication—not just to running, but to the deeper knowledge that the activity is essential to their health and good spirits. The justification, of course, is that both work and family benefit from the vigor conferred by a daily run. Enlightened businesses are beginning to realize that a lengthened lunch hour devoted to a run, pays off in better work performance. As for the family, once they experience the grouchiness of a mother deprived of her normal exercise, they practically push you out the door. "Why are you so upset, Mom?" they'll ask if you blow your top over a little mess in the kitchen. "Didn't you run today?" And they pack you off, with dog, into the evening fog.

Families not only don't object to a running addiction, they learn to use it. Once I returned, exhausted but peaceful, after a weekend 20-miler. My 8-year-old greeted me at the door, with apologies. "I'm real sorry, Mom, I'll be more careful next time." "What'd you do, Jonny," I asked calmly from the depths of the couch, my feet elevated, beer in hand. "Well, you know those new poster paints? I had them on the floor next to the paper, and, well, I knocked one over." "Oh?" said I nonchalantly. "Which one?" Jonny hung his head. "The black. But I cleaned it up a lot." I sipped my beer philosophically. "Well, it could have been worse. After all, your rug is brown. Be more careful in the future."

Crisis past, Jonny could hardly believe it, though he had slyly and deliberately chosen the correct moment to confront me. Nothing seems very upsetting after a 20-miler.

Despite support from work and family, time pressures can undoubtedly be tough. Each runner develops her own tricks for fitting in the run. Those who work usually prefer the lunch break, since they then can avoid the calories and soporific affect of a long lunch, and return refreshed after a run, shower, and (if starving) a snack. Others like to run after work. They are then free to take longer runs, and the activity provides a complete break between work and home—time to leave the business cares behind, or work through any problems which may have arisen. Finally, if there's anything resembling a scenic route to work, you can save gas and get in training mileage by leaving the car at home (or along the way) and running to and from the office. Many people who would like to try this hesitate, because of the unavailability of showers. Ron Hill, the British Olympian who used to run 10 to 12 miles each way to his job, solved this problem by taking a "Liverpool bath"—a quick sponge-off in the washbasin. "You Americans take too many baths, anyway," was his opinion. If you have a closet or locker at work, you can towel off and change into clean clothes, and no one will object—or even know. Dr. George Sheehan and other authorities point out that *fresh* sweat is odorless, anyway, so a daily shower when you get home is plenty. Those who smell (usually men) are those who either object to all showers on principle, or who wear the same sweat-soaked T-shirt day after day.

Women who don't work have no problem running, once their children are of school age. They simply have to resist the multiple demands of cleaning, shopping, doctor's appointments, PTA, Junior League, and Scouts, and set aside their sacrosanct running hour. Such women often become the most avid runners of all, because the run is the only time of the day they are insulated against outside demands. They are also the only runners who can carry on a secret life with any success. Some women, unfortunately, have husbands who "disapprove" of their running. This disapproval may be totally irrational, based on fears of neglect and abandonment, or on an aversion to sweat clothes and liniment, or on TV memories of Russian "female" discus throwers.

Nevertheless, the disapproval is there and a woman must sometimes choose between open defiance of her husband's wishes, or secret indulgence of her running "vice." So many women, immaculate in a flowered robe and impeccable hairdo, pack their husbands off to work, and children to school, then undergo a transformation. Off comes the robe, on go the shorts, T-shirt, shoes, and head scarf—and she leaps out the door like Wonder Woman. She returns in plenty of time to shower, fix hair, apply makeup, and hide the sweaty evidence. Some of the more secretive types I've heard of even wash and dry their clothes, and store them out of sight in the basement, before the family returns. If she avoids bringing home trophies, this "closet runner" can escape detection for years. One woman I know routinely hid her ribbons and patches from a disapproving boyfriend by pinning them on a detachable bulletin board in the bathroom. When he came over, she could slip the evidence out of sight without leaving any suspicious gaps on the apartment walls. After a while, this secretiveness became a bit of a strain, so she replaced the disapproving beau with a running boyfriend. Since the changeover, she has become a much better runner. It *does* help to have support and admiration from those around you.

I am sometimes astounded by how well some women can do *without* such support. "Dipsy," a 35-year-old marathoner from Arizona, is limited to training when her husband is at work and her children in school. She built up her mileage, secretly, as high as 120 miles—in 6 days! Her spouse was home on Saturday, but on Sunday, Dipsy got an hour "off"—and went for a run. Generally, Dipsy runs according to the time available. If she has 2 free hours, she runs 2 hours. If she has 3 hours, she runs 3 hours. It adds up. When does she find time to eat? inquired a solicitous friend. No problem, replied Dipsy. If she feels hungry, she just takes along a peanut-butter-and-jelly sandwich and eats it in the first mile. To me, this revelation implies a cast-iron digestion, to match Dipsy's determination.

Conflict arose once over the "Boston." Dipsy's initial suggestion of a trip to the Hub in April was rebuffed. So she applied (in secret) and was accepted (in secret). Her husband, she felt, would have forbidden her to go. She dealt with this possible roadblock by surprise attack. The Boston Marathon is held on Monday. Sunday morning, Dipsy announced to her astonished husband that she was leaving town, had arranged for a babysitter, and would be back Monday night.

Dipsy then flew off to Boston, ran an "official" 2:58 (including the starting-line delay) and returned to an irate, but outmaneuvered husband. He could do little when faced with a *fait accompli*. He did neglect to ask Dipsy how she'd done. "Can this marriage be saved?" One hesitates to predict.

The running opportunities are admittedly far more limited for the mother of preschoolers. A supportive husband, or a child-care network, or a reliable babysitter are necessary to free such women for longer runs. For shorter runs, one can do without sitters by several methods. Early risers can get in a couple of miles before the husband and babies are up. A nursing mother can reliably catch 20 minutes of quiet time after the early-morning feeding, while baby is sated and somnolent. An alternate method is to bundle kids and toys into the family car and head for the nearest track—preferably at low-use hours. The toddlers can scamper around in the infield, or build sand castles in the long-jump pit, while Mom gets in a couple of miles on the track. The only real limitation here is the boredom that track running often induces. It's hard to think your own thoughts or get into "The Zen of Running" while keeping one eye on the kids. My own effective limit in this situation (I used to try it on weekends, when I was without a babysitter) was 8 to 10 laps—a couple of miles.

Running also is harder to fit into your life when it becomes an obsession. Anything beyond an hour a day, or 50 miles a week, becomes at least partly obsessional. This is far more running than is required for health alone. High mileage is usually either a response to mental stress (job- or marriage-related), a way of achieving peace of mind, or a drive "to excel." This desire for excellence seems to be much more widespread than the traditional "competitive nature." The runner is competing against herself only, testing her capabilities, exploring her potential. If she trains hard enough, she could even become a world-record holder. So a woman who has been moderately successful on "reasonable" mileage, under an hour a day, may often test herself with 80-mile, 100-mile, 140-mile weeks. Until she breaks down, she's going to see what she can accomplish.

Now, running 140 miles a week isn't quite so terrible as it sounds. It translates to 20 miles a day, usually split up into two 10-milers. That's about 70 minutes, twice daily. Physically, not all that tough. Swimmers, gymnasts, and ice skaters put in much longer hours. But that's a lot of time alone, a lot of time moving, and it costs mental as well as physical energy.

Marty Cooksey, who ran record times off of this high mileage, confessed to a certain reluctance that would wash over her every morning. "You wake up and know you've got to go out and do your 10- to 15-mile morning run. Sometimes it's tough."

Most runners who train at such levels have *time* for other things during the day, but find themselves lacking the energy. They spend the interim between training sessions recuperating. Most do not have steady jobs, or full-time ones. They look for part-time employment that will help them conserve their energy for the championship efforts. I have tremendous admiration for the few who have families and manage to take care of them. If I run over 70 miles a week, my kids have to subsist on TV dinners, and the house is in permanent disorder.

152

In practice, obsessional running is a cyclical phenomenon. Typically, a woman who has been training
regularly (Phase A) will begin to have some success at local
races, if she ventures into competition. Curious to learn
just *how* good she may become, the budding star trains
even harder, and has even more success. In Phase B, her
goals are reset at higher levels. From wanting to finish a
marathon at any pace, she now aims for Boston. Once a
veteran of that race, she aims to break 3 hours. Then she
sets her sights on local and national records. Prodigious
amounts of training and self-discipline may be involved.
Injury or another form of breakdown (mononucleosis is
common) eventually interfere. The erstwhile star is
grounded, or trains less. If she still races, she finishes back
in the pack. It can be very discouraging. But take heart,
this is only Phase C! Most runners eventually progress to
Phase D, which resembles Phase A—running as a hobby,
running for enjoyment. Phase E is again highly competitive and successful, like Phase B, but differs in that the
woman has by now (we hope) acquired both experience and
maturity, and may achieve her running goals without the
total obsession needed earlier. For most older women, a
balance must be struck, over the long term, between the
demands of running, family, and work. The choice must be
made by each individual, according to circumstances.

Back in 1974, when the first International Women's
Marathon Championship was held in Waldniel, Germany,
some of us "lone wolves" got together for the first time and
compared notes. U.S. team members Marilyn Paul, Nina
Kuscsik and I were all mothers, with jobs, in our mid-30s.
Over a post-race (or was it pre-race?) bottle of Rhine Wine,
we explored the question of priorities. Why did we all
choose, at that time, to expend so much energy on our
running, fitting our other concerns in around the edges of
our training schedules? The only consensus we could arrive
at was that, for now, we were *good* at our running—good
enough to be on the national team, running world-class

times. Later on, with our lives more organized, we might wish for such opportunities but find the world-class runners had left us behind. It would be too late. *Now* (1974) was our time, we should utilize it. And we did. As we see the world records plunging down at distances from the marathon through the 10 km. (possibly out of our reach even if we trained like those young upstarts), we're happy to have had our time.

Another point to remember about running cycles is that if a woman is temporarily "down" in Phase C or D, you can't count her out. Observation, in fact, suggests that women who move on to Phase E are formidable competitors who are likely to improve on their previous best marks (P.R.s or Personal Records). Nina Kuscsik returned after years of back trouble, and ran 2:50 for the marathon at age 39, versus a 2:55 P.R. years before. Marilyn Paul improved from 2:57 to 2:49. Miki Gorman ran 2:39 (down from 2:46) after time out for a child *and* her fortieth birthday. In the younger age group, Mary Decker, an international star at the 800-meter distance by age 14, returned to national prominence and new records at age 20—following years of obscurity, when everyone said she was "washed up."

Don't count on time and age to eliminate your running rivals! Women runners can always come back, if they choose to. If other matters take precedence for a while, ahead of running, the ability to excel is not lost. It glows there constantly, like a well-banked fire, and may suddenly flare up, just when you're beginning to feel sorry for the "aging star." That "has-been" you were secretly looking forward to beating may actually pass you up in the homestretch. It has happened many times—even to me. My old running buddies Marilyn Paul and Nina Kuscsik, have left me in their dust in their "up" phases. I've paid them back on the next swing of the cycle. If we ever are all "in synch" in Phase E, there will be some superb competition for us all.

Should Children Run? There has recently been considerable controversy about the subject of children running—should they or shouldn't they? Basically, the question is absurd. Anyone who has watched or brought up healthy kids knows that they run *all the time!* Dr. Van Aaken once followed his 7-year-old son around with a stopwatch during the son's routine after-school ball games. He estimated that the boy, and his playmates, ran a total of 9 kilometers (almost 6 miles), interspersed with 400 stops, in the course of a 2-hour game. Dr. Van Aaken was exhausted from the effort of tracking the kids, but they themselves were untiring, and only came inside because of the approaching dark (and their homework). During the game, the individual distances run were at the most 40 to 50 meters—not long enough to build up any oxygen debt. The running in play, then, was essentially aerobic.

What most people *really* mean when they are "against" children running is that they don't feel it appropriate for children to *race* long distances. They see, as in the Avenue of the Giants Marathon a few years ago, a 4-year-old boy "finishing" the race, after running with tears streaming down his face and being urged on by his parents. Or they read a father's story, entitled "My Son, the Running Prodigy," all about a 10-year-old's tearful attempt to break the 3-hour barrier in a marathon.

I would agree that these extreme examples should not be emulated. In my own experience, 4-year-olds have no natural interest in running from Point A to Point B. They'd rather stop and climb a tree, or splash in a puddle, or watch the ducks. After a pause, urged on by their parents, or imitating them, they will resume their jog. But this childlike running, so full of joy in the surrounding wonders, is not compatible with any kind of "racing." The parent who hopes for a fast time for her little one will be frustrated. Worse, she will feel dark urges to "push" the kid a little more, exhorting him or her to run farther. This

155

is the fastest way to kill the spontaneous pleasure children normally have in running—let them do it their way, and only as much as they want.

The older child, say 8 and above, is a different animal. If she is interested, she can maintain basic conditioning and strong legs by regular running, at a time when her classmates may be starting to become sedentary (TV, weather and homework all help to encourage inactivity). If running is a favorite recreation, or one shared with family members, this youngster may even choose to run marathons. The distance is no great strain for a well-conditioned child, and chances are she will finish ahead of many adults who have trained assiduously, but whose bodies are still feeling the effects of many sedentary years. You may see a well-trained child crying in the later miles, but don't jump to the conclusion that she must be the victim of heartless "Little-League" parents. The last miles of a marathon are usually painful for *any* runner, but most of us are too "grown-up" or embarrassed to let our tears show. We just grit our teeth; ignore the leg stiffness, and run on. Kids grit their teeth, cry a bit and run on. If they're running by choice, you can't stop them. John and Mary Boitano, parents of "prodigies" Mike and Mary Etta, who started marathoning at age 6, used to try to persuade their children to quit. No way. The kids insisted on finishing— not to please their parents, but for their own self-esteem and personal goals. Even young children can set themselves important goals. I feel the job of a parent is to help the child establish reasonable goals and help them to train appropriately.

In practice, this is not so easy as it sounds. My younger son, Jonathan, age 10, ran to school several times a week— a distance of 3 miles. Once in a great while he would join me in a 7-miler. Then he decided he'd run a marathon. I discouraged this notion firmly, pointing out that his total distance run, in a good week, was 9 to 10 miles, totally inadequate as marathon training. I wouldn't let him tackle

156

the marathon distance without proper preparation. He pleaded; I remained firm. He began to nag. Every time I entered a marathon, he popped up at my elbow and said, "*PLEASE,* let me run it, too?" Eventually, I grew tired of being nagged and let him enter the Napa Valley Marathon. Somewhere around 15 to 20 miles, I figured, he'd find out for himself the realities of a 26-mile race. He'd hop on the "straggler's bus" and decide to train better next time.

Little do mothers know! I finished the race in 3:02, collected my clothes, refreshed myself, and looked for Jonathan, who presumably would have arrived by then on the bus. Not finding him, I was puzzled. Could he actually be out there, still *running,* more than 20 miles into the race? My eyes filled with tears at the thought of the agonies my little boy must be suffering. I watched for him at the finish line, with a mixture of apprehension and pride. At 4:22, Jon appeared—not limping or in tears, but smiling and running strongly. He sprinted past a few of his agonized elders, crossed the finish line to a rewarding round of applause, and disappeared in search of a lemonade. When I caught up with him, hugged him and asked about the race, he was blasé. "Oh, it was fun," he said. "But I had to walk a little. Can I run Avenue of the Giants next month?" Later, when we arrived back home, Jonathan dashed out to play football till dark.

In a similar vein, I recall seeing a team of kids, ages 9 to 12, from San Francisco's Pamakid Club, compete in the grueling 24-hour relay. In this freaky event, the ten team members take turns running a mile in a specific sequence, for an entire day and night. Adults are successively weary, cold, stiff, and exhausted. They collapse on sleeping bags between turns on the track. The young Pamakids, however, spent their spare moments in a lively baseball game, often dropping mitt or bat to dash off to the track, run a mile, and return.

I tell these stories not to encourage relaying or marathoning on minimal mileage—I *still* oppose it—but to point out that children are incredibly resilient, by adult standards. They can get away with lots of stunts that would ruin older bodies. Kids trip, skin knees, fall off bikes regularly, and rarely, until the advent of the skateboard, did they break anything in the course of play. If running is approached as play, they will not hurt themselves. Unlike many adults, children have enough sense to walk when their bodies tell them to, and to stop if the game, to them, is no longer worth the candle. Parents can give moral support and physical aid (water, sponges, etc.) but should refrain from urging on their children beyond sensible limits. If the motivation doesn't come from within, the child does not belong in a race. I do not believe that any 4-year-old has the desire and self-motivation to run a long race. But many older children do have these internal drives, and should be allowed to explore their limits.

Some orthopedists and pediatricians have expressed concern about the purely physical effects that running long distances may have on growing bodies. They point out that some marathoning kids are in the rapid growth phase that precedes puberty, and worry that constant "pounding" may damage the epiphyses, the growth centers at the end of long bones. Will juvenile marathoners end up as midgets? Does 70 miles/week of training lead to a 50-inch teenager? All I can say is that a few individuals who have run that much since age 8 or 9 (sometimes even younger) are now in their teens, and are towering above their parents, like normal teenagers. Many of the girls, who were "super-stars" at age 11 or 12, have had to make a difficult readjustment to their new, more mature figures. They are heavier, taller and relatively less muscular at 16 than at 10—and they are usually considerably slower, too. The psychological effects of this physiological slowdown may be profound, but there is no evidence of any harmful *physical* effects from long-distance running at an early age.

The potentially adverse psychological consequences of

early serious running are hard to predict, though there has been plenty of head-shaking by observers. One has to beware of making uninformed judgments. One reporter wrote disapprovingly about the parents of a cute 6-year-old he saw running a marathon—or so the reporter thought. The father, running alongside, was congratulating his son on completing 8 miles, and saying, "we're almost at ten, now, that's wonderful."

What the reporter didn't know was that the 6-year-old's *mother* was running that marathon, and her son had leapt in to run, too. The father then had to run to keep the child company—neither had run before. It was a 5-lap course, and after the first 5-mile lap, the father tried to get his son to stop—enough is enough. Feeling fine, the son started out on another lap. The father, swallowing his pain, followed along with encouraging words—hoping 2 laps would satisfy the kid. The 6-year-old finally stopped, proudly, at 11 miles, thus saving his father much grief. The reporter should have written a piece admonishing kids to take pity on their decrepit elders!

I was criticized myself for allegedly "forcing" my sons to run. I'd like to clarify my original public statement, which was apparently misinterpreted. I do "insist" on their running (or walking) to school, a distance of 3 miles. It's far more healthful, in good weather, to go on foot than to take the bus, and I feel strongly that everyone in America— young and old—should be able to propel themselves 2 to 3 miles on foot without making a federal case of it. If we can't condition ourselves to that level of fitness, we'll end up a nation of helpless creatures. In the course of future millennia, our legs will atrophy—wither, and fall off—all from disuse. So my kids, to avoid this fate, run to school. I run with them and generally carry one of the bookbags. Our dog comes along, too, and helps pull us up the hills by her leash.

In the beginning, naturally, my sons complained loudly. They saw a classmate backing out of a garage across the street, riding in state in the back of his mother's capacious station wagon. "Please, Mom," they begged, "let us get a ride with Bobby. He gets driven to school *every day*." I fixed them with an unsympathetic glare—"Bobby is *fat*. He'll probably have advanced heart disease by the age of thirty. I care too much for your health to let you ride." Squelched, my boys complained no more—until the next day! Eventually, despite complaints, they came to enjoy the jog/walk, and they certainly got into better physical condition than most boys of 10 and 11. I consider this amount of "pressure" on children to be acceptable, psychologically as well as physically. It's like teaching them to brush their teeth, or pushing them to get their homework done.

Beyond the 2 to 3 miles that promote physical fitness, however, I think kids should be left alone. If they want to run more, if that's an avenue in which they can excel, and which they enjoy, I think it's fine. I would much rather see a child get involved with long-distance running, even marathoning, than go out for competitive track and cross-country seasons at the same early age. Even boys who compete in high school have traditionally wound up hating the sport, because it's associated with too much pain. Wind sprints and hard races, on inadequate background training, are still the experience of too many young runners, even in our more "enlightened" era of training. How much better it is to see young boys and girls running freely through the woods, enjoying the motion, talking, and "getting in the miles" for long-distance racing. This kind of running should be completely voluntary, and a coach should only provide guidance and training advice, not hard workouts. There's plenty of time for tough training when childhood is past.

The *willingness* of even very young runners to train hard, to do heavy interval loads, and to compete, contributes to the second major psychological problem that may result from early racing. This is the phenomenon of the "burned-out" 13-year-old, the disillusioned ex-runner.

160

Many can withstand pressures from parents and/or coach, but not from within themselves. The athletic world is full of ex-swimmers and ex-gymnasts in their teens. Once they were on top of the world, then they "grew up" and couldn't keep up their early success. Or, having achieved "success," they admitted they hated the sport and never looked at a pool again.

We see a few of these bright, brief careers among young runners, too. Physiologically, as Van Aaken points out, 10- to 12-year-olds are superbly suited to distance running. Their heart volume is larger, relative to body weight, than at any other age—a "strong motor" in a lightweight frame. Their surface area is also relatively large, an advantage in warm weather. And anyone who has ever been passed by a knee-high kid during the hilly "Dipsea" race knows that children, for some reason, are superb hill runners. Perhaps because they have no fear of falling. If the advantages of size and physiology are combined with proper training, the result can be devastating. Young Mike Boitano won the Dipsea race 2 years in a row, at ages 11 and 12, and his sister, Mary Etta, won it the next year, when she herself was 11. Laura Craven, a superb young Eastern runner, placed in the top five or six finishers in several national women's runs when she was 11 and 12, striking terror into the hearts of women old enough to be her mother—or grandmother.

The problem comes in trying to adjust to a larger body and an initially slower pace, after puberty. Fame is fleeting, and this can be a hard lesson for the very young, who may have based their entire self-image on athletic prowess. They may have to redefine who they are. Given the problems that all adolescents encounter in their search for identity, imagine the extra burden of feeling like a has-been, or an ex-child star! I would prefer, myself, to see running among youngsters kept low-key and personal, rather than becoming a road to fame.

Children, of course, are impatient, and a year can seem

to them like an eternity. If you remind them that most top runners have achieved their peak after about 10 years of training, you may have a group of *ex*-Olympic hopefuls on your hands. But more positively, those who go on running without having the carrot of "world records" for 8- and 9-year-olds dangled before them, will be true runners. They will have found, at an early age, the inherent value and joy of physical activity undertaken for its own sake—as play, rather than as a means to fame and fortune. It's a lesson many adults have to re-learn.

Runner and Dog.   Runners can relate to dogs basically in two ways—as nuisances and as companions. We are all familiar with the nuisance dog, who startles innocent runners with loud and sudden barking, or growls threateningly on the pathway ahead, blocking progress. Even a non-hostile canine can be a nuisance if he absentmindedly wanders across your path and trips you up. Dogs often appear totally oblivious to their surroundings. Their minds, or noses, may be elsewhere. Charging along a path after their master, or a fancied rabbit, they sometimes don't notice runners till a second before impact. Then, startled, they blunder right into you as you sidestep to avoid them. When following their noses, dogs appear to have poor eyesight.

An overtly hostile dog can be best diverted by (a) voice—an enthusiastic "*Nice* puppy!" or "Good boy!" throws them off balance; (b) a rock—if you don't have one to throw, even the act of stooping down and pretending to pick one up will suffice; (c) a well-planted kick. But be careful here. My well-aimed (I thought) parries usually miss the target completely and I'm more likely to land on my bottom than to teach the dog a lesson.

Far more important, however, is the companion dog—who generally qualifies as a family member, and thus merits inclusion in this chapter. Most dogs, if trained gradually, can develop into excellent long-distance runners. Breed and size seem less important than enthusiasm and conditioning. The main advantage to having a larger, "endurance"-type dog—such as a Labrador, Husky or German Shepherd—is for its deterrent effect. Even if your family Lab, like my Jenny, has a sweet, friendly disposition, and goes out of her way to avoid a confrontation with a Chihuahua, potential muggers won't know this. Any huge dog, even without slavering jaws, will generally intimidate them, by appearance alone. They'll wait for the next victim, who may be out walking the family Yorkie. No one is afraid of a Yorkie, no matter how stouthearted the little fellow may be; so if protection is important where you run, choose the larger breed.

Training for distance running is best started around age 1. Remember that your dog runs much farther than you do, getting in a kind of canine "fartlek," or "speed-play." He dashes ahead, follows scents, takes side excursions up hills, stops to leave a message, runs to catch up, drops back to search for straggling family members, and generally charges around in circles while you're moving in a straight line. In the beginning, all this activity will tire him quickly, and he may lag far behind you coming home. Dogs have no native sense of pace. If you wish to instill such a sense, you'll have to run him on a leash. He'll drag you along the first mile, you'll tug him back the last—but you'll be exercising your triceps muscle, and he'll be getting into condition. Personally, I prefer running on trails, and dispensing with a leash, even if it means a longer workout for the dog.

Dogs, like people, seem to progress best when brought along gradually and not overstressed. Start with shorter runs—3 to 5 miles—and when Rover is no longer lagging behind, or will still charge off in the last mile if he spies a cat, you can extend the distance. My own dog seems to do best on a hard/easy schedule. Running 10 miles every other

163

day suits her better than a daily 5. She is always eager to go, but seems more energetic if she's had a day off. Be extremely careful about running your dog in the heat—they cannot sweat to cool themselves like humans, and can easily die of heat stroke as they faithfully try, panting, to keep up with you. Even in San Francisco, which is usually cool, Jenny (a Black Labrador) visibly wilts on a sunny day. It's best to leave your dog at home on days when *you* feel uncomfortably warm. I realize that this implies a summerlong layoff for dogs living in the midwest; think of it as the off-season, and resume regular training *gradually* as cooler weather comes. Dogs decondition just as fast as humans.

Humans, of course, take much longer to get into shape, initially, than the average dog. Perhaps you have seen those well-meaning owners who drive along in their cars, letting Rover chase them and thus get in his "daily exercise." Obviously, if the dog needs exercise, so does the owner. It's strange how many people are conscientious about their dog's health needs, while they neglect their own. The dog is always grateful, but can't communicate that he would rather run *with* his master (whom he views as "pack leader") than be "exercised" alongside the car.

Dogs will follow their masters anywhere and are so loyal they can hurt or even kill themselves in their attempts to keep up. Once, when I was training about 70 miles/week, about half of them with Jenny, I took her along with me to high-altitude running camp, as a special treat. The first few days went great—we ran together everywhere, and Jenny loved the new and exciting smells. But I noticed she was sleeping a lot. After a week, we went on a 16-mile road run to a lake. It was a warm day, and with a few miles to go Jenny started to hang back, limping. At the lake, she cooled off with a swim, but she couldn't run more than a mile the next week. Her paws were swollen and sore from the hot asphalt, and the long miles. Unthinkingly, I had doubled Jenny's mileage in a week—a dumb move for any human, and irresponsible for a master. Jenny would have been justified in biting me. Instead, she just looked at me apologetically and thumped her tail as I rubbed liniment on her tender paws. Moral: keep track of your dog's mileage, as well as your own (and beware of hot pavement).

Use common sense: for safety's sake alone, a leash is advisable when running along the roadside. A well-trained dog who usually follows closely in your footsteps may suddenly dash out after a cat, or be startled into the path of a car. My own dog hates sprinklers and has on occasion dodged away from the unexpected water spray, right in front of a bus.

Dog owners must observe a certain etiquette. Dogs are generally unwelcome on group runs, since they have the habit of stopping suddenly to sniff or pee, thus tripping up anyone behind. Only a dog's owner can smile benignly when this happens. Dogs at races are even worse. Dashing along madly in pursuit of their masters, they can overturn several competitors in a crowd. The only exception would be a long race where the crowd thins out quickly and the dog "heels" well. The most famous canine competitor is Ed Jerome's little dog Shelly, who has finished over thirty marathons with her master and has a P.R. of 2:44 (not quite as good as Ed's—he ran *his* P.R. without her). Shelly, a star in her own right, stays out from underfoot and finishes races to loud cheers. At her running club's annual Awards Night, Shelly won a box of "People Crackers" as Dog of the Year. She was thrilled. "Her favorite brand," explained Ed.

Most dogs will enjoy themselves best on solitary trail runs with their master. They can amble along, enjoying the smells, and rest when they feel the need. Races have led to the early, sad demise of several pets—in the excitement of competition, the owners lost track of their dogs, who were run over while searching around for the lost master. Or, even more cruelly, they died of heat stroke from running too hard to keep up on a warm day. If you really care for your dog, leave him at home when you race.

A word about nutrition: running dogs need a constant supply of fresh water, and lots and lots of food. Like all runners, they tend to become sleek and lean—also hungry. Before I started running regularly with Jenny, I felt she was getting a bit soft and fat. So I switched her to Fit-&-Trim, the high bulk, low-calorie dogfood. Months later, when Jenny was up to 25 miles/week, I noticed she was eating constantly, going through bags and bags (the 25-pound size) of dogfood, and leaving huge mounds of excrement all over the backyard. When I complained that Jenny's Fit-&-Trim bill was bankrupting me, a friend looked astonished. "Joan," he pointed out, "*You* may need Fit-&-Trim, but Jenny certainly doesn't." A switch back to regular dogfood quickly solved the problem—for once. Jenny got enough calories to supply her running habit, without going through pounds of diet dogfood.

Like humans, dogs can quickly become addicted to running, and they show withdrawal symptoms clearly. After 2 to 3 days of inactivity, a running dog turns listless, mopes around the house, acts lethargic, and may bark nervously at imagined noises. Such a dog needs a quick 5-miler to restore circulation and zest. Often, as we charge out of the house after Jenny has had an enforced layoff, I'm being pulled along, my leash arm extended. Neighbors wonder who is running whom. And often, as I drag myself unwillingly out of a chair, pull on my running clothes, and shuffle out of the house on a run I would rather skip, just in order to give Jenny the workout she craves, I wonder that myself. She has me well trained.

Chapter Ten: Training

Countless books have been written on the subject of training, and I have listed some of my own favorites in the Bibliography. My own first book, *Women's Running*, gives detailed training advice, and I have no inclination to repeat myself here. However, since all training is a combination of certain basic elements, and since many people still seem confused about the purpose of these various elements, a brief review of principles may be in order.

All "training" aims to condition the body by gradual, progressive adaptation to higher levels of stress. The body is almost infinitely adaptable, given time and patience. If you apply a stress (or workload) regularly, the body adjusts so as to accept the stress easily. Once this adaptation (training) has taken place, a further, slightly greater stress can be applied, and the body adjusts again.

Basic Principles. Two basic principles help in this training process—(1) regularity—the stress should be applied at frequent intervals, not just on weekends, and (2) rest—a recovery day or two between stress loads allows the body to adjust faster. This is the physiological observation that underlies the popular hard/easy training patterns.

For a beginner, then, a weekly schedule incorporating these principles would include jogs (or jog/walks) of 2 miles every other day, with a mile'walk on "off" days. At the Honolulu Marathon Clinic, whose leaders believe in more rapid progression, beginners jog for an entire hour on the 3 "stress" days, and rest completely the other 4 days. World-class runners, using the same hard/easy principle, may run 15 to 20 miles on "stress" days, and recover with comfortable 10-milers on alternate days. The basic methods are identical, only the details of distance or time vary. To show how dramatically the body can adapt, I like to recall that in my first year of running, my longest run was 7 miles, from the gym to the beach and back. This was a supreme effort, and I pushed myself to the verge of exhaustion the two times I did it. By 1974, 3 years later, that same 7-miler was my "easy recovery run." The course hadn't changed, but I had.

Once a runner has progressed to the intermediate or advanced level, she can begin to play around with the other elements of training, while maintaining the basic hard/easy pattern. No one should progress to a more stressful level of running until her body has adjusted to the present level. If your legs hurt, if you have insomnia, a cold, or excessive fatigue, you have not yet adjusted to your current stress level. Wait till you are perfectly comfortable at one mileage/training level before starting something new.

If you are running simply for your health and a sense of well-being, there is no need to progress past a fitness program into competition and heavy training. A half-hour daily, or a 2- to 3-mile run, is all anyone really needs to feel healthy and energetic. Non-competitive types can be perfectly content at this comfortable level. Senator William

Proxmire, one of the nation's foremost fitness advocates, has run 5 miles (to work) each day for years, and feels no urge to run more, or to enter races. This is perfectly all right. I admire the Senator for resisting modern Marathon Mania, for not being swept up in the competitive tumult that now rages through U.S. cities.

Many of us, however, both women and men, enjoy the adrenaline rush of competition. We like to explore our limits, our self-imposed concepts of what our bodies can or cannot do. Racing can add a certain spice to the daily life of a runner. Certainly it is much easier to get out and run on "lazy" days if you are training with a competitive goal in mind. But you should be aware that by racing, or by setting the marathon as your ultimate goal, you are flirting with the danger of overtraining, injury and competitive obsession. Know what you're getting yourself into if you choose to run long, or race.

Now, for those who have been sucked into competition and heavy-duty training, there are ways to run faster and farther. The three basic attributes you want to develop are endurance, strength and speed. Putting these all together, you arrive at what Arthur Lydiard calls "stamina," the ability to sustain a fast pace over a long distance.

Contrary to coaching principles of the 50s, you don't achieve stamina by going out every day and running fast over long distances, or by going out on the track and doing wind-sprints (short, all-out runs) to the point of exhaustion. Stamina is best developed by concentrating on each element separately, and in a specific sequence (see the following section on "Peaking").

Endurance is built by going on long runs. "Long" generally means twice your average daily run—a 4-miler if you usually jog 2 miles, a 20-miler if you're a racer averaging 10 miles/day. The "long" run is most conveniently done on the weekend, and once a week is plenty. Its sole purpose is to build endurance, not speed, so take it

169

easy. Run comfortably. Your leg muscles and enzymes will adjust best if you stay aerobic, talking during the run. Don't *race* the long runs. Avoid competitive companions.

Strength means leg strength. Unless you're a sprinter, there is no need for upper body strength. You develop leg strength for running not by doing leg extensions on the Nautilus or Universal Gym, but by lifting your weight up hills. (Nautilus exercise apparatus is a special kind of weight machine, used exclusively in health clubs. Universal Gym is a competitor to Nautilus; it's the same kind of thing. Both should be used under supervision in a gym.)

Lydiard has a whole system of hill running—with bounding, leg extension, ankle spring, and knee lift all emphasized in various phases. However, you don't have to worry about these variations unless you want to. Any way you run up hills will build leg strength, as will hikes over mountainous terrain. If you don't have hills where you live, you can substitute other "resistance" work to develop leg power—running in dunes, or flat, soft sand, or water, or into the wind. Obviously, if you're working on strength, don't just incorporate the resistance training into your long runs, or you'll end up exhausted instead of strengthened.

Speed is best developed after you have built up endurance and strength. In your first years of running, speed will improve naturally as you run more. As an intermediate, the easiest and most enjoyable way to improve speed is by racing. Short weekend races are available in most areas of the country, by now, and give you an excuse to push harder than on everyday runs. Go ahead, let it all hang out, see how fast you can run when you're working hard, verging on the anaerobic. It will probably hurt, unlike the daily runs, but you may surprise yourself by how much faster you can move. And you'll get a ribbon or T-shirt, maybe even a medal, for your "speed workout."

Frequent racing usually makes daily training seem so slow, in contrast, that you can run faster, comfortably, in

170

training—if you want to. But it's best to keep a clear distinction between *racing* pace and *training* pace for any given distance. Otherwise, your daily runs become like races and may either spoil your enjoyment, or leave you with no extra energy for the weekend efforts. I generally train at least a minute/mile slower than I race. I'm usually urging my running companions to slow down (especially if they are male). Some are disgruntled, then, when I dash past them in races, after telling them to slow down all week. The answer, of course, is simple—I'm well rested, and race enthusiastically. They run hard every day, and are worn out.

If you want to improve your speed, and don't have many local races, you can substitute a weekly interval workout (repeated fast runs, interspersed with jog-rests) on the track, or "fartlek" along the roads and trails. "Intervals" are more for the compulsive types who like to time themselves and measure progress by the stopwatch; "fartlek," which means "speed-play," is for free spirits, who enjoy short bursts of faster running over various distances, during a regular training run. You can structure your own workout on track or trail, according to your own needs and preference. The idea behind all speed-work is to get your body accustomed to faster movement, to develop bio-mechanical efficiency (leg-speed) and the metabolic machinery to tolerate high oxygen demands. Some degree of pain is inevitable in acquiring speed—unlike recreational running, fast running is *supposed* to hurt. A good part of racing is learning how much pain (in legs and chest) you can endure and still keep running. It's not really very pleasant, but some people enjoy the challenge, and it's the only way to set records or win gold medals.

It's always fascinating to me to observe how quickly speed, in terms of biomechanical efficiency, can be developed in an aerobically well-conditioned runner. After 2 or 3 track workouts, each season, times improve dramatically, as you get into the swing, the rhythm of faster running. Runners who try for speed too soon, who do interval-workouts before they build up their aerobic capacity through endurance training, tend to reach a plateau of speed quickly, and don't improve thereafter. It's important to use the proper ratio of speed to distance, as well as the right sequence. Most authorities agree that not more than 10 percent of your total mileage needs to be done fast, in order to race well. From doing 50 miles/week, you can run a good 5-mile race weekly, or do up to 20 fast 440s on the track.

Peaking. When Lasse Viren became a double gold medalist (in the 5000 and 10,000 meters) for an unprecedented second time, in the 1976 Olympics, everyone naturally wondered about his training "secrets." Viren confuses and astounds many people by his ability to reach peak condition in the Olympics—just when it matters. In between gold medals, he runs well, but isn't the same invincible competitor of Munich and Montreal. A few weeks after the Olympics, Viren can again be beaten.

Viren's mastery of peaking caused uncomprehending sports commentators to mutter darkly about "blood doping" and other tricks he might be using in Montreal. But there was no trick. Viren put in more mileage than any of his competitors in the final months before the Games, and used speed-work, or "sharpening," in a deliberate fashion, to ensure that he would be at his best the week of the 5000 and 10,000 finals.

The real surprise, according to Viren, is not that he trains this way (so as to peak for the Olympics), but that no one else seems to. The knowledge of how to train so as to peak during a specific week is public domain; all runners and their coaches have access to it. But very few seem to trust this method, or to depend on it.

The art of "peaking" is one of the most valuable contributions of New Zealand coach Arthur Lydiard. He describes his methods in detail in his (out-of-print) classic, *Run to the Top*. You can also read up on the system in his more recent *Running the Lydiard Way,* or in Ron Daws' American adaptation of the training sequence in *The Self-Made Olympian.*

To "peak" for a particular race, whether it's the Olympics or your local Bonne Bell 10 km. for women, you have to make out a schedule. If you've been running for several years, you should allow about 4 months to go through the entire sequence. If you're a beginner, the buildup takes longer—at least 8 months—and I would recommend, in fact, that you not try an intensive Lydiard program till you've been running and acquiring racing experience for over a year. The stress on legs and general conditioning is simply too severe for novice runners, who risk ending up injured, or sick.

Once you've decided on your "target" race, you simply count back from that date and allot the necessary time to each type of training—4 to 6 weeks of "sharpening" just before the big race, 4 to 6 weeks of hill training before that, and 6 to 12 weeks of mileage buildup before the hill training.

Thus, looking forward from your present state to the target race, you first work on pure endurance, then add hills for strength, and finally step onto the track to develop biomechanical efficiency and leg speed on top of all your stamina. Lydiard's contention, which revolutionized training methods, is that the specific *sequence* of endurance—strength—speed must be followed in order to achieve any runner's full potential. Mixing the three together, by doing high mileage, hills, and speed-work during the same weeks, or racing during the endurance phase, or just doing speed, speed, speed the entire season, won't work. The runner will either peak too soon, winning the early season races but losing the big ones, or she will be injured, or she will be

173

merely a good runner who never lives up to her full promise.

"Peaking" is in some ways a harder concept for road runners to grasp than for track athletes, who have a definite season and championship meets. The road runner is sorely tempted to run hard all year long, to blast each race, not to "lose face" by having an off-season. The runner who wants to peak in November, say, should be doing high mileage, at a relatively slow pace, in July and August. Her endurance will be building, but she'll be slow as molasses. If she steps on a track at this time, or enters a 10-km. race, she should expect to feel sluggish and run poorly. It takes so much ego strength and confidence in the Lydiard system to accept "poor times" with equanimity in the early season, that most women should simply avoid all speed-work or competition in this phase.

Similarly, if you're training with a bunch of people who are not on the same peaking schedule as you are, you have to resist running *their* workouts instead of your own. If you do hill workouts with the gang before you're ready for them, you'll simply get injured. So you must know what phase of the buildup you are in, and resist running with the crowd if it conflicts with your own schedule.

You can see why "peaking" is more complicated in practice than in theory. It is here that a certain amount of pigheadedness can be valuable. If you're not the stubborn, dogmatic type, you might find a coach valuable, one who is also schooled in Lydiard's methods. Then, all you have to do is what the coach tells you. If you insist on racing the 10 km. during your mileage buildup, probably against your coach's advice, the coach can help you look at it just as an early season time-trial, so you won't be discouraged. Or when you try to combine high mileage weeks with 2 tough hill-workouts, your coach can order you to be sensible and cut back.

This kind of coaching advice can be invaluable for the younger runner, who may not yet have sufficient experience or trust in the method to devise and adhere to a "peaking" schedule. Older or more knowledgeable women may resent being ordered around or overruled by a "coach" and prefer to seek out a good "adviser." The adviser can send you workouts or training suggestions from a distance, but only makes comments when asked, and isn't around to check up on you or crack the whip. Ultimately, your motivation must come from within.

Transitions. Yesterday, during a relaxed 8-mile run, my right Achilles tendon gave an unexpected twinge. Unexpected, because never before have I had trouble with my Achilles. It was the one part of my anatomy that had been spared during the past 8 years.

However, thanks to my past experience with injuries, I didn't panic. If you get a pain out of the blue, like that, it usually means something in your routine has changed. So I began the analysis which becomes second nature to most runners, after they've been injured a few times. Speed wasn't the culprit—I was jogging along comfortably at my usual "lazy-day" 8-minute/mile pace. The route wasn't new—I run that same trail several times each week. I wasn't excessively tired, or stiff, or limping—all factors which can lead to a significant change in gait, with resultant pains. So, by process of elimination, I found the culprit that was irritating my Achilles. Alas, it had to be my beautiful new shoes. A $40 model. The latest thing.

Earlier in the week, I had tried on my new shoes with delight. They were a perfect fit, wonderfully cushioned and springy, and lightweight. All in all, a great training shoe. I wore them that day on a 5-miler, then a 10-miler, then, the third day, tested them out on a 20-mile run. Though the shoes did not allow me to sail through the 20-miler without effort, neither did they ruin a toenail (mine are always in a condition of disrepair or regrowth). Two days later, today, my Achilles is sore.

Do I now have to discard my beautiful, expensive new

Super-Doopers? Fortunately not, though maybe I deserve a $40 reminder of my stupidity. Because by now, I should have learned a basic lesson of running: *make transitions gradually*. Whether you change shoes, or running surface, or training methods, or mileage, you should proceed with caution, or you are courting an injury. The injury may bother you for months, whereas it only takes a few weeks to make changes carefully.

It's hard to realize the profound effect on the body produced by very subtle changes in stress. A worn-down shoe can tilt your foot a fraction to the outside. Not very important in itself, but multiplied by thousands of steps per mile, the total effect can be literally tons of extra stress along bones, tendons and joints not yet accustomed to the load. Your body will always adjust to new stress, but it needs time. A day of recovery after each new stress can be helpful. Thus, if you're switching over to new shoes, don't wear them every day, as I did. Even if you've traded in an old, stiff, heavy pair of tennis shoes, not designed for running, for a lightweight, superbly constructed running shoe, and are overwhelmed with joy at how comfortable they are, don't throw away those sneakers just yet. Use them on alternate days, for a week at least. They may be awful, but your body is used to them. It knows what stresses to expect.

The same principle applies when you introduce new training stresses, either quantitative or qualitative. After years of experiencing and observing injuries, I am convinced that most can be prevented by more attention to transitions. Many injuries, especially in new runners, come after a season of road-racing success. This is because the novice racer, encouraged by competitive victories on relatively low mileage, wonders what she might do if she trained harder. So she ups her mileage from 50, say, to 70 miles/week, adds some interval workouts, and begins to "get serious." A few weeks later, she is sidelined with shinsplints, or a pulled muscle, or a stress fracture, or even mononucleosis. This pattern is classic. If you're aware of it, you can avoid it by being conservative. If you're racing well and feeling strong, stick with your successful training schedule. If you modify it, don't increase mileage by more than 10 percent a week, or introduce more than one weekly hill or interval session.

One woman I know, excited by a great marathon improvement on her second try, decided it was time to introduce some hill running to her program. When I saw her a few months later, she was nursing a chronic knee pain which had cut her mileage in half. She had abandoned plans for another marathon that year. Reviewing her history, I suspected the hill training, but Louise didn't agree. She was accustomed to running 10 to 12 miles, and the "hill workout" was really only 4 miles over hills, plus 6 flat miles to the base of the hill and back. I suggested she *drive* (heresy!) to the foot of the hill, and back, next time she started hill work. The hill portion in itself was stress enough, until Louise adjusted to it. Afterwards, she could add the extra flat miles. By keeping hill stress and mileage stress separate for a few weeks, she could make the adjustment painlessly the next time.

If you've never done track workouts, don't run over to the local high school some day and do 20 × 220, fast. Try 4 to 5 × 220, or 2 to 3 × 440 (one lap). You'll be surprised how your legs will protest even this moderate workout, because they are not used to fast running. Much more knee lift is needed to run fast, and you'll probably be sore and stiff in the groin area for a couple of days after your first speed-work. I notice this whenever I return to fast striding after a month or more of just putting in easy miles along the roads. It's helpful to remember the words of a famous sprinter, who said, "A track man is like a flower. He has to bloom again every Spring." Expressed more generally, you cannot shift from one level of running to another instantly. First, you have to allow some time for building up.

In their enthusiasm, runners often forget that the body

has physical limitations. It cannot immediately follow flights of imagination or the demands of willpower. Give it a few weeks. Cut back your total mileage when you start hill training, or speed-work. Limit your mileage when wearing new shoes. The older you are, the more important these precautions become. Children and teenagers can get away with a lot of fast transitions that would leave their parents behind in broken-down heaps. Young bodies are not yet locked into patterns that resist change. Older folks have as much potential for change and achievement—they are not limited physiologically in what they can accomplish—but they do have to take more time with transitions.

Hope for the Reluctant Runner.

What about the women to whom running does not come easily? "I've been doggedly putting in fifteen-minute miles for months now!" wrote one reader, plaintively. "Some of us don't find it so easy to get out there."

I admit, it's far easier to form a running habit if you start, as I did, jogging through a beautiful park and smelling the flowers. A daily jog through the Bronx, dodging cars and muggers, inhaling exhaust fumes, and enduring the jibes of passers-by, requires much more inner fortitude. I doubt that I myself would have begun running under such circumstances. If you saw the TV show, "See How She Runs," starring Joanne Woodward as a middle-aged schoolteacher who takes up jogging, you were treated to a picture of true determination. The heroine persisted, undeterred by darkness, muggers, injuries, dogs and hecklers. I couldn't understand how her run (always too fast, always breathless and apparently painful) compensated for all the hassle. Most women would have quit and taken up a less painful sport.

If you wish to enjoy running, you should try to make the circumstances of running enjoyable. Choose a flat, scenic, beautiful area for your jog—suburban roads or a park, not city streets or a track. Don't start out in midwinter, through the slush, or try to get in shape by slogging up Telegraph Hill in San Francisco. Always use the talk-test, so that you go at a pace that is comfortable for *you,* not for others. Wear loose-fitting, lightweight clothes, and well-cushioned shoes, so that you can feel light and free. Don't wear tight pants and other garments which restrict breathing, or thin shoes that jar your whole body with each step.

Beginners need extra moral support and impetus. In the early days, try to run with friends, at a specific time. Even on days when you feel too lazy or harassed to go out on your own, you're more likely to mobilize yourself to go with "the gang." They expect you, and it's a great opportunity to relax, gossip or compare notes. Later on, when you're self-motivated, you may prefer to spend this quiet time alone, relaxing or working through problems on the run. But as long as the run itself is work, rather than relaxation, it's better to do it with company.

Avoiding boredom while you get into shape is fairly easy, if you see real improvement within weeks. Excitement and improved physical well-being will keep you going. It is necessary to remember that *any* woman, if she jogs regularly, will improve to the point that she can do a 2- to 3-mile run comfortably and easily. And a short, 20- to 30-minute run, 3 times weekly is sufficient to keep you in good aerobic condition (as determined by Dr. Cooper's charts), as well as to improve your lipid (fat) metabolism dramatically. The reduction in serum triglycerides (fats) in those who run about 8 miles/week is almost as striking as that found in hard-training marathoners. In other words, even if you're still "slogging" along at 15 minutes/mile, you are getting many of the physical benefits of running. Speed is far less important than effort and consistency in training. You can be content with your half-hour every other day—as long as you keep it enjoyable. You don't *have* to do more, or go faster.

But what if ambition lurks beneath the surface of this

contented "slogger"? Perhaps she would *like* to go faster, enter some races, excel—but is discouraged because she's not making progress. The miles still seem to take 15 minutes each, and still feel as hard as in the beginning. What is going on here?

It's important to remember that "improvement" can be measured in several ways. You can keep putting forth the same effort, and go faster as you get into condition; or you can keep going at the same pace (15, 12, or 10 minutes/mile), but find the effort easier and easier. The sensation of greater ease would be reflected, physiologically, in a lower "exercise pulse" rate and faster post-run recovery to a pulse of 100 or less. Instead of being out of breath, you'll be chatting easily. In order for this "training effect" to take place, you must run at least every other day. You can't get the effect with one weekend and one midweek jog, or keep improving if you take a week or two off when work gets too pressing. Regular, consistent, but moderate efforts will lead to progress.

If you are following all the rules, training consistently and "doggedly," and do not improve by any of the above criteria, chances are that something is not quite right physically. Nine out of ten times, a woman in this situation is anemic—generally due to iron deficiency. Occasionally, the problem is more complicated—a congenital heart defect, an undetected infection or a hormonal imbalance. Any individual, man, woman or child, who trains consistently and does *not* achieve the appropriate "training effect" should consult a sports-oriented physician.

Though every healthy person will respond to regular training with measurable improvement, this does not imply that the improvement will be identical for all. People are individuals, genetically and physiologically different. No two sets of fingerprints match, nor do physiological profiles. Women with the body-build, lung capacity, and muscle type most suited to long-distance running (see profile on Judy Fox, page 75) will get into shape almost overnight—the activity exploits their natural talents. If you are overweight, or stocky, or large-busted, not to mention anemic, flat-footed, or a smoker, you may struggle for years to achieve the 8-minute mile which the "natural runner" can do—untrained—the first day out. Console yourself with the thought that if you were both thrown into the sea, you could swim happily to the nearest island, whereas the lean "runner" type would shiver and sink like a stone.

No matter what your natural physique, or how poor your starting condition, you can improve. The heart, lungs and muscles are all quite trainable. The time required, and the absolute magnitude of the change achieved, are the variables. The goal is first, as Dr. George Sheehan says, to "be a good animal." But as he points out later on, "You'll be your own kind of animal"—whether it be a mouse, a fox, a lion, or a hippo. At least, you can try to become the "best of species."

Chapter Eleven: What to Wear

The woman runner used to be in a quandary when setting out to run. What could she wear that would be warm (or cool) enough, wouldn't chafe, could prevent bouncing, and still look decent? Cut-off blue jeans were popular for years, or baggy gray sweat suits, but the former chafed and the latter definitely lacked grace and chic. Men's shoes were okay, if your foot wasn't too narrow, but men's running shorts just didn't suit the female build.

Fashions in Running Gear. Fortunately, times have changed. Jogging outfits are stylish, colorful, and comfortable. They are available to fit all female builds, from sylphlike to voluptuous. Some are much too nice to actually jog in. I'm thinking of the $80, soft velour outfits which no one would dare call "sweat suits" anymore. Sweat would ruin them. Even "jogging suits" or "warm-ups" would be misleading. I think the really chic togs should be clearly labeled "Après-Jog" attire.

Among women, nylon seems to be the most popular material, with soft, stretch terry cloth a close second. Several lines of running clothes are now designed by women runners, who know precisely what women want and need, and won't sacrifice comfort to chic. The new running clothes are functional as well as attractive. And the market is booming.

Color Coordination. In California, the availability of colorful running gear, and the wide choice, has led to a new concern among the women runners—they want to be color coordinated! If you wear green shorts and a blue top, you'd definitely complement them with a pair of blue-and-green shoes, and socks with blue trim. Generally, the choice of outfit is determined by the shoes, which in turn are dictated by the terrain. If the run is to be 10 miles on trails, you'd have to wear a waffle-type shoe, and your only pair may be, say, gray and blue. Shorts, therefore, would be blue, the shirt gray, blue, or green, and ankle socks one of the above. One could not appear in red shorts with yellow socks and an orange shirt. It just isn't done. After a while, such color clashes offend the eyes and bring reprimands from fellow runners.

The only drawback to this color fetishism is that shoes are often coveted for their color mixes rather than for cushioning and comfort. And a pink T-shirt, otherwise very attractive, may languish in a drawer unworn, because it wouldn't go with navy/red or blue/yellow shoes, not to mention yellow shorts.

California may be ahead of the rest of the country with regard to color coordination. Certainly, in the Boston or New York marathons, no one seems to mind shocking his neighbor's visual sensibilities. And gray sweat suits can still be found in parts east. One woman who lives and runs in "mellow Marin" county, north of San Francisco, complained that people *stared* at her when she went for a run in Cambridge, Massachusetts. "I was wearing my usual clothes," she explained, "my dark blue/light blue Nike sweats (it was cold), matching white/blue TRX-Comps, white socks, blue hair ribbons, and in case it got warm enough, a matching T-shirt, and people looked at me as if I were some kind of *snow-bunny!* They couldn't believe I could look that matched and actually *run!*" Cambridge residents, according to this woman, still favor torn sweatshirts, faded pants, and muddy shoes—and they are even inclined to wear different socks on right and left feet, *neither* of which goes with the shoes. One suspects that some kind of reverse snobbism must prevail in Cambridge, Massachusetts. No one, insists my Marin friend, could be that unmatched by accident.

The classic feminine concerns with appearance and fashion may pop up unexpectedly, and from the male viewpoint, inappropriately, in training sessions. Our own West Valley Track Club women's coach, a young marathoner named Darryl Zapata, found this out after several weeks of group workouts. The women had turned out gamely for tough hill drills and time-trials in cold, wind and rain, never complaining. Then one Tuesday, since half the team had run a marathon 2 days earlier, Darryl decided to substitute an easy "fartlek" run over trails for the usual pace-work on roads. It had been raining and the trails would undoubtedly be muddy. Darryl hadn't considered this aspect, but his suggestion of a trail run brought an immediate and loud protest from the women. "Trails!" said Irene. "They'll be muddy. And I'm wearing my white shoes!" Judy pointed out that four of the ten women present were indeed wearing white shoes while two others hated to get their canary-yellow Nikes muddy. "You should have warned us, Darryl," she said accusingly. Darryl stared at us in disbelief and exasperation. "Well, you can *WASH* your shoes afterwards!" This suggestion didn't mollify Pat, who grumbled that her car would still get dirty if she drove home with muddy shoes. Our coach was heard to sigh, "Whoever told me that coaching women was just like coaching men?" However, in the end, we yielded to Darryl's point of view and ran happily through the mud for an hour—and washed our shoes later.

This brings me to a useful tip for cross-country racing. Many runners hesitate to take the most direct (and muddiest) path, trying to avoid soiling their shoes/clothes as long as possible. Better to go roll in the mud *before* the race, so the damage is done. Then you can run out aggressively and take an early lead. You can always shower and clean up, but there's no way to win a cross-country race and still end up looking like a fashion plate.

Some male reporters have done a great disservice to women runners by commenting on appearance, which has no relevance to racing performance. After the famous Russian distance runner Lyudmilla Bragina ran a world record for the indoor 3000 meters at Madison Square Garden in 1974, one AP newsman managed to corner her for an interview. Did he ask about her tactics or training? Not a chance. His article stated only, "She looked a sight—flushed face, wet hair sticking up in spikes." I was appalled. No one thought of describing the appearance of any of the male runners of that evening—none of whom had set a record. Imagine an article about Bill Rodgers or Henry Rono written in similar style. "Billy (or Hank) was breathing hard and looked a sight—face all covered with sweat, *dripping* wet actually, tank top wrinkled and hanging over his shorts," etc., etc. Any reporter who covered men's sports in this style would be laughed out of the profession.

Obviously, appearance is important to both men and women runners; we all like to be attractive. A colorful running outfit with matching shoes can boost a woman's self-image on the run, just as a man likes to show off a good build. But these matters are secondary or even inapplicable to the racing situation, and women are just as oblivious as men to peacock displays during competition. Any woman who finishes a race calm, unsweating, and with hair unruffled, has not run close to her limit—and will certainly not set any records, world or personal.

The Burning Bra Question.   The appearance of thousands of new woman runners on the roads has finally been noticed by the bra manufacturers. It's about time, frankly, that someone took note of our need for good underpinnings. For years, we have had to make do with the various inadequate commercial models available, or go without, an uncomfortable proposition for most of us. Nothing was designed with the active sportswoman in mind. In 1979, however, several leading bra companies jumped into the competition for the runner's dollar by coming out with special "Running Bra" models. But just how good are these bras, and do they meet the real needs of the women who are asked to buy them?

The search for the perfect bra—that non-visible, but essential part of the female runner's ensemble—is one that concerns women even more than the search for the perfect shoe. In part, this anxious concern must stem from the Myth of the Sagging Bosom. Bra companies, echoed by girlie magazines and surprisingly even some woman doctors, proclaim authoritatively that "jouncing" will invariably lead to—horrors!—sagging breasts. They make dire references to "ligaments" that can be stretched irreparably if you don't wear the proper support bra.

As I have stated repeatedly, this myth has no basis in anatomical facts. I was trained as a pathologist, and can assure you that the so-called ligaments are merely bands of fibrous tissue that do not offer any "support." There are no built-in ligamentous bra-straps that can stretch or snap with bouncing. Instead, the breasts are supported mainly by their own content of glands and fat. "Sagging" occurs

186

because of age and hormonal changes, which reduce this supportive filling. Sports are not the culprit.

Nevertheless, the motion of running does cause considerable up-and-down bobbing of the breasts. This can feel distinctly uncomfortable (and looks it). The larger the cup size, the greater the momentum, and hence the discomfort. For the sake of comfort, rather than fear for their figure, most women with more than an A-cup will choose to wear a bra. Those with smaller problems can rejoice, and get along with Vaseline or a Band-Aid over the nipples, to prevent chafing—the only *real* hazard from going braless.

For the bra-wearers, which is the bra of choice? This question was asked in the locker room following the 1977 Women's National Marathon Championship. If anyone knew, surely these women did, reasoned *The Physician and Sportsmedicine* magazine, which conducted the survey. But, of the twenty-seven women interviewed, all but four wore a bra during the race, and none was entirely satisfied with her own model. In fact, some couldn't even recall it. Frances Caldwell, the interviewer, wrote me that she found the results ". . . really crazy. They were all opinionated about what they wanted to see in a sports bra, but they didn't have the slightest idea what they were wearing."

Frances interpreted this to mean that "since their need isn't great, their interest isn't great." My own feeling is that since none of us has yet found the ideal bra, we don't focus on the brand names of inadequate makeshifts.

Most of the marathoners *did* agree on the characteristics they would like to see in an ideal bra. In runs longer than 8 to 10 miles, chafing is the major problem. So first of all, the bra should have no potential friction parts—no metal fasteners, hooks, loops, Velcro or wires. Preferably, no raised seams at all. It should be an all-stretch, molded-cup model, pulled on over the head, made of a soft, comfortable material such as cotton or nylon knit, but still giving

187

enough support so that bouncing is restricted to a comfortable level.

Obviously, the support (generally reflected by the percentage of spandex) should be greater for the C and D cups than for the A and B. Equally obviously, most marathoners are a B cup or smaller. Researchers at the Aerobics Institute in Dallas have found, in fact, that cup size is the best single indicator of body fat content in women runners. They have not yet found anyone with less than 18 percent fat who was troubled by excessive mammary size. Perhaps lean women who are amply endowed do exist, but don't become runners because they can't find the proper bra. Write to the researchers in Dallas if this is your case!

Some women I know are reluctant to train hard and lose body fat for fear of losing their "figure" too. But a small decrease in cup size (usually only one notch) can be offset by building up the pectoral muscles with push-ups and similar exercises.

Back to the ideal bra: there probably is no model which could suit all runners from 32 AAA through 40 DDD. Even spandex won't stretch that far. But two basic models should cover the territory adequately, one for the "competition" sizes (sub-B) and one for the "joggers." Since I first listed the features runners look for in a bra, several models incorporating these suggestions have become available in running stores. My own favorite now, recommended by many women who wrote to me, is a Danskin bra—either their all-nylon dance model, or the polyester/cotton leotard bra. These are supposed to fit everyone up through 36 C. Except for slight chafing under the front seam in very long runs (20 + miles), I have found these bras very comfortable. A bit of Vaseline over the offending front seams even prevents the 20-mile chafing.

For the more amply endowed, who until now have suffered in quiet with their underwire bras or ace bandage wraps, there is the new innovative "Jogbra." Designed by two women runners in Vermont, this bra is supposed to work like a jockstrap, by "holding its contents close to the body." All "hardware" has been eliminated and all seams are stitched to the outside. While this bra, with its wide bands and straps, is a bit too confining for my own taste (and needs), it should be a real boon to those with C and D cups.

What are the big bra-makers coming up with to support women athletes? Unfortunately, all the big-name models I have examined thus far are obviously not designed by runners. They are the traditional bra, with hooks, rings, and seams that rub, simply modified with new materials, etc., to "meet the needs of the active sportswoman." While these bras can be quite comfortable for an hour or so of active sports, they are not suitable in the long run. All those potential friction points become actual irritants. The seams are stitched on the inside, for a neat appearance at the expense of the runner's skin. A loud protest from the runners should be heard. Look for the runner's bra made by Formfit Rodgers, supposedly designed in conjunction with New Balance, the running wear company, to be modified first, if NB has as much influence as it should.

Those who cannot find the Jogbra or Danskin models locally may choose to order Sears "Step-in Sports Bra" from the handy Sears catalog. While not perfect, this bra at least is a pullover type without hooks.

I look forward to the day when the running-wear people design and market their own models without relying on the giant companies that manufacture bras, who are rather too set in their ways. Their products are designed for the 99 percent of American women who are more concerned with their appearance in a sweater than their performance in a marathon. Runners have special needs, which are more likely to be met by Nike (they could market "The Bra with the Swoosh") or Adidas (naturally, a three-stripe model) than by Maidenform. A final suggestion: like the optional blue Jogbra now available, all bras made for runners should be made in opaque fabrics, color coordinated with shoes and shorts. Then we, like the men, could casually discard our T-shirts in warm weather and feel chic rather than embarrassed.

Shoes. Several years ago, when running was still in its infancy, I suggested that runners in search of a bargain check out some of the "cheapies" sold at Sears, Penney's and similar stores. If you knew what features to look for, you could often pick up the equivalent of a $30 running shoe for a third the cost—in fact, less than it would cost to resole your old favorites.

I no longer feel that bargain-basement shoes have anything to offer the runner, whether beginning or advanced. This is because even the best of the "cheapies"—those that were lightweight and flexible, with adequate cushioning—have been left miles behind by the newer models of specialized running shoes on the market. Virtually every large company offers at least one model which is a "class" shoe, worth the extra cost in the stresses averted from feet, knees and body.

Naturally, I myself have not been able to test all the new models available. Over 100 models were reviewed in the latest *Runner's World* survey. Still, my room looks like a shoe junkyard, littered with thirty or so pairs I'm actively running in during any season. Non-runners have a conniption when they see this display. They tend to think that a couple of pairs of "sneakers" should be plenty for any runner—after all, I'd have to have a spare pair to run in when the other pair is being washed, or dried or repaired.

I patiently explain that there are different shoes for different purposes. I need a training pair for short trail runs, one for longer trail runs, plus their racing equivalents. Then, there are the shoes for running on pavement: short runs, long runs, and races. A special lightweight marathoning shoe, the advertisements claim, can save you over a *ton* of weight lifting during 26.2 miles of striding. Of course, some of that weight saved is at the expense of cushioning, and each runner has her own individual compromises to make, depending on running style, lightness of movement, etc.

So you can see that 20 pairs of shoes are not excessive, though spartans can get by on fewer. It also indicates to some extent the enormous market that manufacturers of running shoes are competing for. Twenty million joggers, at least three pairs of shoes each, every year . . . you figure it out.

With so many new and different models available, and with my own limited sampling, all I can do is indicate, again, what features to look for in a good shoe, and some of the models that I consider the best. This is a very individual evaluation. Bear in mind that my own favorite models may not fit your foot at all, and may be too soft or too hard for your own comfort. My best advice would be to try out as many of the recommended models as you can find before making your decision. At $40 or more a shot, it pays to be choosy!

I also want to make it clear that I am not a consultant or adviser for any of the shoe companies. I happily accept any and all shoes that are given to me (as do many well-known runners) to evaluate, and I give in return my honest opinion. If the shoe seems too rigid or heavy to me, I'll let the company know, and you won't find it listed here. My own built-in bias is toward good cushioning and light weight.

Here then are my *personal* favorites in the general categories of training and racing shoes.

Training: Nike LDV (and "Daybreak"), Nike Tailwind, Brooks Hugger, Vantage and Texan, New Balance 320 (road) and 355 (trail), Adidas TRX Trainer.

Racing: Nike Elite, Adidas TRX Competition, Adidas Marathon-80, Brooks Texan, New Balance Cross-Country.

And here are a few more details about these shoes (and

companies) to help you evaluate other models and brands. New models are being introduced yearly (almost monthly, it seems) and it helps to know what to look for. The search for the perfect shoe is unending!

Adidas is a giant in the sports-shoe field. Back in 1972 and 1973, their SL-72 and SL-76 were the best shoes available. Alas, the company began playing around too much with a good thing—adding layers of sole, new tongue, and cushion material, etc. The old, lightweight SL-72 grew heavy and stiff. Meanwhile, other companies forged ahead with innovative shoes, leaving Adidas behind, with only two somewhat clumpy training models ("Runner" and "TRX") to sell. Then in late 1978, Adidas jumped back into the competition with the two outstanding racing shoes listed above ("TRX-Comp" and "Marathon-80"). Both are extremely light and extremely expensive. These shoes should definitely be reserved for racing— no sense wearing down such expensive shoes in training! Despite their light weight, these models are very well cushioned with good foot and ankle support, and ample toe room. After seeing the success of these racing shoes, Adidas in late 1979 came out with the training equivalent, by adding a bit more cushion. Adidas quality control tends to be good.

Nike is an American company founded by and for road-runners. It has consistently shown real concern for runners' needs and an innovative, experimental approach to the field. Nike was the first company to introduce the flared heel, the waffle sole, and the moccasin toe, which is generally roomier than conventional seamed toes. Some of their "experiments" have been tremendously successful, others less so. The LD-1000, with a greatly exaggerated heel flair, went overboard with a good idea—it caused more knee problems than it cured. But a later modification, the LD-1000-V (later the LDV), restored a more acceptable heel and introduced a superb cushion layer, which gave

192

most runners the feeling of "running on pillows." Using the same straight-last upper (an upper which is unsuitable for the 25 percent of people who have banana-curved feet), Nike then came out with the "Tailwind," a model with compressed air pockets in the sole. Theoretically, this should improve cushioning and prolong shoe life, since the cushion layer would not be permanently mashed down by use. We shall see. Despite its remarkable comfort, the Tailwind may not be ideal for everyone: the lack of a firm surface, plus extra foot mobility can cause leg stress for some users.

A note of caution about my own favorite racing shoe, the Nike Elite: a runner whose gait shows excessive *pronation* —flattening of the arch and inrolling of the ankle—should not wear this shoe, as it has very little inside support. The runner who pronates should either wear customized orthotics in her shoes, or a "varus wedge," or race in a shoe with more heel support.

Nike seems to use different lasts for different shoes, so the size and shapes of various models can differ considerably. For instance, I wear a size 8 Elite, but a size 6½ Sting. Their moccasin-style shoes are more suited to me than their original "Waffle-trainers," because they have a wide toe and narrow heel. Many women need this narrower-in-the-heel shape, rather than a shoe which is narrow throughout its length.

In keeping with its inventive, young image, the Nike company often tries out rather unconventional color combinations, and you may be the first on your block with a pair of silver-and-purple or canary-yellow-and-turquoise racers. If you have comments or requests, feel free to write to Nike, since they have a well-earned reputation for being responsive to runners' comments and suggestions.

Brooks, a relative newcomer in the business, burst on the scene in 1976 with their excellent and inexpensive Villanova model—at that time, the cheapest "quality" shoe available. Since then they have found favor with several other models, including the Vantage, a well-cushioned training model which features the "Varus Wedge," a built-in 3-degree cant which is recommended for runners who pronate excessively (a fairly common problem). Several of their newer models have a "soft-support" system which cups and molds to your foot. It feels weird at first, but as you run it squooshes down in the right places and provides comfortable support. The Brooks shoes, even the racer "Texan," tend to feel a little heavier and stiffer than their counterparts in other lines, but they have excellent toe room and cushioning. Their newest "Hugger" model is an outstanding training shoe.

The one big problem with Brooks shoes has been quality control—though company spokesmen assure me they're aware of this complaint and working to change it. Still, many of the Brooks shoes on the market have subtle defects which should qualify them as "seconds"—torn nylon mesh, heel tilted in instead of out, fast-lace loops in a zigzag pattern instead of across from each other, etc. Be sure to examine each pair carefully. You may have to go through several boxes before you find a pair that passes muster, cosmetically speaking.

New Balance, headquartered in Massachusetts, has had a great "gimmick" for years. It makes shoes in a huge variety of widths, from AAA to EEE. Recently, New Balance introduced identical models aimed especially at women in that the heel is narrower than the toe. Some women, like myself, need this duck-footed style rather than just a narrower shoe overall.

The top New Balance models are light and well cushioned, but I can't wear them. At least, not without considerable stretching of the toe box, and even then, not if any of my toes are hurting. The main problem with New Balance (*every* company seems to have one big problem) is the toe box, which seems to be made for creatures with wedge-shaped toes, tapering to a very shallow end. If you

194

have rounder toes, you have to compensate for this peculiar toe box by buying your shoes a full size too large. This still leaves an inch of too-shallow toe room ahead of your toes, and you may find yourself tripping a lot.

The New Balance shoe designers swear they keep asking for a higher toe box, and a less pointed foot, but the shoes still come out in the familiar non-foot shape (I don't know any Earthling with a foot or footprint shaped to the New Balance last). I suspect, myself, that it's a question of economics as much as New England stubbornness and resistance to change. I think New Balance started off with pointed, street-shoe lasts—the form on which the shoe is constructed—and is unable or unwilling to switch over to new lasts with a more realistic shape.

New Balance has the ability to make outstanding shoes, and the ones they make now would rank much higher on most lists if they fitted more feet (the shape, not the width). Once New Balance custom-made a pair of shoes for my big toes and wide forefoot. They were soft, light, beautifully cushioned and fit like a glove. Delighted, I tried to get several more pairs—in various color combinations—for future use. But the last (or specifications) which had been used for my customized pair had been lost. I hope it turns up again soon, as I'd like to try the latest New Balance models without suffering from black-toe disease.

Others. This far-from-exhaustive review leaves out several sizable shoe manufacturers, including EB-Sports International, Etonic, Saucony, Tiger, Puma, Pony and Converse. If you know what to look for and what your foot needs, it is possible to get excellent shoes from all of these companies. Don't get too locked in to what any other runner wears and recommends—your feet are your own. If in doubt, get advice from a knowledgeable running-shoe salesman.

Don Kardong, a 2:11 marathoner who was fourth in the 1976 Olympic marathon, owns a running store in Spokane. In 1977, when Don and I were at running camp together, he complained jokingly that women were coming into his store to be fitted, then rejecting the model he recommended because it wasn't top-rated in my first book. I solved this problem by giving him a note, now prominently displayed on the store's wall; "I hereby authorize Don Kardong to overrule the shoe recommendations in my book, if necessary, to achieve a better fit based on his examination of your own feet."

Women's Shoes. Traditionally, running shoes have been made only in one set of sizes—men's. The men's size is approximately one less than the women's—thus, if you wear a size 8 street shoe, you should try a size 7 running shoe. Men's shoe models provide enough variety so that most women will feel comfortable in some model. The narrowest last is probably Tiger.

A small percentage of women with very small and/or narrow feet can't use the men's shoes at all. The men's shoes just aren't made that small. Until recently, such women had to get by with children's shoes (inferior), or heavy socks—sometimes in layers.

Several companies have now introduced special women's shoes. Tiger brought out the baby-blue "Tigress," Nike introduced the stylish yellow- and-turquoise, "Lady Waffle Trainer." These shoes are simply slightly narrower versions of their men's shoes, with more attractive colors. I even bought a pair of the Lady Waffle Trainers because I liked their appearance—though they are a bit narrow for my duck-foot.

If you buy a women's shoe, make sure it's a true match for the men's shoe you like. In the past, women were treated like children. We weren't taken seriously, and special shoes for us tended to be cheaper, stiffer, heavier— then distinguished by some fancy name ending in "-ette." Choose the model of men's shoe you want, first. *Then* see if you can find it in a version that fits your foot.

While some companies have appealed to the female

market by featuring springlike "feminine" colors and pastels—Nike even added a sexy ankle bracelet in one highly successful ad campaign—other companies seem appallingly ignorant of the woman's mind. I recall one company that asked me to try its new super-shoe—one that had received rave reviews for wear, comfort, etc. I must confess I did not wear that shoe often enough to evaluate it properly—because it only came in black with neon orange trim. What women would be caught dead in such a shoe— except on Halloween? Which was indeed the first time I wore it, to go with my orange and black sweat suit. I relegated this very comfortable and promising model to the back of my closet, where it languished between rare excursions into muddy bogs, which would have dirtied my pretty canary-yellow shoes.

The moral for shoe companies would be, just because running involves a certain amount of sweat, dishevelment and (sometimes) mud, don't assume that we women don't like to look pretty, clean, even *dainty*—or at least elegant—while running. A smart company would simply dye half its regular shoe line colors that would match the seasonal fashions. No need to spend large sums on R & D (Research and Development); the female foot is not different, really, from the male foot—just somewhat smaller, on the average. And most women runners can save themselves time by skipping the lengthy evaluations of "women's shoes" that appear in various magazines. It's hard enough to keep up with advances in Unisex shoes.

Chapter Twelve: When You Can't Run

There comes a terrible moment in every runner's career, when you realize you can't run—not just for a day or two, but for weeks, possibly months. If you're addicted, panic sets in. You wonder if you'll go to pieces mentally, how you'll cope with everyday strains and stresses, the kids, the house mess, the job. You've heard dire rumors about the physical degeneration that occurs when runners are grounded—perhaps you should just retreat to bed and stay there until you're healed.

It's better to look at this crisis calmly. First of all, it's quite possible that the grounding is unnecessary. After the initial few days, very few running injuries are cured by enforced rest. You may be the victim of a too-conservative doctor who doesn't recognize the difference between overuse and traumatic injuries, or the principle of healing through continued activity. If you're uncertain about whether a suggested cast or layoff is necessary, get a second opinion! By the third or fourth opinion, you may find a doctor who thinks you can keep running. If not, the grounding is probably justified.

When Not to Run. The acute injuries that require a few days to a week or more of rest include muscle pulls, sprained ankles, and any traumatic injury that has torn or ruptured body structures—blood vessels, ligaments, bones or muscle fibers. These injuries should be immediately treated with ice, compression and elevation for up to 24 hours, but modified activity can usually be resumed after 3-4 days. Don't go out and run a marathon the week after a muscle pull, or even a fast 800 meters, but gentle half-hour jogs are usually well tolerated.

More serious layoffs can result from chronic overuse injuries, which often seem to push the body into deadends of pain and disability. Sometimes a judicious retreat is in order, which can include as much as 3 to 4 weeks of curtailed activity. I doubt that any injury requires a complete layoff of more than a month.

Some of the most stubborn problems are chronic, recalcitrant inflammations—"shinsplints," Achilles tendinitis, chondromalacia (pain under the kneecap) and other knee problems. Treatment includes correcting basic biomechanical problems, stretching, aspirin and reduced activity. If the basic cause of the problem has been treated (run-down heels on shoes, for instance), and the pain persists, complete rest *may* be required. My rule of thumb about whether or not to pamper injuries is simple: if you can't run without a limp, don't run at all. Running on a limp, gritting your teeth, will only cause you to favor the part that's injured, and lead to a potentially worse problem elsewhere.

Withdrawal Symptoms and How to Avoid Them.
There is no more pitiful sight than a totally grounded runner. She may be seen at local races, sighing and

handing out finishing sticks with a brave smile to those who can still run. Or she may be out walking the dog on the fringes of her favorite running turf, with a lump in her throat as she waves to former running companions.

At home, the grounded runner is not easy to live with. She rapidly becomes moody, irritable, downright bitchy. She tosses and turns all night, disturbing the household, and is tired and grouchy by morning. She loses her temper over trifles, barks at the children, and inexplicably bursts into tears. She may be plagued with constipation, headaches and twitches as well as insomnia.

These withdrawal symptoms are so common among runners that they lend support to the view of running as a true addiction. Several years ago, a research team wanted to study the physiological changes that occur in people who are accustomed to regular running, and stop. They asked for volunteers to stop running. No one volunteered, nor could the researchers bribe any of the regular runners to stop for a month, for a thousand dollars. So they had to settle for 3-times-per-week joggers, who were not yet addicted.

When I speak of "grounding," I refer only to cessation of running due to *injury*. There are certain illnesses which the runner should not "run through," including any disorder accompanied by fever. When the running hiatus is caused by an infection or other generalized ailment, the runner generally feels lousy anyway and has no desire to run. In this condition she shouldn't force herself. Bed rest may be indicated. Running can be resumed as the desire and energy return.

Substitute Activities. The pathetic non-runner is the one who is full of health and enthusiasm, but hurts with each running step. Fortunately, withdrawal need not be total. A methadone-like substitute is available in the form of other aerobic sports and activities. While these substitute sports do not usually give a running addict the same "high," they do serve to preserve cardiovascular conditioning and muscle tone during the off-season. And occasionally, a grounded runner will become so intrigued with the substitute sport that she switches fields, becoming a skier, cyclist or race-walker permanently. The most popular substitute activities, in fact, seem to be those that are out-of-doors, like running, and have their own competitive networks. Cross-country skiing, cycling, and race-walking fall into this category. Others, less competitive but which still condition you and alleviate withdrawal symptoms, include swimming, hiking, and just plain walking.

Some runners try to maintain strength in specific muscles by exercising on the Nautilus or the Universal Gym (competitors in exercise apparatus, used under supervision in a gym), or by "running" in the deep end of a pool, with a life jacket providing buoyancy. If you can survive the basic boredom of confinement to pool or gym, go to it! Personally, I prefer an hour's brisk hike in the hills to an hour of "intervals" in the deep end.

The best substitute activities are those that not only maintain cardio-respiratory (aerobic) fitness, but also exercise the injured part. It may seem paradoxical to exercise the part that is being "rested," but in fact, movement promotes circulation, which in turn leads to faster healing. Slow, rhythmic, non-weight-bearing motion is well tolerated even by an inflamed, aching part. What you want to avoid is heavy, sudden, jarring movements, which can lead to further irritation. For a sore knee or ankle, walking is preferable to jogging, since it is smoother, and bicycling is better than either, since both ankle and knee are in constant motion, but do not bear weight.

To a large extent, convenience and opportunity dictate what sport you choose. If you live in a hilly city, uphill walks are better than cycling; if you have a pool, you can swim all day long; if you're injured during a midwestern winter, you can ski to work and back.

201

Whatever activity you decide upon, the principle is to spend the same amount of time each day as you would ordinarily be running, at an equally vigorous level. If your activity is less demanding, for instance walking or cycling on the flat, you should spend longer at it. Those who want to quantitate their effort in "equivalency" units can utilize Dr. Kenneth Cooper's point system for various sports. The point charts, found in all of Cooper's books on Aerobics, take into consideration both the metabolic demand of each activity (swimming is more demanding than golf or bowling), and the time spent. You can earn points either by covering ground faster (greater effort) or by spending longer periods of time. It's a very neat system, though runners, who may be earning 100 points in 3 hours per week, are often discouraged to find out how long it takes to earn the same 100 points with other activities. But take heart, Cooper believes that as little as 30 points weekly can keep you in excellent aerobic condition, if not in top racing form.

If you don't have the Aerobic point charts available, or aren't so quantitative in your approach, you can gauge your effort quite accurately by how hard you are breathing and how high your heart rate goes. All sports are not exactly equivalent in heart and lung involvement, however. I find, when pedaling uphill or propelling myself up an incline on cross-country skis, that my heart is pounding along near maximal effort while my respiratory rate lags behind. In general those sports which demand more muscular strength cause a rapid rise in heart rate, while those that demand greater circulation, without equivalent muscle power, increase pulmonary ventilation more. The former is said to put a "pressure load" on the heart, while the latter type causes a "volume load." You needn't worry about these distinctions in practice; if you feel you're working very hard, you probably are.

A few details about the most popular alternative sports for runners may be helpful:

CROSS-COUNTRY SKIING.

If you're injured while there's snow around your home, you're in luck. Cross-country skiing is by far the best substitute for running, demanding the same qualities of endurance, cardiovascular conditioning, and leg strength that runners need. In addition, skiing demands a certain grace and balance that are optional in running, as well as considerable upper body strength, which most runners lack. Thus, while cross-country skiing is easy to learn and fun to do, as well as inexpensive (no lift tickets or fancy clothes needed), it ends up being even more demanding than running. In fact, cross-country skiers regard running as a second-best alternative to their own sport, something they practice only in summer, to keep in shape. Even then, they prefer to do their hill-bounding with poles, so their shoulder muscles don't dwindle away to nothing.

Almost all running injuries respond well to skiing, because the gliding movement eliminates jarring while exercising muscles and joints. Just be careful not to stop by running into a tree. If you want to stop suddenly, just fall into the soft snow. Cross-country skis are thin and lightweight, boots are as light as running shoes, and the foot is only attached to the ski at the toe. So if you fall, you are not liable to twist or break your leg, as in downhill skiing.

Cross-country skiing is a sport for families that like the outdoors; it is currently enjoying a "boom" comparable to running, and ski centers with well-groomed trails are now available in all parts of the country. These centers usually sponsor frequent "Citizens' Races," low-key participation events, if you want competition during your running layoff. But trails and races are not necessary for conditioning; you can keep in shape by setting your own tracks through local parks, meadows and woods.

Even if you're a hotshot runner, you can be quickly humbled by some of these skiing "tigers." One year, on my way to a medical conference in Aspen, I stopped for a couple of days at Devil's Thumb X-C Ski Center, site of a summer running camp. Feeling in the mood for a nice easy 10-km. "run," I found two young women, Lee Tillotson and Peg Newman, who volunteered to take me around the "Black 10" ski trail. They looked both slim and strong, but disclaimed any expertise. "We're just Citizen's Racers," they said modestly meaning they entered low-level competitions. That's like saying, "Oh, I just jog a few miles." In fact, Peg and Lee wiped out all us poor runners on the "Black 10." "Are we halfway yet?" I gasped after struggling up hills and swooping down for what seemed an eternity. My shoulders and arms ached, my butt was icy from repeated falls ("stops") in the snow, I couldn't catch my breath in the thin air (8500 feet up). "Soon," replied Peg soothingly. "Try to relax on this next downhill." Lee came along behind me, trying to keep me from slipping backwards as my herringbone and wax both weakened. The "Black 10" took this intrepid marathoner about 2 hours, and I subsequently learned it was really only 9 km. Fortunately, I wasn't injured either before or after. But I was awfully stiff the next day.

So if you switch from running to skiing, don't try to do your usual mileage (especially at altitude). Judge your workouts by elapsed time, instead (mine was a 2-hour, not a 10-km., effort). And beware of smiling, slim "Citizen's Racers" who will cheerfully ski you into a total frazzle, while finishing fresh as daisies themselves.

SWIMMING.

Many current runners started out as swimmers, and initially took up jogging to get in better shape for long swims. The fact that most of the movement is from water to land, rather than the opposite direction, is a clue to the main drawbacks of swimming. You can't be as gregarious in the water, and swimming long distances can be dull. There's not much to look at, and laps can get monotonous. One tends to lose count. Therefore, if you choose to swim when injured, it's best to swim continuously for a set time, rather than try to keep track of *distance* covered. If you're swimming laps in a pool, be sure to stay in your own lane (keep your eyes open underwater), and try to swim at odd hours, so you won't be crashing into other lap-swimmers. Just paddling around at random, or sitting around gossiping in the shallow end, won't keep you in good aerobic condition. It has to be a continuous, vigorous effort.

You can use any stroke you like in swimming your 20 or 40 minutes. Many people use an individual medley. If your knee is injured, however, you should avoid the breast-stroke. The whip kick (frog kick) is very hard on knees, and in fact "swimmer's knee" is as common in breaststrokers as "runner's knee" in joggers. You don't want to combine the two.

Certain muscle injuries, too, can be aggravated by brisk leg movements against water resistance. If you experiment a bit, you'll find out which strokes provide you with a good, painless workout. You can even work hard enough using arms alone, just dragging your injured legs along behind. Your heart, lungs and arms will be strong, even if your leg muscles are neglected.

Some coaches and competitive runners utilize the resistance and weightlessness provided by water, to devise special training methods. Some injured runners will be leaping around in the shallow end, exercising thigh and calf muscles without jarring. Another trainer puts a life jacket on his injured athletes and sets them to "running" interval workouts, while they are supported upright in the water. Most of the running motions can be duplicated in this way, while the heart and lungs stay in optimal condition, since the demands are the same. Jacqueline Hansen "ran" an hour a day in the deep end when she had a stress fracture, and was able to race 5 miles without strain as soon as she got back to running on dry land.

BICYCLING.

Cyclists in general tend to have powerful quadriceps (thigh) muscles and excellent cardio-respiratory endurance. Unless they are injured and can't cycle, they also tend to avoid running. Cyclists are a group apart. There is a great overlap in conditioning benefits, between cycling and running, so each makes an excellent substitute for the other. The only real barrier is mental. Cyclists would rather be cycling and runners would rather be running. A few hardy souls try to combine the two sports, with varying degrees of success.

At least two excellent women runners were cyclists first. Natalie Cullimore, who astounded the running world in 1970 and 1971 by finishing a 100-mile road race, only did so because she had injured her neck and couldn't cycle for a while. She couldn't turn her head to look out for cars, so figured she'd be safer running while her neck healed. She progressed rapidly from 5 miles to marathons, and did her first 100-miler in a world record time of 16 hours (the men's record is 12). The following year Natalie was a bit slower, 18 hours, but won the race, with the only male finisher straggling in 4 hours later.

Louise Burns, a 38-year-old mother of two who is also a 3:12 marathoner and jogging instructor, also made an easy transition to distance running because of her cycling experience. For fun, Louise used to cycle "Centuries" (100-mile events) and even "Double Centuries," apparently whipping a lot of men in the process. Many male cyclists in the San Francisco Bay Area are relieved that Louise has transferred her endurance and energy to the running scene. It gives them a better chance at victory in the long rides.

Injured runners, especially those with non-weight-bearing problems like stress fractures and sprained ankles, can find relief in a daily, vigorous 1- to 2-hour ride. Unless your bike ride is all uphill (requiring more effort and thus less time), you'll have to pedal longer than you would run—maybe twice as long, so that an hour's (flat) bike ride would equal a half-hour of running. If you'd rather use distance equivalents, figure that 3 to 4 miles on a bike equals 1 mile of running. Coasting downhill doesn't count at all. I've even passed some "Sunday bike riders" on the *downhill,* when I've been out running. One of these middle-aged males looked surprised as I ran past (he wasn't even pedaling) and said, "Say, you folks never get to coast, do you?" I could tell he felt sorry for me.

The point is, as in swimming, you can put a great deal of energy into cycling, or coast along using none at all. Obviously, if you're trying to get training benefits or aerobic points for your ride, you have to go fast enough so it feels like an effort. If you prefer to stay indoors and use an Exercycle, set the resistance high enough to get your pulse up to your usual exercise level (120 or higher for most people, though it varies with sex. As you get older, it gets lower). To combat boredom on the indoor cycle, try setting it up in front of the TV. One member of our fitness program assured me that *Monday Night Football* was good for over 20 miles on his Exercycle.

Certain problems of runners will not respond well to cycling. Tendinitis around the knee, or "chondromalacia" (pain under the kneecap), may be aggravated by pedaling as much as by jogging. Foot imbalances can be as severe in cleats as in Waffle Trainers. If your pain gets worse, rather than better, when you bicycle, you should switch to another substitute.

WALKING, HIKING, RACE-WALKING.

It's amazing the number of people who swear they "can't run," but who have no hesitation about walking. They'll walk for miles, up over mountains, down into the Grand Canyon, or to the grocery store, but hesitate to jog a step. This hesitation is illogical, because basically walking and running are just two variants of the same kind of locomotion—using your feet. Running is usually, but not always, faster than walking. Technically, the difference is that in running, both feet are off the ground at some point in the stride, whereas in walking, one foot must always be in contact with the ground. If you're a race-walker, you're disqualified if the judge sees daylight beneath both feet at any time. Race-walkers must also straighten the knee when pushing off. Recreational walkers have no such style restrictions.

Running and walking are equally natural motions, and the impulse to break from a walk into a run is universal among people who are in a hurry. For some reason, though, walking is more socially acceptable. Perhaps adults feel that running is too playful, too childlike—inappropriate for the more mature. Whatever the reason, many older folks prefer to achieve and maintain fitness on a walking program, rather than "on the run." This preference is okay. The only drawback to walking is that it takes longer, generally, to go a specific distance. And if you're working off calories at the rate of 100 per mile, for instance, you'll only walk off 300 to 400 calories every hour, whereas runners can burn off twice the calories in the same amount of time (by covering 7 to 8 miles). If your time is unlimited, you can catch up with the runners by walking 2 hours while they only run one!

Walking is simple and requires no special equipment, though a good pair of well-cushioned, lightweight running shoes would be a great gift for any avid walker.

A major advantage of walking, for both the elderly and the injured, is that it is a gentle kind of movement. Because you don't ever leave the ground, you don't descend heavily, either. Jarring and joint stress are minimized. Almost every kind of running injury can be safely and comfortably walked on.

How strenuous walking is depends on both your pace and

your basic conditioning. An overweight individual just beginning to walk for exercise may achieve near-maximal heart rate within 20 yards, and have to stop to catch his breath. A well-conditioned runner may have to stride briskly up a steep hill to generate the equivalent amount of stress. Keep in mind that you must learn to judge exercise equivalence by your own sense of effort and hard work, rather than by pace and distance only.

Walking can also be used effectively as part of treatment, as in Dr. Ernst Van Aaken's favorite "jog and walk" prescription. With many injuries, you can keep in shape by walking till warm, jogging (gently!) till your injured part protests, walking till it feels better, jogging again, etc., etc. You can cover 3 to 5 miles briskly in this manner, and alleviate most of the common "withdrawal" symptoms (while earning up to 15 aerobic points).

Once when I was grounded by a calf-muscle pull, I walked 2 brisk miles each day—1 before my jog, and 1 after. The first mile got me moving and warmed-up, stretched the aggravated muscle gently, and let me practice my "push-off" without limping. Then I would "jog" a gentle, slow mile, my feet *barely* leaving the ground. One more brisk mile walk, and I was cooled down. The whole session took 45 minutes, for 3 scenic laps around the lake.

Competitive runners often turn to race-walking when injuries keep them from running; walking is definitely less traumatic, but offers competition at all levels, including the Olympics. Some fast walkers shy away from racing because they think the typical hip waggle looks peculiar; however, this gait is a natural consequence of walking at maximum speed, and looks especially fluid and graceful when done by young girls (who also tend to be fine natural runners). Many former runners stick with race-walking long after their injuries have healed.

Race-walking may also be a fine outlet for the older woman who likes to compete, but feels awkward jogging.

One of the most enthusiastic proponents of this alternate sport is Phyllis Sears, a Phoenix woman now in her 50s. Phyllis had a triple handicap a few years ago. Not only had she been sedentary for over 20 years, she also smoked 3 packs a day and had managed to pack 184 pounds onto a 5-foot, 5-inch frame. Lesser women might have been discouraged and quickly smoked themselves into an early grave, perhaps hastening the process with alcohol. But Phyllis was determined not to let her husband jog off alone into the Phoenix sunset. She joined behavior modification groups, cut down on both calories and cigarettes, and started jogging on the last day of her stop-smoking program.

Now a trim 130 pounds, and well conditioned, Phyllis has started a jogging/race-walking club for women in the Phoenix area. She feels that many older women, who may hesitate to start jogging, especially if they are overweight, can ease into sports more comfortably through race-walking. And her club provides an automatic haven for the injured jogging contingent.

For more information about competition and/or Masters programs in the substitute sports, you can contact the following groups.

Swimming, Race Walking: Your local AAU office
Cross-Country Skiing: United States Ski Association and its regional offices
Bicycling: U.S. Cycling Federation (and its district representatives)

(A faster way to learn about local events is to visit your local sport shop and pick up announcements there.)

Chapter Thirteen: Medical Matters

Menstrual Irregularities. Several "scare" articles have appeared recently in newspapers around the country, with lurid titles such as "Can Running Harm Women?" and "Running—Does It Cause Sterility?" These articles call attention to a phenomenon—menstrual irregularity—which has been around a long time, but is suspected to be especially frequent among long-distance runners.

I was aware of this problem as early as 1974, having been asked about it by many outstanding women runners throughout the U.S. and Europe. Each thought her own lack of periods was unique, and was reluctant to consult a non-running, male gynecologist about the matter. Hearing all these identical stories, I began to suspect a relationship between running and amenorrhea (complete absence of periods for months or years). Most of the women I talked to were in their 20s. Earlier, Dr. Ken Foreman of Seattle surveyed a younger group of distance runners at the 1971 and 1973 Women's Cross-Country Championships, and

211

found that eleven out of forty-seven had "very irregular" periods. Since most of these girls were teenagers, who have notoriously irregular cycles anyway, Foreman's data were suggestive rather than conclusive, while my own, of course, were what is termed "merely anecdotal."

In 1979, more quantitative data were published by a group of researchers in Atlanta, who took advantage of the 1978 Avon International Women's Marathon to survey a large number of national-caliber women runners. The runners had significantly fewer menses per year (8.1 versus 11.4) than either athletic (non-running) or sedentary controls. They also had significantly lower body fat. Since past oral-contraceptive use was similar in both groups, this did not appear to be a factor in the "runner's amenorrhea." Irregularity was less common in runners who had previously borne children, but among the non-mothers, it affected an astounding 51 percent.

So those of you who have experienced scanty, delayed, or absent periods since you took up distance running can now be assured that you are not unique, and that this change probably is related to your running habit. To judge by my mail, this is probably the single most important concern among woman runners. I have received countless letters from women in their 20s and 30s, most of whom report that they feel great, are running well, but are worried about whether their bodies are "functioning a hundred percent." This worry has driven many of them to their gynecologists for reassurance, which is unfortunately rarely forthcoming. Some women with completely normal physical examinations have been subjected to expensive diagnostic studies, hormone treatments and even surgery, in a misguided attempt to restore them to "normality," defined as monthly bleeding.

To understand how this can happen, you have to understand the mental "set" of your average gynecologist. A "normal" woman, in his view, is the typical American

212

housewife who forms the backbone of his practice. She is generally sedentary, and has at least 30 percent body fat. She also has periods like clockwork, every 28 days or so. This average woman is not only the "norm," she becomes the ideal. The gynecologist's aim, then, is to restore any aberrant females to this physiological "norm."

Enter our typical woman marathoner—lean, graceful, exuding health and energy, but a bit worried about her lack of bleeding. An enlightened gynecologist would do an examination and conclude: "Ms. Smith, you are outstandingly fit and healthy with a normal physical exam. Therefore, your absence of periods must simply be a reflection of your good condition, for reasons we don't understand. Don't worry one second more about it!"

But such enlightenment is rare. Most doctors haven't been trained to recognize good health. They keep trying to find out what is *wrong*. Anything unusual is considered a problem, almost by definition. In medical terms, any physiological aberration must be pathological.

Women should not become paranoid and feel that this situation is sexist, representing a tyranny of the predominately male medical profession over women. Male runners experience similar difficulties when they seek consultation about heart murmurs, bloody urine, etc.

Confronted with the need to make a diagnosis, the traditional doctor thinks in terms of known diseases or disorders. Most gynecologists have never heard of "runner's amenorrhea," which is not in the textbooks. Many women have asked their doctor, very sensibly, whether there might be some connection between their recent running habit and their recent menstrual disturbances. This logical suggestion is usually dismissed as nonsensical since it is a new concept. After many expensive tests, the worried runner who persists in searching for answers is generally given a misdiagnosis from the textbook. There are two popular misdiagnoses for women runners without periods: (1) anorexia nervosa or (2) Stein-Leventhal syndrome. Let us examine these maladies to see if they fit the runner.

Anorexia nervosa is a condition seen mostly in young girls who are concerned about being overweight; their ultimate solution is to stop eating. Naturally, they become thin, even emaciated. With starvation comes lack of periods and other symptoms of distress. Some of these young women also manage to run—at least until their growing weakness stops them. But in practice there should be no problem distinguishing an "anorexic," even one who runs, from the runner with benign amenorrhea. Appetite is a giveaway. The typical runner eats like a pig; consumption of food may be way over normal, and ice cream, pastries, etc., are considered delicacies. By contrast, the anorexic will pick at her food and look slightly nauseated at the thought of apple pie or lasagna. Physically, there are many differences, too. The anorexic loses muscle along with fat. She can be weak and skinny and still have well over 20 percent fat content. The runner with amenorrhea tends to be older and leaner (12 percent or less fat), but strong, because she has not dieted away her muscle protein. You don't *lose muscle* by running, only by dieting. By analyzing fat and muscle content, eating habits and energy level, the doctor can avoid the misdiagnosis of anorexia nervosa.

Stein-Leventhal syndrome is the other popular misdiagnosis, and seems to be reserved for amenorrheic runners with hearty appetites. This "syndrome" consists of a cluster of physical findings—besides amenorrhea, the chief hallmarks are obesity and hirsutism—abnormal hair growth and distribution, usually in a more masculine pattern. The syndrome is thought to be due to hormonal disturbances related to presence (found at operation) of ovaries with an abnormally thick, fibrous capsule, and multiple cysts formed by unreleased ova (eggs). Treatment is by surgical "wedge resection"—cutting a wedge out of the thickened

214

capsule—or more recently, by use of fertility drugs such as Clomid.

Now, obviously, the woman runner who develops amenorrhea while running 80+ miles/week and dropping her body fat down around 10 percent does not fit this description. She will be far from "obese," and I have yet to see any runners with the associated "hirsutism." So the only explanation I can think of for such a gross misdiagnosis is desperation on the part of the doctor. He feels compelled to come up with a diagnosis, preferably a treatable one, and in view of his patient's gargantuan runner's appetite, he has ruled out anorexia nervosa. Stein-Leventhal syndrome is all that is left, according to the books.

This sounds laughable, but in practice, a misdiagnosis can lead to much grief. One woman wrote me after having already undergone hormone treatments and a wedge resection. Since the operation (understandably) had not restored her monthly periods, the doctor was suggesting a repeat operation! Another gynecologist, a very eminent specialist, assured a world-record holder with amenorrhea that she suffered from Stein-Leventhal syndrome and had less than 1 chance in 10,000 of ever becoming pregnant without hormonal or surgical treatment. I advised this friend that since she was neither obese nor hirsute, she had been misdiagnosed and was probably not infertile either. But on the basis of the eminent specialist's advice, she dispensed with birth control—and a few months later, found herself unexpectedly pregnant. I trust the eminent gynecologist took care of her free of charge.

This sad story brings me to the main reason women—not their doctors—are concerned about not having periods. Are they infertile? Can they ever have children?

All the evidence is reassuring to would-be mothers. The absence of periods is not permanent and does not indicate sterility. In fact, a woman who is having irregular or no periods should never assume she is infertile and depend on this for birth control. I have known several women runners who became pregnant without having a period. Obviously, the absence of menstruation does not mean that ovulation is not taking place at all, only that it is occurring at irregular and unpredictable times. Other tests used to determine if a normal (28-day) ovulatory pattern is present—temperature charts, endometrial (uterine) biopsies, etc., will show the same irregularity and are of no help. Hormonal tests of a few runners with prolonged amenorrhea have low levels of certain hormones (LH and progesterone) necessary to a monthly cycle, and less pronounced cyclical variation in pituitary FSH (follicle stimulating hormone), which acts on the ovaries—but note, the *hormones are still there,* ready to spring into action at unpredictable moments. If you don't want them to spring into action, be sure to take precautions.

Since amenorrhea is so common in fit, healthy young runners, whereas clockwork-like menstrual cycles are more frequent in the sedentary, plump population, I have developed what I call my "anthropological theory of the origin of monthly cycles." We doctors traditionally see our epoch, even our decade of historical time, as the physiological norm. We assume, therefore, that it is normal to have menstrual periods, normal to be 25 percent fat as coeds and to get fatter as we get older, normal to suffer from atherosclerosis, etc., because that's all we know. But perhaps we are looking at life backwards, and our little pinpoint of time is the aberration. Perhaps menstruation, like atherosclerosis, is a degenerative manifestation of a sedentary life-style!

Consider primitive man—wandering in tribes around the planet, never staying long in one spot, hunting for food, running away from predators. Our species was a "hunter-gatherer" for millions of years. We only settled down in villages and became agricultural creatures about 10,000 years ago. The carriage and automobile, which reduced our aerobic activity to virtually zero, have only been around for a fraction of our human history.

How inconvenient, then, for active nomadic females to *bleed* for several days each month. How doubly inconvenient to be pregnant for 9 months out of every year, while in the "sedentary" pattern. Think of the liability to a group which lives and eats almost literally on the run, of having a large number of pregnant or nursing or menstruating women around (not to mention their babies) at all times—slowing down the group, inhibiting its hunting, *luring* predatory animals by leaving a bloody spoor.

Anthropologically speaking, monthly periods and yearly pregnancies do not make sense—they are a liability to an active species. So my astounding theory is that menstruation is a relatively modern (10,000 years?) physiological aberration which can only flourish in a settled and inactive society, which can afford to have its women effectively immobilized much of the time.

Therefore, you needn't panic if you simply revert to a pattern much more appropriate to healthy women who are very active. In periods of decreased activity, heavier eating and more fat accumulation, you will undoubtedly revert to the "normal" monthly pattern of a sedentary society.

This "anthropological" theory of mine fits in well with the little that is known—or speculated—about the causes of runner's amenorrhea. Young girls, who are the majority of cross-country runners, tend to be irregular anyway for several years after puberty. Moreover, it is well known that a variety of stresses—travel, change of climate, change in sleep habits, sudden plunges into vigorous exercise, even mental distress—can cause temporary amenorrhea lasting months or even years. Some young girls in the most susceptible age group, 12 to 20, may get their bodies so mixed up that they have two periods a month rather than none. Their hormones have not settled down.

Some doctors, myself included, feel that the most significant factor in amenorrhea may be the decrease in body fat found in most women runners who train seriously (60 or more miles/week, usually). These women often have less than 12 percent body fat, and in countries where the population is leaner than ours (India, for example), menstruation starts at a much later age—15 or 16 versus 11 in the U.S. Whatever the cause of low body fat, it seems to be associated with low pituitary FSH production. It is as if the pituitary "knows" that body fat is below optimum level to support a pregnancy (in case of low food supply) and thus is reluctant to stimulate ovulation. The body has its own kind of wisdom.

Finally, it is not rare for women who use birth control pills to have amenorrhea when they stop taking the Pill— and the lack of periods may persist for months or years. These women should be excluded from any studies of runners, as a different mechanism may be involved.

My advice to runners with amenorrhea is, don't worry about it. Enjoy the relative freedom you' have, and the savings on tampons. If a pill were invented which would simulate runner's amenorrhea—stop periods temporarily, with no undesirable side effects—it would make a fortune. As all women realize, amenorrhea is convenient! Don't be frightened into thinking that a woman has to bleed monthly to be healthy.

If you wish to become pregnant, and haven't had a period for months or years, I'd suggest the following. First, discontinue birth control measures for a year or more (the longer interval may be necessary for former Pill-users). If nothing happens, or if you are getting impatient, cut down your stress level and/or increase your fat percentage by reducing running mileage to a level which is easy for you. Eat adequately. If you haven't been menstruating anyway, you may not realize for a while that you are pregnant. Early symptoms include dropping things, fainting and vague nausea, also frequent urination. If in doubt, try one of the new home pregnancy tests before seeing a doctor (it's cheaper).

As a last resort, you and your spouse can go have a "fertility workup" by a gynecologist, and if necessary, take pills to induce ovulation. Don't be overanxious and take too many pills, or you may find yourself the first running mother of quadruplets!

The Pregnant Runner. An estimated 5 million women in the U.S. now run or jog, many of them 5 to 10 miles daily. Since the vast majority of these women are in the "childbearing years," 15 to 50, it is not astounding that many of them become pregnant each year. Nor is it astounding, given the addictive nature of running, that the pregnant women wish to continue running as long as possible. Some even hope to keep up their training for an important event—the Olympics, the Boston Marathon, a local championship race, etc.

Whether or not the mother-to-be remains a runner throughout the pregnancy depends mostly on luck. If she meets with encouragement, or even a neutral attitude, from her obstetrician, the road is clear. But many women still depend on conservative obstetricians who frown upon "excessive" or "strenuous" activity during the pregnant state. Faced with a conflict between their own physiological needs (including a daily run) and anxiety over the health of their baby, most women look around for a second opinion—from another local doctor, or frequently in sending a letter to me.

Obstetricians themselves, having no established guidelines for prescribing exercise during pregnancy, look for special advice. The newsletter of the International Correspondence Society of Obstetricians and Gynecologists, published one such query in 1978, along with answers from five doctors (including myself). Surprisingly, the "experts" all agree on the advantages of continued vigorous activity in pregnancy, with the provision that all walking/jogging/running be done at an "aerobic" pace—slow enough and comfortable enough to allow conversation. The most conservative of the experts—Dr. Kenneth Cooper—suggests switching from jogging to walking in the last trimester. He gives no medical reason for the switch, so presumably the recommendation simply reflects Dr. Cooper's generally cautious views on exercise for women. The other four doctors all see no contraindication to running right up to term, as comfort dictates. So if your first obstetrician is the disapproving type, it's worth shopping around to find one who will be more supportive.

My own sons were born in 1967 and 1968, years before I ever thought of running. I did bicycle in the early months of both pregnancies, but stopped, scared when I had some spotting in the first one, and when some cruel person slashed my tires in the second. So my own pregnancies were the traditional, sedentary kind, and from being deconditioned to start with, I sank to being heavy, fatigued *and* deconditioned. I thought this sluggishness was an inevitable part of pregnancy. Now, having met many pregnant runners—some in races—I see that I was wrong—that pregnancy need not detract from health or limit a vigorous life-style—though it *will* slow you down!

Pregnant women at races were still a great novelty in 1976, when I saw my first example. Following a half-marathon in Dallas, local friends pointed proudly to a group of women finishers chatting about the race. "Mary Jones, over there, is due in a couple of weeks," they claimed. "Where? Which one?" I asked, since all four women looked equally slim, in back view. Then Mary turned around to be introduced, and I noticed that she did have a considerable bulge in front. So that no one would think she was simply fat, she wore a sequined T-shirt with the word "Baby" and an arrow pointing downward. But there could be no confusion, anyway. Mary looked strong, slim and radiant. She had just finished the half-marathon (13.1 miles) in 2:10, a 10-minute-mile pace. Less than 3 weeks later, baby Amanda arrived. "Amanda's disposition is unequaled by any other baby's I have ever met," claims her mother, and less biased observers agree. It must be an advantage to the developing fetus to live in an environment that is calm, healthy and well oxygenated.

For the mother-to-be, the benefits of exercise are well known. Regular aerobic activity helps to reduce water retention and weight gain, improves muscle tone, and accelerates postpartum recovery. The continued psychological benefit to the mother may be equally important. According to Mary Jones, even in the final weeks of the pregnancy (after the half-marathon) despite spending "a lot of time lying on my back with my feet in the air . . . I somehow felt better jogging than doing anything else because I could get into a comfortable rhythm which seemed to soothe me."

Most pregnant women (and their doctors) are aware of these benefits. Their questions tend to be about the health of the fetus. "Won't all that bouncing around hurt it?" is a common question. Kathie Samuelson, who described her own experiences in an amusing and informative article entitled "Schlepping through Pregnancy," complained about well-intentioned comments such as "Does your doctor know you're doing this?" and "You're going to kill that baby!"

It helps to remember that the fetus is not something like a backpack, an external mass that bounces around. The fetus is encradled in its own watery, warm internal environment. I like to compare it to fish in a fishbowl—as you move the container around, the fish float happily in place. The fluid cushions against most shocks.

Of course, it is advisable to avoid the possibility of more violent shocks, even though these would tend to do more harm to the pregnant woman than the fetus. I heard of one horsewoman who insisted not only on continued riding, but on show-jumping, despite her advancing pregnancy. In her seventh month, she missed a jump, sailed headfirst off her horse, and landed (fortunately) in a mud puddle and (unfortunately) right on her growing belly. Somewhat shaken, she agreed to abandon jumping—but not riding—in the final months. The fetus was unharmed and emerged healthy at term. Nevertheless, I wouldn't recommend risk-taking of this sort. Nor would I recommend sky-diving, hang-gliding, pole-vaulting or ski-jumping either. But in general, a pregnant woman should be encouraged to keep on with her usual exercise program as long as she is comfortable. The aerobic exercises, those that promote blood flow and increase oxygen consumption, are really most beneficial—the "big four" are jogging, bicycling, swimming and cross-country skiing. In making this recommendation, I am assuming that the pregnancy is normal. Certain conditions—an "incompetent" cervix, tox-emia, maternal diabetes, etc.—require restriction of exercise and very close obstetrical supervision.

If running can be so beneficial in a normal pregnancy, why do so many concerned onlookers and "experts," i.e., doctors, frown upon it? I think their disapproval, which ignores the known facts, rests on certain traditional myths about pregnancy, and misconceptions about the nature of running.

The first of these myths is that pregnancy is some sort of an illness, or an abnormal (pathological) state. In the nineteenth century, doctors prescribed bed rest not only during pregnancy, but even for menstruation and other "ailments" related to the reproductive functions. All of the woman's energies, it was felt, had to be conserved and directed toward propagation. Even higher education for women was discouraged on the grounds that intellectual endeavors could "unsex" them, by diverting precious blood flow and energy away from the reproductive organs.

Although women were allowed greater activity during pregnancy in the twentieth century, childbirth itself remained a concern of the hospitals. Even after normal deliveries, women were confined to bed for 2 weeks or more. My own mother recalled, with a sigh, how she was finally allowed to "dangle" her legs over the side of the bed a few days after I was born (in 1940)!

Like many medical advances, the contemporary shortened hospital stay and early ambulation after childbirth came about by accident. During World War II and the Battle of Britain, bombs were falling all around London hospitals. To their horror, the hospital staffs realized that even new mothers would have to get out of bed and *walk* to get down to the deep air raid shelters. To the astonishment of their doctors, these mothers not only did not suffer— they *thrived* on the movement. Recovery was much faster than under conventional treatment.

The explanation is simple. Any activity stimulates uterine contractions, and returns things to the normal state faster. There is less pooling of blood and a much lower incidence of phlebitis and pulmonary embolism (blood clots in the legs and lungs, a major hazard of prolonged bed rest). Nowadays hospital stays for delivery are down to 2 to 3 days or less—thanks to the Battle of Britain!

The traditional medical conservatism about pregnancy is compounded by the view held by most non-runners about running—that it is a "strenuous" activity. Perhaps this idea stems from watching reruns and dramatizations of the Olympic games. Or, perhaps it is a misinterpretation of the open-mouthed grimace which is the usual expression of a non-conversing jogger (it maximizes air-intake).

Of course, the extent to which jogging is "strenuous" depends primarily on conditioning. My first attempted ¼-mile around the block when I was *out* of shape was more "strenuous" than my best marathon when I was *in* shape. So a wise obstetrician should advise women to use their heads about what is strenuous and what is comfortable. A caution against overexertion and fatigue is in order, rather than a blanket condemnation of running.

It is helpful for all runners, and especially those who are pregnant, to remember that running is a completely *natural* activity for human beings. Our species did not survive millions of years of a nomadic life-style—on foot— by cautioning its members not to run, or by confining women to the home cave for weeks out of every year. Our bodies have evolved so as to permit running without harm to the unborn. Like all mammals, we carry around with us our watery environment for fetal development. If it were that fragile, human beings would have been extinct long ago. As a species, and as individual animals, we are more endangered by an unnatural, sedentary way of life than by vigorous activity.

To come down from this anthropological plane to more practical matters, what amount of running is permissible in pregnancy? Obviously, the exercise prescription must be individualized. For every Mary Jones, training 320 miles during her seventh month, there are a hundred who find themselves unable, in the later months, to jog a single mile without walking breaks. That's okay. Do whatever you can, as long as it's aerobic and regular. Don't judge yourself by what others can do.

Kathie Samuelson, who was able to run 5 miles continuously when not pregnant, found herself limited to 2 miles, walking and jogging, in the last week. Any attempt to do more brought on immediate symptoms of overstress— fatigue, a headcold, grouchiness. "At times I really wondered what was the matter with me. If those others could do it, why couldn't I? But, the plain fact was I *couldn't,* and I had to discipline myself to remember this." Her suggestions: "Don't try to emulate the Bionic Woman. Let your body guide you."

You are not a Lesser Mortal just because you have to

slow down as pregnancy progresses. That slowing-down occurs naturally as the pregnancy inevitably results in making you anemic about midterm. Unless you work *much* harder—uncomfortably hard, even to anaerobic levels (a no-no), you *can't* go as fast. So throw away your stopwatch, and just cover the distance. And be sure to take iron supplements.

If you seriously wish to continue marathon training during pregnancy, it's possible. We really don't know what the limits are. Several women in the early 1970s, when "serious" runners always did "intervals," were at the track training when labor began. They did have time to get to the hospital (by car). Long mileage is also possible, if you stick to a comfortable pace.

All the women who have run in pregnancy speak of certain discomforts caused by their condition. Lower abdominal pain caused by round ligament stress is common, since these structures help support the growing uterus. One woman found that a wide ace bandage wrapped around the abdomen was helpful; another ran *faster* to alleviate the pain (by reducing sway, she speculates). They recommend urinating *before* the run, with "pitstops" along the way if necessary. A tree-lined route is helpful. One woman even mastered the art of peeing standing up (try loose underwear and a wide stance)! Elastic stockings can help subdue the varicose veins which can appear late in pregnancy.

Babies born to running mothers almost universally receive high marks (Apgar scores)* for alertness, color, and good disposition. Some have a special love for backpack rides and swings.

One of the advantages of running is that it increases

*"Apgar scores" are marks for alertness, color, etc., in the newborn. All newborns are scored this way within minutes. Dr. Virginia Apgar invented the scoring scale used.

oxygen uptake, the consumption of air by muscles (as opposed to *intake*—the consumption of air by the lungs). When you run, your heart rate increases, cardiac output more than doubles, and oxygen consumption can soar to 8 times the "resting" level. Despite these facts, some doctors fear that jogging in pregnancy might *reduce* oxygen supplies to the fetus. Though studies have not yet been done, I fail to see any logic behind this fear. For one thing, *decreased* fetal oxygenation during activity would be suicidal for the species. Mother Nature can't work that way. And anyone who observes the general alertness and health of babies born to running mothers must be convinced that they have received their full share of the extra daily oxygen.

The mothers report fast recoveries and returns to running (within 2 to 3 weeks generally, a month after a Cesarean section). Mary Jones ran the Boston Marathon 4 months postpartum.

CLOTHING.

Bras: Even if you were once a sub-A cup, you will need a larger and more supportive bra when pregnant. Try the Jogbra or similar styles designed for runners.

Abdominal Support: Use a wide ace bandage (adjustable to your requirements) or a special maternity panty-girdle—avoid anything that binds the thighs.

Chafing: Use liberal applications of petroleum jelly over all friction points, and between the thighs.

Shoes: As weight increases, cushioning and support become more important. Treat yourself to one of the top-rated models with these features.

There is a growing suspicion that a 9-month "time-out" from a serious athletic career, for these running mothers, may actually be beneficial in terms of performance. Many women runners have improved their times greatly after motherhood. Fanny Blankers-Koen, the great Dutch Olympian of the 40s, was the first to make a "comeback" after childbirth. Many examples can be given, now, of similar breakthroughs. Following childbirth, Judy Ikenberry (1st National Women's AAU Marathon Champion) ran 2:54 in the marathon, Madeline Manning Jackson was the first U.S. woman to break the 2-minute barrier in the 800 meters, and phenomenal Miki Gorman ran a 2:39 marathon—at age 40!

Recent East German studies reportedly found that women who had given birth were able to tolerate higher workloads than their peers. Therefore they encourage their women athletes to have a baby sometime in the 2 years before the Olympics. It's not specified who will take care of the baby, the husband and the house during training— presumably the state will provide!

If these reports are accurate, it is interesting to speculate what the physiological basis for increased work tolerance after childbirth might be. I suspect the clue may lie in Miki Gorman's comment: "Compared to having a baby, the marathon is *easy!*" Certainly pregnancy puts a huge physical and psychological burden on most women. And labor itself, while not inevitably painful, is undeniably hard work, as the name implies.

Another explanation may lie in the unavoidable anemia of pregnancy. Because of the increased maternal blood volume and the iron demands of the fetus, all mothers-to-be become anemic somewhere around midpregnancy, and childbirth results in the loss (via baby and placenta) of huge amounts of iron. If training continues throughout pregnancy and resumes shortly after delivery, the mother is experiencing the same effects as in altitude training— less oxygen is available to the working muscles. As the iron and red cell counts return to normal, the identical workload will become, subjectively, much easier. Or the athlete can even undertake a heavier workload with the same amount of effort.

Whatever the explanation, observation and some scientific studies tend to be reassuring to the pregnant athlete. Not only will she have (generally) an easier labor and faster recovery than inactive women, but maternity will probably enhance her athletic capacity in future years. Perhaps the benefits even compensate for a 6-month interlude in one's racing career!

Stress Incontinence: Many women are handicapped or discouraged in their jogging careers by the common affliction known as "stress *incontinence*." This term refers to the involuntary leakage of urine caused by sudden increases in intra-abdominal pressure—when laughing, coughing, sneezing or (alas) jogging—especially if your movements or breathing are excessively jerky while jogging. Developing a smoother running style and regular, unforced breathing definitely help the situation. Unfortunately, some women are so distressed by their problem that they avoid sports altogether. "I'm not athletic," they will smile apologetically, watching tennis or fun-runs from the sideline. Actually, they would love to participate, but don't, for fear of embarrassment.

These potential stars of Masters' running may take heart from knowing that they are not alone. Stress incontinence is one of the most common problems reported by women over 30. It definitely overshadows "Runner's Knee" and other popular orthopedic ailments. Most of the women bothered by incontinence don't run enough to develop Runner's Knee. And most of them are also too embarrassed to seek help, so they remain sedentary.

The usual cause of stress incontinence is stretching and laxity of the perineal tissues surrounding the bladder neck, together with weakness of the urethral sphincter muscle. The stretching generally results from childbirth and is aggravated by inactivity and poor muscle tone. To make a brief obstetrical digression, I recall that my own medical school instructors advised *routine* episiotomy and the use of "outlet" forceps in normal deliveries, with the intent of reducing the incidence of stress incontinence in later years. "The baby's head acts as a battering ram against the perineum in second-stage labor," explained the resident. "By preventing such tremendous stretching now, we hope to reduce the number of women coming in ten or twenty years later for repairs." While I, myself, applaud the main aim of "natural" childbirth, to keep the mother "awake and alert," the body undrugged—I have to agree with the resident that a totally uncontrolled birth, "out under the bushes," as he said, might cause unnecessary stretching or other maternal damage, especially in prolonged deliveries.

But back to the older woman, generally a mother, who runs in place for a few steps and finds that she has to go change her underwear. Obviously, sports are not for her, unless certain measures are taken. A survey of suggestions sent to me by readers shows three different approaches that can be used: (1) protection (2) strengthening (3) surgical intervention.

Protection is the most obvious. Many women with only minor leakage can get by with a mini-pad. If you empty your bladder just before running, this should be adequate for the initial jogs, at least. If you progress to racing (with greater stress) and/or long runs, a maxi-pad may be needed. One woman marathoner swears by Pampers, with their greater capacity and waterproof outer layer. If it works for a toddler, why not for his mother?

Strengthening is a more hopeful alternative. Not all women who have given birth develop stress incontinence. Those who do not, tend to have better muscle tone (or less damage initially—as with smaller babies). Athletic individuals—even those who start later in life—gradually build up the perineal musculature as they increase muscle tone generally. So some mild problems of incontinence will clear up spontaneously as you continue to run (months, not days, are required). You can greatly speed up the strengthening process by doing specific exercises—the same ones, in fact, that are taught to men who have had prostate operations and need to restore bladder control. The exercises ("Kegel") are very simple, mostly just alternate tightening (squeezing) and relaxation of the muscles of the perineum, which surround the bladder neck and vagina. Practicing them can not only help incontinence, it also may enhance your sex life! (An added bonus.) One other exercise that helps strengthen the bladder sphincter itself involves tightening the sphincter several times during urination, interrupting the flow. A couple of weeks of these exercises can give dramatic improvement.

Surgery is, of course, the most drastic (and "unnatural") solution, but may give the fastest and best results. The most common operation (a "Marshall-Marchetti") is quite simple and trouble-free, though it may not be appropriate in all cases. Check with your own gynecologist about this. One young mother I know (definitely young, since she's my own age) started appearing in local runs last year, after years of watching from the sidelines. She shaped up, got faster and improved her endurance greatly within months. "Why did you wait so long to get started?" I asked curiously, since she wasn't the type who simply follows fads. "Incontinence!" proclaimed my friend loudly (several nearby women in the race pricked up their ears). "I finally went and had a repair, and I wish I'd done it *years* ago," she elaborated. "Now, I feel liberated, I can do anything I like." With that testimony, you may not wish to depend on Pampers throughout your running career!

A problem related to stress incontinence is that of the "prolapsed uterus," in fact, the two conditions generally go together. The woman notices stress incontinence; the gynecologist examines her and says her problem is a prolapsed uterus (with bladder prolapse as well—the structures are connected). One Chicago gynecologist caused a mild furor recently by announcing that uterine prolapse results from jogging; he cautioned women against the sport, concluding sadly that because they are constructed too "loosely," they are not suited for running.

This statement is shockingly sexist and untrue. In fairness, one must assume that the doctor was either misquoted or misinterpreted. Stress incontinence and prolapse of pelvic structures can result from (1) overstretching during childbirth and (2) disuse atrophy of pelvic musculature and generally poor muscle tone. Symptoms (like incontinence) are much more pronounced in the first group. In the second group, there may be no symptoms whatever unless the woman is subject to sneezing or coughing fits. Naturally, women who have been sedentary for years often take up jogging and begin to notice some urine leakage. Naturally, too, they consult their doctor. If he is unfamiliar with runners, who usually have tight, not loose, pelvic musculature, he may come to the erroneous conclusion that jogging has *caused* the prolapsed uterus, when in truth, it has just become noticeable through the unaccustomed activity.

If a man has watched TV for years, developed a beer belly and potential hernias, then starts to jog and notices the hernia, he too may visit a doctor. You can bet your life, however, that the doctor won't inform him that the male body is unsuitable for running. A smart M.D. will counsel the man to lose some weight, build up muscle tone through continued jogging, and then if necessary have a hernia repair. Which is exactly what the Chicago gynecologist should have advised his female patient.

I am distressed by the myth, commonly heard, that women's wider pelvis results in looseness and bouncing of the pelvic contents—both excretory and reproductive—and represents an inherent weakness. If we're talking of "looseness" or lack of intrinsic support, surely the structures most at risk are the male genitalia, which bounce around totally external to the pelvis. But do any doctors warn

231

against this hazard, or make ominous predictions about elongated testicles, sterility or impotence as a result of jogging? Of course not. Yet the actual momentum imparted to male organs by each running step is far greater than that affecting the female parts, which are cozily protected *within* the body. Increased muscle tone can support them even better, while no amount of exercise will improve the bouncing condition of the male. If momentum (and jarring) were indeed a problem, you would see a far greater dependence on jock straps than is commonly observed. In fact, most experienced (male) runners prefer to "swing free," and no doctor has yet sounded an alarm about this practice. No dire warnings about "scrotal sag," testicular atrophy, or prostatitis. In short, medical "experts" who discourage women from running on grounds of alleged anatomical inferiority are simply letting age-old prejudice against women athletes overwhelm logic and consistency. Ignore them.

There is another kind of urinary incontinence which can affect men as well as women and should not be confused with the problem discussed above. This is the temporary loss of sphincter control that can occur with extreme exhaustion. Be happy if it's only the *bladder* sphincter that's involved! This sudden, unexpected leakage can happen to anyone, particularly nearing the finish line of a very demanding race on a very hot day. Your mind may be willing to push you on, but your body suddenly rebels— hopefully, not until you've crossed the finish, since such urinary leakage is a sign of total exhaustion. If you find yourself suddenly beset with involuntary leakage (often accompanied by chills and/or palpitations) while you're still racing in the heat, you're in trouble. It's an advanced danger signal. Stop racing at once and walk to the finish, or just sit in the shade under a tree till you recover. Don't risk your health!

Skin Care. Running is popularly believed to keep you young-looking as well as young at heart and of body. Certainly there are many runners in their 40s and 50s who appear 10 to 20 years younger than you would expect. I think that this apparent youth is owing more to general health, vitality and animation than to any mysterious capacity of running to prevent wrinkling of the skin. Certainly, the improved circulation and oxygen flow that running brings to the face should help to maintain good skin tone and quality. But circulation isn't everything. Runners are outdoors a lot, and the environment is not always kind to skin. If you look closely at a 40-year-old runner you mistook for her daughter, you can usually find the telltale wrinkles and laugh lines.

Certain factors can actually work *against* a youthful appearance in runners. The hollow cheeks and leanness so coveted by "serious" runners, as a sign that they are fit and tough, imply a lack of subcutaneous fat. It is this same fat which fills out the skin of teenaged girls and lends them that unwrinkled "bloom of youth." When the fat disappears, skin lines show up more readily.

Dehydration can have even more striking effects, though only temporarily. Check out marathoners (male and female) after a race. If they haven't replaced their fluids along the way, they may look like wrinkled old men at the finish. The loss of moisture from the tissues causes the skin to droop, unsupported. A few beers will restore the apparent 50-year-old to his 30-year-old face.

Remember that the greatest enemy of skin, young or old, runner or sun-worshiper, is the *sun*. Ultraviolet light penetrates unprotected skin, breaks down elastic fibers and damages collagen. In the fair-skinned, ultraviolet light causes freckles, blotches, and other patchy melanin deposits. If you're lucky, it will cause an even tan, which is an evenly distributed increase in melanin content.

The luckiest runners, when it comes to preserving youth, are those whom nature has protected with an inborn melanin layer—Blacks, some Hispanics, some Orientals. If you lack this natural protection, it makes sense to cover up when you run in the sun. Wear a visor to shield your face (and nose), and invest in a huge bottle of sunscreen lotion. Use it liberally before you go out. Look for something with PABA in an aqueous solution (oils don't work so well). A good lotion will soften the skin somewhat and adhere longer than an oil, though both tend to wash off with sweat. The protection is *not* as good as that afforded by a dark skin. On a hot day, I have an overwhelming urge to dunk my head in streams and wash my face with the cool water. Naturally, this washes off the sunscreen, too. But at least I make an effort. I use up bottles and bottles of a lotion that I first encountered as a (tiny) free sample at a women's race, showing that it pays to distribute useful products to runners. Unless PABA is someday discovered to be carcinogenic—which is not likely—my face will be in better shape 20 years hence than if I ran unprotected against the elements. But if you really want to avoid all the sun's adverse effects, you'd better run in the fog, or at night. Running, by itself, will not preserve you.

Chapter Fourteen: Controversies

"Athlete's Heart." You will frequently see reports in the local papers that "experts disagree . . ." about the value of running—for men, women, children, those with weak hearts, confused minds, arthritis, etc., etc. In fact, though a good reporter can dig up contrary "expert" opinions on almost any topic imaginable, running is currently a far less controversial issue than in the recent past. No medical authority any longer believes that running can damage a healthy heart. Even Dr. Meyer Friedman, the most vehement critic of competitive or "strenuous" activities, is primarily worried about the effect of such sports on people who already have severe heart disease—but may be totally unaware of it. The classic example is the middle-aged male who goes out to shovel snow and drops dead of a heart attack.

Most genuine "experts," meaning those who not only have an M.D. degree, but are also personally familiar with runners and running, actually agree that the body benefits from any continuous, aerobic activity. Running, cycling, swimming, walking—all clearly lead to a sense of well-being, a lower pulse rate, a more efficient heart, greater exercise capacity, endurance, and enhanced resistance to fatigue. These effects have been documented repeatedly. The real controversy these days is not *whether* the heart benefits, but to what extent, and how?

At one end of the spectrum are Bassler, Scaff and their colleagues, who like to promise virtual immortality to marathoners—or at least absolute immunity to fatal heart attacks—though you can still die of cancer, or get hit by a car (not an uncommon demise among runners, unfortunately). Those with less radical views ask for proof, rather than mere "anecdotal" evidence, and are often involved in research which seeks to collect such evidence. Virtually all the doctors involved in these controversies are on the side of the angels; that is, they are all runners, and hope to demonstrate that their chosen addiction is as healthful as it is enjoyable. Aware of this bias, they try to be scrupulously fair and quantitative in their assessments.

The late Dr. Paul Dudley White was an early exercise enthusiast, and a familiar figure on his daily bicycle rides. Twenty years ago, this famous cardiologist helped to debunk the early myth about "athlete's heart." This was the notion that the "enlarged" heart characteristic of well-conditioned athletes was similar to the "enlarged" heart of little old men admitted to the hospital with congestive heart failure. Both hearts looked big on X rays, after all, and "common sense" in those days dictated that anyone who would run long distances must be straining his system terribly. Also, it was a common observation that ex-athletes went downhill fast, often succumbing to heart attacks. Medical myth attributed their demise to "athlete's heart." But in 1960, White and his colleagues managed to examine (after embalming, unfortunately) the heart of Clarence DeMar, "Mr. Marathon" himself, the long-dis-

236

tance runner who had won the Boston Marathon 7 times by 1930. He continued to run until months before his death—of cancer—at age 70. Autopsy of this ultimate "athlete's heart" didn't show the expected chronic damage; instead, White reported, it looked like the heart of a man in his 30s. The coronary arteries were especially impressive—wide of bore, and virtually free of atherosclerosis. The doctors concluded that "running long distances for many years does not appear to have damaged" DeMar's heart—a strikingly conservative comment from our modern point of view, but quite radical at the time.

What happens to ex-athletes, then, if their hearts aren't damaged? Apparently, they revert quickly to the unconditioned state of their sedentary neighbors, and their formerly strong, healthy, slow beating hearts become weak, flabby, pitter-pattering organs again. The heart muscle atrophies, in effect, so the heart *should* get smaller. But, the heart is surrounded by fat, and if the ex-football player continues to eat like a linebacker when he has retired to the armchair, his heart may still be large—with fat, rather than muscle. If he maintains his weight, instead of losing pounds, as the once muscular body reverts to flab, he'll be an excellent candidate for a heart attack. I believe this is how all the warnings about the perils of athlete's heart got started. A sensible ex-athlete is no more imperiled than the rest of the population. The truly sensible ex-jocks, of course, take up running or some other regular exercise to maintain their health.

Recent studies which attempt to document the advantages of exercise are mainly of the epidemiological or statistical variety. This is because it's hard to put human beings into a long-term, randomized, and controlled study. And experimental studies on randomized groups of rats, say, or pigs, aren't very convincing to humans.

Epidemiological studies usually compare two groups which are quite similar in all respects except activity level:

bus drivers (who sit) versus bus conductors (who dash around), or postal clerks versus peripatetic postmen. All such studies suffer from the criticism that the more sedentary groups may have chosen to be that way, have eased themselves into the less active positions, because they were predisposed to sit. In other words, the groups weren't really comparable—the more active may be basically healthier to begin with.

Dr. Ralph Paffenbarger's recent studies skirted around this particular pitfall, and provide important evidence that high caloric expenditure (in work *or* play) is associated with a lesser incidence of cardiovascular disease (heart attacks, angina, or stroke). "Paffie," as he is known to friends, is a Harvard alumnus, and a professor of epidemiology at Stanford. He also happens to be a long-time runner and an ultramarathoner, who has twice completed the ultra-rugged, 100-mile Western States Endurance Run in less than 24 hours (in his 50s). Yes, his heart is biased toward running, but his statistical methodology is sound.

Paffenbarger's retrospective analysis of 17,000 Harvard alumni suggests that recreational energy expenditures totaling 2000 calories weekly provide measurable protection against the cardiovascular diseases which plague twentieth-century Americans. The 2000-calorie level is easily obtainable by most joggers, figuring about 100 calories/mile, or 20 miles/week. This protective effect appears to be statistically distinguishable from the beneficial effects attributable to diet, lack of smoking, lower blood pressure, and lower blood lipid levels. If you improve *all* these risk factors simultaneously, as do most runners, you stand an excellent chance of eventually dying of something *other* than heart disease.

Useful as Paffenbarger's quantification of the "beneficial" level of exercise may be, it is far from the prospective, randomized study that many skeptical doctors demand. In practice, of course, "randomization" of treatment is virtually impossible. The nationwide "MR. FIT" study is a good example of the pitfalls that can plague a rigorously controlled study on humans. "MR. FIT" stands for Multiple Risk Factor Intervention Trial, and is an attempt to determine if "intervention," aimed at reducing certain "risk factors" in persons considered prime candidates for coronary artery disease, actually has any effect on their eventual development of disease. The idea is to identify a number of males 35- to 50-years-old, who (1) have high blood pressure, (2) smoke cigarettes, and (3) have high cholesterol and triglyceride levels. Candidates for the study are then randomly assigned to "intervention" or "control" groups. The "controls" are then neglected, receiving no advice or medication, while the lucky others get medicine to lower blood pressure, stop-smoking programs, and advice on dietary and exercise measures that can help lower cholesterol.

If you were a patient referred to this program by your doctor, and alarmed to hear that you were in a high-risk group because of your dismal health and habits, how would you like to be assigned to the control group? Would you make no attempt, on your own, to stop smoking and lower your cholesterol? Would you refuse your doctor's medication to lower blood pressure? Probably not. In fact, sheer stubbornness might impel you to change your life-style more drastically than your fellow patients in the "intervention" group, who may be lulled into complacency.

In sum, humans—unlike rats—tend to object to being randomized, especially if they're assigned to a "let nature take its course" group. If they're motivated to a join the study to begin with, they're also anxious to *do* something. So a rigorously controlled prospective study of the influence of exercise on heart disease is simply not feasible.

Data comparing people who already run with those who remain sedentary are much easier to come by. We know, for instance, that distance runners are leaner than the average American, seldom smoke cigarettes, and tend to have normal or low blood pressure—in other words, they are in the "low risk" group. Studies at Dr. Kenneth Cooper's clinic in Dallas have demonstrated that aerobic fitness ("good" or "excellent" level) is a separate factor lowering the risk of coronary artery disease.

Your chances of a heart attack, then, are statistically minimal if you are a young female, run daily but non-competitively, avoid cigarettes, keep your weight and fat content low, and have low blood pressure. You may, of course, alarm your doctor if he is not familiar with the powerful heart of a young woman athlete. But you know better. Keep your heart athletic, your resting pulse slow—and watch out for cars. The prudent doctor, rather than waiting for absolute proof to be in, would give you the same advice.

Cholesterol and HDL.

Runners are always eager to demonstrate how healthy they are. They leap at the chance to take treadmill tests, give blood samples that will demonstrate their superior metabolism, and generally try to impress the doctor. Sometimes this eagerness can back-fire: several Masters runners, themselves M.D.s, discovered signs of coronary artery insufficiency when striving for new treadmill records at a medical meeting. Such incidents are, fortunately, rare. Most researchers who wish to study runners are assured of an adequate supply of superhealthy volunteers. As a result we are learning more and more about the features that distinguish active people from their sedentary counterparts. The new data quickly find their way into the popular press and running seminars.

One recent study has established that runners have high "HDL-cholesterol" levels. You always thought high cholesterol was bad for you, right? Well, apparently this was an oversimplified idea. As Dr. Bassler expresses it, we now know there is "friendly" as well as "unfriendly" cholesterol.

To understand the HDL story, which was pieced together

by Dr. Peter Wood and his colleagues at the Stanford Heart Disease Prevention Program, you have to understand how fats travel through the bloodstream. Fats, or lipids, are insoluble in water and aqueous solutions, like blood. So all fats, whether ingested (dietary) or locally produced (endogenous), travel in suspension, in little globules. If blood is drawn shortly after you have a fatty meal, you can see all these suspended lipids with your own eyes—they give a shimmering, incandescent, yellowish tinge to the blood, and render the plasma portion opaque. They also mess up laboratory instruments, which is why doctors prefer to draw blood from people in the fasting state.

The lipid globules come in various sizes. The largest, from ingested fat, are called chylomicra. The rest are classified according to density—from the largest, balloon-like "very-low-density lipoproteins," or VLDL, to the smallest, "high-density-lipoproteins," or HDL. In between, of course, are the plain LDL ("low-density"). As the name "lipoprotein" implies, these globules contain protein as well as lipid; the protein molecules help form an interface with the surrounding aqueous solution (blood) and keep the lipids in suspension. The fat molecules, being unwelcome by their naked selves, cluster together in the middle of the globule. Cholesterol, which also travels in these particles, is found mainly in the shell.

An eminent lipid researcher, Dr. Richard Havel, has pointed out that the cholesterol/triglycerides (small fats) *ratio* in the plasma is determined largely by the geometry of spheres. The larger the particle, the less "shell" (surface area) there is, relative to the core. In a simplified diagram, it would look like this:

Cholesterol	Cholesterol	Not much room for TG inside
TG	TG	tg
VLDL	LDL	HDL

So if a person has elevated cholesterol *and* triglycerides, her blood will contain lots of the larger particles. If her cholesterol is high, say 200 to 250, but triglycerides low—about 50—she naturally has more of the smaller (HDL) particles.

All this is of great interest to lipid chemists, but not, until recently, to the rest of us. High cholesterol was considered bad, and probably worse in conjunction with high triglycerides, but we let the doctors worry about such things. (Unfortunately, some doctors never even worried till blood lipid levels reached incredibly dangerous heights, like 300 or more for both cholesterol *and* triglycerides. Personally, I would consider a cholesterol over 180 and triglycerides over 80 uncomfortably high.)

A few years ago, HDL leapt into prominence from the obscurity of the lipid journals. It was discovered that individuals in line for a heart attack have lower HDL-cholesterol levels than normal—less than 20 percent of their total cholesterol is in HDL, to be exact. Conversely, *more* is in the LDL particles, which explains why these people usually have high triglyceride levels as well as high cholesterol. "Normal" levels of HDL cholesterol are 20 to 30 percent of the total.

What of runners? Dr. Wood's research, mainly on male and female runners over age 30, showed that they are even better than "normal." Many have 50 to 60 percent of their total cholesterol in the form of HDL. Among sedentary controls, only young women show such high HDL cholesterol—and young women seem to be protected against coronary artery disease. Great excitement in the medical community! Rejoicing among runners! Perhaps this is the mechanism by which running protects against heart disease!

With the discovery that your total cholesterol level is not so important as the HDL level, HDL tests became very popular with health-maintenance clinics, and runners.

Many runners, who had avoided cheese and ice cream for years because of "high" cholesterol (above 200), returned to gluttony with a sigh of relief when they discovered they had 55 percent HDL. Those who believe diet to·be more important than exercise tended to reserve judgment, and stuck to their brown rice-and-vegetables regimen.

One question that has not been resolved by Wood's research is the old bugaboo of self-selection. Perhaps running doesn't *cause* protective HDL levels, perhaps it's just that people who naturally have higher HDL like to run. What we need is a good before-and-after study of runners (several are in progress at present). The aim is to establish whether people who *start* to exercise late in life can elevate their HDL cholesterol. Of course, it is already well known that regular aerobic exercise lowers trig-lyceride levels. If you refer back to the sphere chart, you will note that decreasing triglycerides implies lowering VLDL and LDL levels, and thus would automatically increase the *proportion* of HDL particles. If nature is at all consistent, we can anticipate that well-controlled before-and-after studies will eventually demonstrate that run-ning increases "friendly" cholesterol.

Wait a minute, say the diehard TV watchers and beer drinkers. Maybe there's a way to get protective HDL levels without doing all that nasty, unpleasant exercise. One solution, of course, is to be a young female, hardly a universal option. But, hold on—*other* researchers have discovered that alcohol ingestion will raise HDL! Yes folks, sit back, put your feet up, drink more beer, and you may die of cirrhosis—but at least you'll have a nice, high HDL level.

In fact, it doesn't work out that way. Sloth is not rewarded to the same degree as virtue. More research on HDL shows that there is not only "friendly" cholesterol in these particles, but a "friendly" subfraction. Further split-ting of the HDL fraction of serum reveals 3 electrophoretic

243

"peaks," cleverly labeled alpha, beta, and gamma. Gamma is the good guy, and is elevated in those "low-risk" groups, young women and runners. In sedentary normals, and middle-aged males, the HDL that is present is largely alpha and beta type, and apparently non-protective. In alcoholics, it is these non-protective alpha and beta peaks that are increased.

As research now stands, then, you are better off running than drinking. And if you're a young running female, you have it made.

Diet vs. Exercise.   Even among doctors who agree that exercise is wonderful, healthful, and life-restoring, there is ample room for disagreement. Arguments and controversy add a great deal of spice and interest to otherwise dull medical meetings. One of the most heated and continuous arguments centers around the role of diet—is a certain pattern of eating essential, helpful, or irrelevant? Some running doctors advocate continuous hydration by beer, others warn against any alcohol ingestion. The advocates of megavitamin programs are challenged by nutritionists and studies claiming that supplements to the normal diet are useless and a waste of money. Those who maintain you can eat whatever you like, as long as you run enough, are denounced by other experts who believe that even marathoners must steer clear of eggs, butter and steak.

If you are not already sufficiently confused by controversy among the experts, and you wish to follow these colorful conflicts in detail, let me suggest you read the *AMJA Newsletter,* which features wild testimonials by Dr. Bassler and others, countered by equally vehement and wild-eyed proponents of opposite viewpoints. Sometimes the bemused, general readership is moved to comment. "Enough is enough!" wrote one of these "neutral" running doctors in mid-1979. "These absurd attacks and counterattacks are . . . the workings of obstinate children." He

244

suggested the arguing physicians recall that most of us run for enjoyment, "for the pleasure, not for the longevity."

If anyone wishes to know where *I* stand on all the above issues, let me reiterate briefly that I am (a) *for* running, (b) *against* alcohol ingestion on the run or while driving, (c) *against* vitamin supplements, in general, (d) *for* iron supplements for women (e) *for* a vegetarian or low-fat diet. I have given detailed reasons for all these opinions in the past, and have no intention of doing so again.

Just because I have opinions doesn't mean that I always adhere to them. I enjoy wine, and love ice cream. Pastries and whipped cream can always tempt me. Chocolate is irresistible. And once, having run out of iron tablets and being too cheap to buy more, I found myself suddenly anemic.

I have a nagging feeling that for optimal health I should be living on sprouts and brown rice. But not being sick, I'm not sufficiently motivated to make drastic life-style changes. I hope that those who believe that marathoning excuses a multitude of sins will turn out to be right.

Our own data at the Institute of Health Research, however, suggest that diet has much more influence on blood chemistries, specifically on lipids, than does exercise. Among our 2000 healthy research subjects are a sizable number of vegetarians of all types—some sedentary, others active; some "ovo-lacto" eaters, others purists. A total analysis of their blood "profiles," broken down according to type, has yet to be completed. But, "eyeballing" the results of blood tests on these people over a period of 6 years left me with several distinct impressions. If you look just at the cholesterol and triglyceride levels, the lowest—and presumably the most healthful—values were found among running vegetarians. Next, a close second, came the results among non-running vegetarians. Not quite so outstanding were the nonvegetarian runners, who had admirably low and well-controlled triglycerides, but somewhat higher cholesterol values. Finally, trailing behind in dismal last place, were our "normals"—the typical, average, non-sick American who is neither very active nor a vegetarian. True "meat-and-potatoes" types, especially the sour-cream lovers, were probably underrepresented among our normals, since high blood lipids were grounds for exclusion from the program.

These findings provide good support for the concept that diet may be just as important as exercise in the battle against coronary artery disease. But the foremost advocate of the dietary approach, an engineer by the name of Nathan Pritikin, has even better data. Pritikin, an extremely well-informed "layman"—he has no medical degree—leapt into the vacuum left by doctors too cautious to give diet therapy a try. He founded the Longevity Institute, now located in Santa Monica, where victims of advanced atherosclerosis, diabetes, and related disorders can come for a month of strictly supervised therapy and reeducation. The Pritikin diet is drastic by American standards, but palatable, even ingenious. It contains about 80 percent carbohydrate, 10 percent protein, and less than 10 percent fat. Comparable values in the average American diet are 30 percent, 30 percent, and 40 percent respectively.

Pritikin achieves dramatic results—but precisely those that one would expect with such a diet and a highly motivated group. (Not only are they grasping at a last alternative to open-heart surgery or death, they also pay $4600 for the month-long program.) Blood pressure drops; cholesterol, triglycerides, and weight are lowered significantly; insulin requirements decline, sometimes to nil. If I or one of my loved ones suffered from atherosclerosis or related ailments, we wouldn't hesitate to take up immediate residence at the Longevity Institute. The results are virtually guaranteed. And the wealth of careful data being collected by doctors at the Institute is beginning to win

246

over the most skeptical group of all, the surgeons—whose usual approach can be summarized as "a chance to cut is a chance to cure."

The Pritikin Program may emphasize diet, but not to the exclusion of other contributory health measures. Smoking is Out—no "cheating" allowed, and exercise is definitely In. Most patients at the Institute are walking or jogging 6 to 10 miles daily by the time they leave—even if they couldn't cover 100 feet without pain, on arrival. Pritikin, of course, would argue that reducing atherosclerotic buildup within arteries, by means of diet, leads to greater exercise tolerance and improved circulation. Diehard exercise buffs would rather believe that the long hours spent in aerobic exercise result in better circulation and healthier blood lipids. The debate continues, though both sides welcome the results.

Pritikin himself hedges his bet. He adheres religiously to a low-fat diet, but runs 5 miles a day with his wife. On weekends, they often go 10 miles. Whatever the mechanism, he has reduced his own cholesterol from over 300 to a value around 120. He also looks and acts extremely fit. Trim and dark-haired, with sparkling eyes, he resembles a man of 45 rather than the 65 he claims. I was introduced to Pritikin at a recent running symposium, and promptly dropped my pen as I asked for his autograph. Before I could bend over (stiffly) and retrieve it, Pritikin demonstrated superior agility by bending over gracefully and scooping up the pen almost before it hit the ground. I was impressed. Lunch that day consisted entirely of vegetarian gourmet delights from *The Pritikin Program,* an excellent cookbook. We feasted on rice, green vegetables, whole-grain bread, and salads with low-fat dressings. For those who were not hard-liners, however, butter, coffee and tea were available. I felt a bit guilty sitting next to Pritikin and questioning him, while I blatantly stirred my second cup of coffee and had a telltale coating of butter on the delicious whole-grain bread. Pritikin graciously avoided comment on these lapses. Across the table, podiatrist Steve Subotnick virtuously ate his bread plain—or so it appeared. When I complimented Subotnick later on his ability to dispense with fatty spreads, he confessed that he had buttered his bread on the *bottom,* so Pritikin wouldn't notice.

Such is the response of most marathoners—they concentrate on exercise, but try to be at least *prudent* about what they eat. And if they "cheat" a bit, whether with butter or a piece of blueberry cheesecake, their gustatory pleasure may be tinged with guilt—as if, perhaps, diet *may* be important, too.

Carbo-loading. In quotes, this phrase actually refers to the masochistic practice of carbohydrate-*depleting* for several days. Then, when one is thoroughly weakened by continued hard training in the absence of carbohydrate intake, one dives into the high-carbohydrate goodies for 2 to 3 days, allowing one's carbo-starved muscles, in essence, to gorge themselves in relief. Technically, this diet should be called carbohydrate-*over*loading, since its demonstrated effect is to increase the amount of glycogen stored in the muscles.

I have modified my views somewhat on the subject of "carbo-loading." It has never been proven that loading up on extra glycogen does anything positive for an athlete's performance. The sizable weight increase (due to the large amounts of water bound by glycogen) could actually be detrimental in a race. The original Scandinavian study of runners using the "overloading" diet did *not* provide clear-cut results. The greatest improvement was observed in a few relatively untrained subjects, who would tend to be more glycogen-dependent than experienced distance runners anyway. Also, the distance raced in the test was only 30 km., or 18.6 miles, too short for anyone to hit the infamous "Wall" which is believed to signal total glycogen depletion in a marathon.

Although I myself have never encountered the Wall, I used to play it safe and "carbo-overload" anyway, just in case. But doing it even once or twice a year proved too much for my feeble willpower. I would wake up weak and cold on day two, drag myself up a flight of stairs, heart pounding, trip over the rug, and wonder how I could ever summon the energy to run my workout. In the past couple of years, I have quietly abandoned dietary manipulation as a means to better performance. I have detected no difference in my ability to run marathons. I continue to have good days and bad days, on an unpredictable basis—just as I did on the runs for which I "loaded."

Many other, better marathoners, who used this diet regularly in the mid-70s, have dispensed with it now, often after a bad experience of heavy legs or "loginess." The only world-class marathoner I know who still utilizes the full "classic" regimen is Don Kardong (fourth in the 1976 Olympic marathon), who thinks it's a useful crutch when he doesn't believe he's in top shape yet, or when he feels he's lacking in long training runs (and thus, more glycogen-dependent than he'd like). His successes—as in the Olympic Trials in 1976 and the Honolulu Marathon, in 1978—may reflect an individual idiosyncrasy, too. Don's known to have more "fast-twitch" fibers or "sprinter's" muscle than other 2:11 marathoners. Perhaps he has a special need to feed these "speedy" fibers, to keep them happy.

In general, I'm reluctant to advise any drastic changes in normal eating habits the week before a big marathon. If practiced properly, the carbohydrate-"overload" diet will play havoc with your fat and muscle metabolism, with unpredictable results. And, remember, women may have even less use for this diet than men, if Van Aaken's theory of superior fat utilization (by female muscles) proves to be correct. However, if you insist on trying it, here is the proper way, in preparation for a big race on Day 8.

DAY 1:

Run 2½ hours or more, to deplete your muscles of glycogen. The faster you run, the faster you'll deplete, so a 2-hour race may be as good as a 3-hour slow run. Drink only water during the run, tea or coffee after. No juices, beer or soft drinks (even diet drinks have some carbos).

Lunch: Cottage cheese and shrimp.
Dinner: Steak and a lettuce and mushroom salad, oil and vinegar dressing. No dessert.
To drink: Lots of water—you'll need to keep your kidneys flushed out.

DAYS 2 AND 3:

Continue regular training. You'll probably feel horrible and be slower than usual, so don't time yourself.

Breakfast: Herb or mushroom omelets, cottage cheese, black coffee or tea are allowed. You may get tired of boiled eggs, but eat as many as you like.
Lunch: Again, a small salad with no-carbohydrate ingredients is good, plus cottage cheese.
Dinner: Try fish or chicken—broiled, with herbs; or Rock Cornish game hen; or turkey. But, *no* stuffing allowed, no thickened gravy; and of course, no mashed potatoes. A small helping of a green vegetable—broccoli or asparagus—is permitted: beans and carrots have too much carbohydrate. For "dessert," try a cottage cheese and shrimp cocktail. By the evening of Day 3, you will probably feel nauseated, and tempted to sell your soul for a baked potato or a piece of toast. Hang on until . . .

DAY 4:

Get up and run out the door before your body has time to object. This is transition day. After the pre-breakfast run (remember to drink water first), you can hit the carbohydrates again. A feast! I usually have toast with jam, English muffins with honey, granola with a banana, etc. Did I mention that fruits are *verboten* during the depletion days? Now you can eat them all—they're juicy bags of good carbohydrate.

Some very disciplined persons stick to the original schedule of 4 days of depletion and 3 days of loading. I prefer the reverse, and "expert" opinion suggests the amount of extra glycogen stored by this diet is the same whether you deplete 3 or 4 days. As long as you're feeling weak and slow, the first few days, your depletion has been adequate.

DAYS 5 AND 6:

Loading Days. Bliss for the poor depleted runner. "Complex" carbohydrates such as whole-grain breads and cereals, potatoes, fruits and pasta are preferred by nutritionists. Junk-food freaks, however, can peacefully turn to pies, cakes, chocolate, and ice cream. One outstanding marathoner I know munches candy bars the last few days before a big race (I think her idea of depletion is to abstain from candy the first few days). In short, *any* kind of carbohydrate will do—it all turns into the same glycogen.

Once your liver has a good supply of carbos again (and you feel "fed," if not stuffed), your muscles load up their share. You can actually feel the change in your leg muscles on this diet. During the depletion phase, they feel soft and pliable. When they've loaded up (by Day 5 or 6), they'll be firm and solid—sort of like a salami. Are you really sure you want to do this?

Naturally, while your muscles are busy storing up all this glycogen for use in future runs, you don't want to drain it off again. So you must be very slothful for the last few days. Avoid any demanding activities or moving fast. Run about 5 miles on Day 5, 3 miles on Day 6, not at all on

251

Day 7. Jog slowly and stay completely aerobic, so your muscles don't start to consume those precious glycogen stores. You should do so little running that you feel guilty and a bit nervous about it.

Day 7:

A rest-and-eat day. But eat lightly and avoid roughage, spicy food, etc. Pizza and salad may be fine carbohydrate sources, but they have messed up the best-laid plans of many runners when ingested the night before a marathon. Any roughage eaten up to 24 hours before a marathon may cause the runs during the race. Instead of your usual granola breakfast, try a sweet roll or toast. Lasagne, manicotti, etc., are great for supper. All kinds of pastries are easily and quickly digested (unless they're loaded with whipped cream).

Day 8 (Race Day):

Rise at least 3 hours before the race if you want to eat (I advise it), and have your last solid food 2 hours before the start. I always eat toast or an English muffin with jam or honey, and I drink tea instead of my usual coffee, because tea is easier on my stomach. Eat whatever *you* can digest quickly and easily—the simpler the carbohydrates, the better. For instance, white toast is more processed, hence digested faster, than whole grain. Don't put butter on your toast or cream in your coffee, because all fats slow down digestion and may still be around in your stomach when the race starts—an undesirable situation.

High-carbohydrate diet.

Most high-mileage runners burn so many calories that they can eat like pigs and not put on weight. From 80 miles a week on up, such runners can be recognized, at rest, by the combination of a lean frame and conspicuous carbohydrate consumption. Their *daily* diet resembles the loading phase of the special "carbo-overloading" regimen. They simply never bother with the depletion diet, since they are depleting their muscle glycogen continuously on the run.

Don't ask these runners if they "carbo-load" (they'll say yes), when what you really want to know is if they depleted several days before loading. Their schedule doesn't give them time for dietary depletion. Generally, world-class women marathoners I have known tend to be less extravagant in their pursuit of carbos than their male counterparts. Marty Cooksey, for instance, is a vegetarian who eats lightly the day before a race and not at all the morning of the run. She likes to feel lean and mean, and is hard to catch with a pastry in hand. I have yet to see Marty "pig-out" in classic style.

Men, even the best, are different. Once when I was in Spokane for their annual "Lilac Bloomsday Run," the race sponsors sensibly decided to forgo their spaghetti feed for the invited runners the evening before the race. Instead, they went right to the heart of the matter with a pre-race "dessert" evening. I was in ecstasy. Spread over table upon table, in room after room, were trays of gourmet delights for the dessert-minded: cakes, pastries, etc. I positioned myself happily beside the pastry table after sampling the intervening cake and pie rooms, and proceeded to eat while talking. Engrossed, it took me a while to notice that another arm was snaking out from the other side of the table and grabbing the most decadent cream puffs, éclairs and napoleons just as I reached toward them. Annoyed to find myself so consistently outmaneuvered, I looked to see what pig belonged to the arm that was raking in even more than I could have eaten. The culprit was none other than Bill Rodgers, the Boston Marathon winner, who appeared as undernourished and frail as ever. Even I was amazed and awed at the way he could shovel in those pastries. Bill did not suffer from his indulgence; he won the race the following day in record time. Perhaps, if I ran over 160 miles each week, I too could handle a few more éclairs.

If Rodgers is the King of the Simple Carbohydrates, Jack Foster, New Zealand's over-40 Olympian, is still the King of the Complex Carbos. Jack admits that he doesn't "do the diet," he just loads all the time. I didn't realize the implications of this statement until I saw him return from a bountiful buffet table in Honolulu, his plate heaped high with mashed potatoes. Like kids, Jack had mashed down the center of the pile with a spoon to make a huge lake for gravy. Instead of gravy, he had filled the depression with a small mountain of spaghetti. My mouth dropped open in astonishment. Jack caught my expression and explained a bit sheepishly that he liked potatoes and would go easy on the rest of the buffet (until the desserts). Jack was one of the first world-class runners I observed at the trough, but he still qualifies as the best two-fisted eater I have known. He manages to remain lean, even on relatively low mileage (seldom over 100/week).

A word of caution to women is definitely needed here. A little restraint is in order. Even if they pile up similar mileage, women cannot eat like their male counterparts and still stay lean. The reason is that women have less muscle and more fat than men have, and the muscle is the metabolically active tissue that burns up all those ingested calories. A man who runs 60 miles weekly may be 45 percent muscle and 5 percent fat. He may weigh the same as his female running partner who is only 25 percent muscle and 15 percent fat—but he can consume (and burn) many more calories than she can. This is one of those sex differences that can make women despair, but take heart. The other side of the coin is that if you're training together, 60 miles weekly, you'll probably leave him behind at the 20-mile mark in your first marathon.

Chapter Fifteen: Fat: Friend or Foe?

Changing the Body. The best women runners compare very favorably with their male counterparts. Running at submaximal effort on the treadmill, men and women consume equivalent amounts of oxygen; i.e., their "aerobic demand" is the same. Women achieve equally high maximal heart rates, have similarly low blood fats (and admirably high HDL cholesterol)*, and certainly look at least as graceful as male runners. But in most race distances, the top women do not yet run so fast as the top men. Champions such as Grete Waitz and Marty Cooksey, it is true, finish ahead of 90 percent of the males in any race, but by and large, the best men don't yet have to worry about female competition. Why not?

The answer may lie in lowly fat. If you look at male and female runners, both 5 feet, 10 inches and 130 pounds, for example, both world-class runners, the man is likely to

*See Chapter Fourteen.

have about 5 percent fat, the woman 10 percent. The difference may seem very little, but since maximal aerobic power ($\dot{V}_{O2}$ max.) is expressed as ml. of O_2 consumed (used) per kilo per minute, and only the working muscles are using the oxygen taken in, a 5 percent surplus of fat translates to about a 5 percent lower $\dot{V}_{O2}$ max.

Otherwise expressed, the woman has less *lean* weight than the man—he may be 40 percent muscle compared to her 25 percent (average figures). When $\dot{V}_{O2}$ max. is expressed in an alternate fashion, as ml./kg. of *lean* weight, the figures for top men and women runners are comparable. Unfortunately, this theoretical equality does not extend to actual races, where the woman has less muscle to propel the same mass. Her extra fat is not particularly useful at short distances like the marathon. Over a few hundred miles, it would be a valuable extra source of fuel. In fact, women's traditional ability to survive shipwreck, starvation, Dinner party disasters, and long marches, while the men around them are dying off one by one, probably reflects the edge given the women by their supplementary fuel. Especially when you consider that the average coed contains 26 percent fat, the typical 30-year-old closer to 35 percent. That can be a tremendous aid to survival on a life raft, or in a concentration camp. Even the average young male is much leaner, at 15–20 percent fat.

Even though the best women runners may consume slightly less oxygen (at maximal effort) than male champions, and be a touch fatter, they still appear strikingly lean to eyes more accustomed to the average. While our aesthetic perceptions have evolved considerably since the days of Rubens' plump, pink and pillowy goddesses, illustrations in *Playboy*, three centuries later, still emphasize the ample in bosom and buttocks. In between, the poor Playmate is expected to be slender, even willowy, reflecting the more modern ideal of beauty. Since it is physiologically extremely difficult to deposit extra fat on the mammaries while reducing it elsewhere, the aspiring Playmate must often resort to modern technology to fool Mother Nature. She is usually neither so lean as her waist would suggest, nor so fat as other parts imply. On the average, possibly 25 percent fat and 4 percent silicone.

The true runner generally prefers to run faster, and carry less weight everywhere. The women distance runners studied by physiologist Jack Wilmore and his colleagues averaged 16 percent fat, with a low of 6 percent. Cup size, a good indicator of overall body fat, was mostly A, with some B's and sub-A's. Because of the generally modest amount of subcutaneous fat, and the muscle tone that running develops, you can generally notice that women runners possess real muscles—their outlines can be discerned, whereas the average American woman, if all her muscles haven't atrophied from disuse, has them buried deep and invisibly under a thick layer of adipose tissue.

When I'm training hard, trying to rein in my appetite and lower my percentage of body fat, I look anxiously in the mirror to see if any new muscles have been revealed during the night. I'm proud of my deltoid, when it finally emerges from the lard that hid it. Others may be jealous. Once, after the Honolulu marathon, some woman friends and I were recuperating on Kauai, and rumors of our running hobby spread rapidly through the resort. As we walked to lunch one day, we overheard one middle-aged lady in a chaise longue point us out to her friend. "Look, there go those runners! Aren't they nice and thin!" "Yes," replied her friend with a sniff, "but, my dear, they look so *masculine.*"

Knowing that they referred to our carefully cultivated arm muscles, newly revealed, we smiled with satisfaction and moved on to the buffet table.

The sedentary resort ladies might not have been so snotty if they had realized that we runners were not born slim. In fact, all three of us had "weight problems"—when not running. Like many others, we run, in part, so we can afford to eat what we like and not worry about dieting.

Personally, I would much rather reduce by running more than by eating less. Somewhere around 70 miles/week I go into negative caloric balance. Unfortunately, as your running becomes more efficient, and you lose pounds, you also burn fewer calories per mile—so the mileage needs may escalate. As a beginner, I lost inches on 20 miles a week; later, I needed 50, now 70. Life is unfair.

Very few of the top women runners who look so slim, graceful and gazelle-like in action, started out with perfect bodies. Some of the leanest and the best were once "fatties," who started running expressly to lose weight. Cheryl (Bridges) Flanagan, who ran a world record 2:49 marathon way back in 1971, slimmed down from 155 pounds to 115 (at 5 feet, 8 inches). At her athletic peak she had the lowest fat content (6 percent) and highest $\dot{V}_{o2}$ max. (74) ever measured in a woman. Patti Lyons, an outstanding marathoner and 30-km. record holder, went from 150 to a low of 96 pounds before stabilizing around 108. Somewhere along the way, she also stopped smoking. Weight loss, if it reflects decreased *fat* rather than loss of muscle tissue, almost always leads to dramatically improved performance. If you remember that fat content and $\dot{V}_{o2}$ max. vary inversely, it's easy to see why running is much easier when you're lighter.

Many women (and men) are terribly confused about the nature of weight loss. It's no wonder they're confused, in view of the glut of diet books on the market. A good way to distinguish the genuinely helpful (and healthful) diets from the quack types is by what they say about exercise. If the book suggests you can achieve a new, svelte, girlish figure by sitting around eating grapes, or protein, or nothing, don't buy it. If you want to lose *fat*, as opposed to weight, and stay fit while you diet, your decreased caloric intake *must* be combined with regular aerobic exercise. If you go to the grapes-and-bed-rest route, you will urinate away a lot of poundage, but you'll be too weak to enjoy yourself, and your clothes will just hang on the new, scarecrow you. The explanation is simple. If you lose weight by dieting alone, you lose water, muscle and fat—very little fat. If you diet (properly) and exercise an hour a day, you're better off in two ways. First, a *bad* diet (the high-protein, low-carbohydrate type especially) reveals itself quickly, because you'll soon be too weak to exercise. Heed your body signals. Secondly, exercise has a muscle-sparing effect—weight loss may be slower than on a crash diet, but it will reflect true fat loss—and you'll grow leaner. I'm a case in point. When I started running, I lost only 2 to 3 pounds in the first year (I wasn't very "overweight" nor dieting very assiduously). But I quickly went from a size 14 to a size 10.

An opposite, very sad, example is that of a fortyish woman who, although she was jogging 1 to 2 miles daily, felt dissatisfied with her 134 pounds. At 5 feet, 8 inches, she was scarcely chubby. Nevertheless, she went on a very low-carbohydrate diet, and soon found herself too weak and tired to jog. Still confused, she gave up the exercise and continued the diet. When she came for a checkup, she was delighted to find she weighed only 112 pounds! She looked awful. All bones and flab, no visible muscles. No strength, either. We popped her into a water tank to find out how much she'd lost. She was astonished to learn she still had 34 percent fat, and only 76 pounds of "lean weight"—virtually no muscle to drag her 112 pounds and 5 feet, 8 inches around the house. No wonder she was unable to jog! I was surprised she could even walk. She had lost 22 pounds, virtually all of it in the form of muscle.

Nutritionist Covert Bailey, author of *Fit or Fat* (Houghton Mifflin, Co., Boston, 1978), suggests that we'd all be better off throwing away the bathroom scales. It's not over*weight* one should worry about, but over*fat*. Muscle is lean, compact, dense, he points out. It adds to your weight. Fat isn't heavy at all—it takes a much larger volume of fat to make you heavy. By the time your scales register all those extra pounds of fat, your clothes have been getting tighter for months. Fat is bulky, but light. "Fat is *ethereal*," Covert informs his fascinated audiences. Covert is a humorous and accomplished public speaker. "Fat floats." Pause for reflection. "Oil slicks float, too." Prolonged pause. "Why, a fat man is nothing but an oil slick in a bag!" Somehow, the image sticks. The audience collectively resolves to go out the next day and start jogging.

Bailey also likes to show before-and-after slides of a young female acquaintance of his, wearing a skimpy bikini. The concept may be sexist, but it makes a point. Before, we see an attractive, if somewhat spindly-looking blonde. She is slender, but underdeveloped—thin calves, weak chest, and on the hips—gasp!—CELLULITE. All that dimpling. She weighs 118 pounds and is 24 percent fat. In the "after" shot, the young lady is transformed into Miss Blonde Bombshell. Excellent shoulder and bust development. Strong, well-proportioned legs. Slim hips. No "cellulite" left. Miss Bombshell is now only 17 percent fat, but . . . she weighs 126 pounds! She has, fortunately, discarded her bathroom scales and did not succumb to panic as she *added* 8 pounds. The moral is simple: weight and fat are not the same thing. In losing fat, one may actually put on weight. This is more likely to happen in women than men, however.

Men are basically muscular creatures, unless they have been brought up in a closet, and restrained from sports. They develop strength and muscle bulk in their teens, as puberty floods them with androgens. After age 20, whatever extra weight they add is due to fat (unless they are bodybuilders). So a middle-aged man who takes up jogging usually loses pounds as well as inches, as fat retreats. Governor Jerry Brown alarmed his aides, in 1979, by losing 25 pounds in 7 weeks (by running 5 miles daily and adhering to a Pritikin-type diet). Already skinny, the governor began to look gaunt. His PR adviser suggested he should quickly put 10 pounds back on, so he'd look his best "for the tube," nationally.

Women, of course, know very well that cameras add pounds to one's appearance, and would rather *lose* weight "for the tube." The typical woman who starts jogging will improve her muscle tone and strength—not by adding *bulk* but by reducing fatty "marbling" within muscles. The pounds added in muscle may counterbalance the pounds lost as fat. The resultant figure, however, is much improved. A quick calculation shows how this works. Take a typical sedentary, harassed 30-year-old mother. She is about 5 feet, 10 inches and 140 pounds—not fat, but a bit "puffy"-looking, size 14 and spreading rapidly. If weighed underwater, she would probably contain about 30 percent fat (42 pounds), and only 98 pounds of "lean" weight. She takes up running, hoping to reduce spread and preserve sanity. After a few months, clothes are loose, and she can fit into a size 12, then a 10. After 2 years of steady jogging, she is reweighed underwater. Her initial disappointment at still being 140 pounds (on dry land) dissolves when she finds she is now 15 percent fat, and 119 pounds lean weight. In other words, she has lost 21 pounds of fat (think of this as 84 sticks of butter—that represents a lot of inches). And she has added 21 pounds of lean, which is far more compact. Not all the lean weight is muscle, though she is much stronger and firmer than 2 years earlier. Some of it is increased blood volume, more capillaries, etc.

Some women worry about adding lean weight. They fear they'll acquire "bulky, unsightly" muscles. Simple observation can set their minds at rest. Distance runners tend to develop long, slender muscles, not short, round ones. Women running the 1500 meters in the Olympics do not resemble those putting the shot.

Muscles do not all look alike, just as they do not all act alike. And female muscles do not develop the same way as male muscles, since their hormonal environment is quite different.

Doctors Jack Wilmore and Harmon Brown were among the first researchers to study the effects of weight training on women. They ran into an image problem at first, when they advertised a course in weight-lifting for coeds. Only a handful of rather tough-looking, heavy girls applied. To improve recruitment, Wilmore and Brown changed the title of the class in the college catalog. It became "Body Shaping and Slimming with Weights." I think the "with weights" part was in small print. In any case, dozens of eager coeds enrolled in the renamed course, and were soon hard at work in the school gym, doing curls and bench presses.

The doctors made several interesting observations. First, most women have good leg strength, comparable to men, but woefully underdeveloped upper body strength. At puberty, when boys go on to run faster, throw harder and jump higher, aided by their new surge in muscle development, the girls retire. Unable to measure up in brute strength, they stop honing their skills, exercising their throwing arms, climbing trees and ropes. They become proper young ladies. Their muscles, in fact, *regress* from earlier levels. "Lady-like" has traditionally meant "weak and fragile."

But Wilmore's class showed that all is not lost; strength can be regained, even increased remarkably. Some of the young coeds doubled their strength after a few months of workouts 3 times a week. All improved at least 50 percent. And, as Wilmore's slides demonstrate, they did not acquire "bulky, unsightly" muscles—just strength. The greatest increase in arm girth measured was ¼ inch. Most women showed no increase in girth—the loss of fatty layer more than compensated for any growth in muscle size.

Two factors explain how women get improved strength without bulk. The first is that muscular "hypertrophy," or increase in size, requires the presence of large amounts of androgen, the "male" hormone. (While women do produce some androgen, it is in far smaller quantities than men. And men produce some estrogen, but much less than women do . . . it all balances out.) The system is not perfect, and once in a while a woman with somewhat higher androgen levels than the average will start "bulking up." If she doesn't need the extra strength, such a woman may prefer to abandon weight work.

The other factor in a woman's not getting a bodybuilder's appearance is to avoid the *training* of a bodybuilder. "Powerlifting," which tends to promote strength *and bulk* (in men), emphasizes very heavy, near-maximal loads, and few repeats. Endurance strength is better developed by doing many repeats (and "sets") with relatively light weights, well within almost any woman's ability to lift. I know one woman who found a conventional barbell too heavy. She could lift the bar by itself, but even with "sleeves" and "collars" on, much less weights, the load was a bit of a strain. So this resourceful woman marched off to the department store and bought a set of smaller weights for kids. "I'm sure your son will be thrilled," gushed the saleslady. "I don't have a son," replied my friend calmly. "These are for me." After working out faithfully with her "kid stuff" for a month, she eventually progressed to "grown-up" weights. But her approach was absolutely right. If you wish to improve your upper-body strength, start with a weight that you can lift comfortably 20 to 30 times—not some incredible load that you struggle to raise 3 or 4 times. Most experts advise doing your "repetitions" 3 times per week, rather than daily. You should also realize that there is no such thing as "spot reduction" of fat. By exercising your triceps (back of arm) or your thigh muscles, you don't "work off" the overlying fat deposits. Some ads seem to suggest that if you jiggle the fat around enough, it will get tired of all that motion and go away, or at least go elsewhere (the most popular alternate site is the chest). Don't be fooled by such claims. Exercise spas and figure salons may be great places to relax or enjoy a social life, but the only way you're going to get rid of fat in a particular area is to reduce your fat content *everywhere*. (To review, you do this by aerobic exercise plus a low-fat diet.) The subcutaneous fat layer is an accurate reflection of total body fat. For this reason, researchers who do not have access to a tank for underwater weighing can use multiple skinfold (subcutaneous fat layer) measurements and estimated body fat from the total thickness. It is *very* hard to do the multiple skinfold test yourself. You need special calipers and the measurements have to be done at *exact* points. You can buy calipers that have instructions with them, but generally it is best to have the measurements taken in a lab or doctor's office.

This brings me back to the subject of "cellulite" and all the promoted remedies for same, which I consider another consumer fraud. Obviously, if you tell women that they're not *fat*, they only have a "cellulite" problem, you're going to make them very happy. They will even buy books with detailed instructions on how to lose that unsightly "cellulite"—of course, if it's not just plain *fat*, it won't respond to counter-fat measures like exercise and diet.

Here's the sad truth. Remember that I was trained as a pathologist and have cut into a *lot* of fat in my past career. Cellulite is *die-hard*, "depot" fat. It looks dimpled because in order to be stored in large quantities on thighs, etc., it is interlaced with supportive fibrous tissue. Without the fibrous tissue it would just hang loosely, in great gobs. "Cellulite" tends to be deposited early, as the slim teenager evolves into a young matron. First to come, it is also last to go. It probably is more inert, metabolically, than fat which is constantly being used, as for fuel. I'm sure cellulite comes in very handy if you're shipwrecked and short of food—but it *is* sort of a final reserve. Jogging doesn't cure cellulite like magic. Once I received a plaintive letter from a 30-year-old woman. She had been jogging 1 to 2 miles, 5 days a week, for a *whole month,* she complained, and she *still* hadn't gotten rid of her cellulite. She was getting discouraged. I advised her to be patient, up her mileage and write back in a year. These things take time.

Runners, however, even those who were once young or

even middle-aged matrons, *can* lose their cellulite. Covert Bailey, with his slides of Miss Bombshell, points out that *her* cellulite disappeared when she went *below* 19 percent fat. At 19 percent it was still there, at 18 percent it was gone. The actual cutoff point may vary among different women—some may have to get down under the 15 percent fat level—but it's quite apparent that the best distance runners don't have the problem. And they didn't all start out looking like gazelles.

Lay opinion tends to agree with Bailey, that running and fat loss are a cure for cellulite. A fireman acquaintance of mine, a cyclist and sometime jogger, went to watch the annual San Francisco Bay-to-Breakers race a few years ago, when about 12,000 runners participated. He was amazed at the number of women racing past—until 1970, they were not allowed, and for a few more years they were rare. Now, he saw thousands. "Good-looking women, too," he said admiringly. "No tapioca there." Obviously, he is a leg man.

It is important to realize that you *can* reshape your body to an incredible extent. Women, of course, are somewhat less moldable than men because their low androgen levels prevent them from building huge muscles. But then, few women would want to look anything like Arnold Schwarzenegger anyway. But women have a great range of variability, and can reshape themselves to suit their sport. You are not always stuck with your teenage development. Nor is the progression always from lean to fat, as so many assume. In fact, our whole society accepts as inevitable the addition of a few pounds each year, or 40 pounds in 20 years—all fat, I might add. This is *not* inevitable; it is a sign of self-neglect, overeating and lack of exercise. No one need accept such a fate. At any race, you will see hundreds of people—women and men both—who have reversed this supposedly "inevitable" increase in bulk with age, and are slimmer than ever before in their lives.

Besides changing from slim to fat and back again, the

body adjusts in other ways to the imposed demands of sport. Gymnasts, who need overall muscular strength combined with extreme flexibility, have perhaps the most beautifully balanced development of all—their bodies are symmetrical and graceful. Swimmers tend to develop powerful arms and shoulders, coated with a layer of fat which is an advantage in their sport, since is provides both buoyancy and insulation. Long-distance swimmers, especially, tend to have much higher body fat than other women athletes, since it helps them adapt to icy channel waters.

Figure skaters have highly developed buttocks and leg muscles, downhill skiers tend to be heavier than cross-country skiers (weight adds to downhill momentum), and sprinters have powerful legs. The next time you're at a track meet, see how many of the runners you can assign to their proper event just by looking at their build. Among the men, the 400 runners tend to have the most powerful physiques, as do the 100- and 200-meter female sprinters. After 800 meters for men, 400 for women, there is an abrupt change to endurance-type builds—long and thin, rather than powerful.

No one, however, is stuck in an unchanging body. The different physiques reflect *training* and *use,* not just genes. By selectively building up or trimming down various muscle groups, through training, the hurdler can become a marathoner, the marathoner a swimmer. The world-class 440 runner may never become a world-class marathoner, but she can certainly train to break 3 hours for the distance.

In our running club we have an Olympic bronze medalist in the discus, Dave Weill, who is about 6 feet, 6 inches, and weighed close to 300 pounds at his (throwing) peak. When Dave retired from competition in the discus, he took up jogging, looking a bit like a fast-lumbering elephant as he towered above the pack in fun-runs. Dave was always fast on his feet, being blessed with both power and momentum (or mass). But after an initial fast mile or two, he would fade. This bothered him, and he slowly began to work on endurance. His huge bulk melted away gradually—from 280 pounds to 250, to 230. Dave tried some marathons, eventually breaking 4 hours, quite an accomplishment for such a large man. Spurred by growing competition with the "heavyweight" division of local races. Dave trained harder and got down to 220. His cheeks looked hollow, friends called him "Skinny." He ran under 3:30—but was not old enough to be qualified for Boston (the standard then was 3:30 for men over 40, but 3:00 for youngsters under 40—Dave was only 33). Undaunted, Dave kept on marathoning and ran 3:11—nowhere near Olympic caliber in his recreational sport, but a testimonial to the adaptability of the body. Another powerhouse who became a marathoner is Alan Page, long-time star of the Minnesota Vikings. Endurance training enabled him to drop 30 pounds of fat and run an impressive 3:57 marathon. Unfortunately for the Vikings, their management does not distinguish fat from lean weight (bulk is bulk on the field, they maintain), and traded away the rejuvenated and far healthier Page.

Old myths die hard, and it will take an entire nation of sports participants to revise some of the entrenched notions. As Page discovered, men have always loved to equate weight with strength (even if most of their mass is in the paunch), when in reality, 100 pounds of fat don't add an ounce of power. As for women, the long-legged beauties used in ads for resorts and cruises, or bathing suits, or even *jogging* gear, are obviously underdeveloped. They have skinny, useless calves, not a hint of muscle disturbs the smooth, unbroken line of arm or thigh. To my mind, this apparently inactive creature with totally non-functional limbs is singularly unappealing—one wonders how she can *hold* the tennis racquet long enough to be photographed. Perhaps it's suspended on a wire?

I don't believe the ad-makers are aware of the new, more

athletic ideal of American beauty. Margaret, a local woman runner who is extremely slender, with a gorgeous mane of brown hair, huge brown eyes, and very photogenic features, was being considered as a model in an ad for running shorts. The ad-men, somewhat titillated at the notion of having an actual *runner* in the ad, checked out Margaret's legs before making the final decision. "Sorry," they sighed, when Margaret stepped out in her running shorts, "your legs aren't thin enough." In fact, Margaret's legs are both slender and well shaped. What the ad-men needed were *unshaped,* unused legs. Eventually, they had to settle for a non-runner.

Another woman, though delighted that running had helped her slim down, stop smoking, and get new energy, complained that her knee-high boots didn't fit anymore. She tried on every pair of boots in the store, trying to find a replacement, and nothing would zip up over her calves. I looked at her legs, thinking she might be one of those women with enough androgen in their blood to make them "bulk up" excessively. But no, her legs looked fine, and she had lost inches from the thighs. I told this woman that her legs weren't the problem, the boots were. They were made for the average sedentary woman with skinny calves, whose broadening beam has caused airlines and auditoriums to widen their seats over the years. Once enough of the public are active and complain (about boot fashions, not the seats), we'll be able to buy boots that fit. In the meanwhile, the woman had to either stop running and let her legs atrophy a bit, or forget the boots. I think she rebelled at being a slave to outmoded fashion and kept on running.

Fat as Fuel. In our drive to lose fat, to slim down, to maximize our oxygen consumption and performance, we often forget that fat can be useful. It's not always just excess baggage. During periods of food deprivation (starvation), fat is broken down and used to manufacture a continuous supply of blood sugar (glucose) for the brain, which is a rather fastidious organ, dependent upon a single fuel. This process of making glucose from fat (and protein) is called "gluconeogenesis," to distinguish it from the usual production line, in which glycogen is broken down into single units of glucose. Glycogen, or muscle starch, is a storage form of glucose—the small glucose molecules are polymerized, strung together in long chains, to await future use. When you fast overnight, or go on a long run, your muscles and brain are easily supplied as long as the muscle and liver glycogen stores hold out. When the glycogen is depleted, fat and protein are utilized to make more glucose, which is sent off to the poor, dependent brain.

The muscles are much less particular. Once the glycogen gives out, they can burn fatty acids, other lipids, even lactic acid. The heart muscle, which is the principal endurance muscle of the body, since it never gets a chance to rest (while you're alive), burns anything it can get as fuel. It actually prefers fatty acids and lactic acid to glucose. The skeletal muscles, which support and propel you on a run, will burn fats if they must, but usually prefer glucose, if given a choice.

The infamous "Wall," which some unfortunate marathoners encounter around the 20-mile point, is thought to reflect total glycogen depletion. The skeletal muscles, forced to switch from caviar to meat and potatoes, protest loudly. They cramp up, cause pain, refuse to contract rapidly. The runner who has hit this "Wall" can keep on going, but has to jog slowly, or perhaps even walk.

The Wall, however, is only a hazard for the untrained runner, or for those who have unwisely run too fast at first, and "deplete" with a bang. Even Bill Rodgers would hit the Wall if he was so foolish as to dash out at a 4:40 pace for the first 18 to 20 miles. The *trained* skeletal muscle, contracting aerobically, isn't so exclusively geared to glucose fuel. It becomes more like heart muscle, calmly continuing its labors, utilizing fat as fuel. It has learned this technique during miles of training, and through long runs, which wean it away from dependence on glycogen. Since more oxygen is required to produce energy from fat, compared to glucose, fat-burning is only feasible at aerobic levels of effort. Anyone who relies heavily on anaerobic processes (sprinters through milers) can't use fat. You can run marathons on fat, but once your glycogen is gone, your "kick" is non-existent.

In human muscle there are at least three separate fiber types, with different physiological characteristics. Researchers can debate endlessly about the exact number and specifications of muscle types, but the information useful to runners is fairly simple. One main kind of fiber ("fast-twitch") is best suited for short, explosive efforts; the other ("slow-twitch") for prolonged, less intense muscular work. There is probably some overlap in such subtle matters as glycogent content, enzyme complement, and "twitch" pattern.

Using muscle-biopsy techniques, exercise physiologists compared jumpers, hurdlers and weight lifters with long-distance runners. Not surprisingly, they concluded that the athletes who use short, powerful muscle contractions have a preponderance of "fast-twitch" fibers, while those who go in for distance running have more of the "slow-twitch" ones. There are occasional exceptions—Don Kardong, fourth in the 1976 Olympic Marathon, has only about 50 percent "slow-twitch" fibers. (Researchers say this explains his good performance at 2 to 3 miles.) But as a general rule, there is a nice symmetry to muscle-typing—the fast-twitch guys sprint, run anaerobically, and burn glycogen; the slow-twitch guys like marathons, run aerobically, and burn fat.

The original Swedish experiments on fat utilization during exercise showed that several factors increased the proportion of fat to glycogen burned: length of experiment, type of diet, and—surprise!—amount of training the subject had done. This would imply that the glycogen-dependent sprinters could train themselves to run marathons without "hitting the Wall." The "anatomy is destiny" school of exercise physiologists tend to point (a bit gloomily) to their muscle-biopsy results and conclude that you'd better stick to shot-putting if you're born with 80 percent "fast-twitch" fibers. Conversely, if you're 99 percent slow-twitch, as I suspect of myself, you'll probably never break 16 seconds for the 100-yard dash.

But no longitudinal studies have yet been done, so we don't know yet to what extent training can alter inherited muscle patterns (if at all). Ideally, we should do fiber-typing on thousands of 5-year-olds, then train them for different sports for 15 years and re-biopsy the same muscle to see if the distribution of fiber types has changed. This experiment may be feasible in Eastern Europe, where sport is considered an important concern of the State, but in America it's out of the question. Since East Germans are extremely secretive about their sports-training methods, they are unlikely to enlighten us. The question remains unanswered, at least as far as humans are concerned.

Fortunately for science, we still have animals. Some of the most intriguing studies, by Hollosczy and his co-workers, utilize endurance-trained rats. Your basic sedentary lab rats are divided into experimental and control groups. The control rats continue to vegetate in their cages and eat; the experimental rats are remolded into athletes. For some, it's "Sink or Swim"—they are trained to swim for hours daily. Others run on a treadmill for varying intervals. After several weeks or months of conditioning, the animals are checked for muscle changes. In fact, their muscles can be not only biopsied, but ground up and analyzed for biochemical changes. Rats are expendable.

Hollosczy's results are fascinating. Put briefly, the endurance-trained rats actually develop the enzymatic appa-

271

ratus required by the task—they learn to metabolize fat efficiently and their muscles change visibly (more "dark" meat) as well as chemically. The metabolic and oxidative pathways of their skeletal muscles come to resemble those of heart muscle.

Drawing conclusions from rats and applying them to animals is always hazardous, but at least these results are "suggestive." They imply that metabolic changes in the body in response to training may be just as dramatic as the structural alterations discussed earlier. If a muscle biopsy from former discus thrower Dave Weill could be compared with a similar biopsy from the present, 3:11-marathoner Dave Weill, I suspect strongly that one could both see and measure significant changes in oxidative capacity of the fibers. Knowing how extremely adaptable the body is in its shape and size, we should expect that biochemical adaptation also occurs.

If indeed top distance runners are distinguished by their ability (inherited or acquired) to burn fat efficiently, are there any sex differences in this capacity? Dr. Van Aaken believes there are. He points to the greater ease with which women run the marathon distance, at least compared to male runners of similar ability. Since women obviously have different fat metabolism than men (resulting in different fat distribution and higher fat content), it is reasonable to suppose that the visible differences reflect functional ones. His theory is that women's muscles do *naturally* what men have to train theirs to accept—using fat as a fuel. There is as yet no laboratory evidence to support Van Aaken's theory, nor to refute it.* Acting in accordance with his beliefs, however, the doctor doesn't advise his female protégées to go on the 40- to 50-km. long

---

*Though recent studies by Dr. David Costill, a leading exercise physiologist, showed no difference in fat metabolism between *trained* male and female runners.

runs so necessary for male marathoners. Both Christa Vahlensiek, former women's world record holder (2:34) and her compatriot Manuela Angenvoorth (2:38 best) train the Van Aaken way, and never run the marathon distance as a workout. Manuela shuddered in distaste when I told her, somewhat proudly, about my weekly 22-milers. "My God, how can you stand it?" she said. "Thirty km. [18.6 miles] is more than enough for me." When training hard, she does that distance once a week, but under protest.

Grete Waitz, who set a women's world record of 2:32:30 in the 1978 New York City Marathon (and 237:32 in the 1979 one), was a newcomer to the distance. Primarily a track runner, her longest previous run had been 10 miles. Because of her inexperience, she deliberately stuck close to veteran Christa Vahlensiek for the first half of the marathon, covering the 13.1 miles in 1:17. Apparently finding the pace too slow, she then struck off on her own and ran 1:14 for the second half. Although she complained afterwards about leg fatigue and sore feet, Grete did not appear to encounter any mythical Wall. Perhaps Van Aaken's theory is correct, and the muscle metabolism of a woman adapts naturally to endurance activities.

Even more striking examples can be found among long-distance swimmers. At a time when only four men had finished the two-way English Channel swim (the fastest one taking 30 hours), a young Canadian girl—the first *woman* to give it a try—accomplished the same feat in 19 hours. A few weeks later, an American girl knocked an equivalent time off the two-way swim of the Catalina Channel. Her time was 20 hours, smashing the previous record (held by a man) of 31 hours. Endurance swimming requires the muscles to utilize fat almost exclusively (glycogen stores are depleted in 1 to 2 hours), and the extra body fat of the female is an advantage in the water, where it adds buoyancy and insulation.

Running women, of course, do not need extra fat. The

273

desirability of using fat as fuel should not be construed as a license to gorge on hot fudge sundaes. Since fat is so efficient a fuel, a little will take you a long way; unless you're embarking on a 300-mile hike without food, 3 percent body fat should see you to your destination easily. A woman with 13 percent body fat, then, doesn't need that extra 10 percent (except for appearance, and cushioning when sitting on hard benches). It just adds weight, and lowers the measured $\dot{V}_{O2}$ max. This handicap of higher fat *content* may offset the advantage of better fat utilization, and (along with lack of experience) account for the fact that Grete Waitz did not win the *open* division of the NYC Marathon—an honor taken by Bill Rodgers, for the fourth time in a row. The leanest runner is still the fastest, other factors being equal.

Several years ago, in a talk on muscle metabolism during exercise, I naturally discussed Van Aaken's theory about women's natural advantage. His theory struck the fancy of a local newspaper reporter, who proceeded to misinform the public in an article called "Fatter Is Faster." The implication was that I (not Van Aaken, whose name is even harder to spell than my own, and is frequently omitted) think fat is great, and promotes athletic powers. For a while, I was known locally as "Fatter Is Faster" Ullyot, and I haven't been able to eat a hot fudge sundae in peace since. Any fellow runner who sees me stoking up, smiles and says, "In training for another marathon, Joan?" In fact, Van Aaken thinks I should lose 10 to 15 pounds, and *then* we'll see what my endurance-trained, female muscles can do!

Appendixes

Sample Training Schedules

The first "beginner's schedule" is the one I usually suggest.
Those who are thoroughly out of shape should walk briskly
the first few weeks; others can jog/walk as breathing needs
dictate.

The second "beginner's schedule" is that used in the
Honolulu Marathon Clinic, it presupposes that you jog *very
slowly* in one direction for 30 minutes, then turn and come
back. If it takes you more than 30 minutes to get back (or if
you have to walk), you went out too fast!

I define an "intermediate," arbitrarily, as one who can
jog *comfortably* 20 to 30 minutes—at any speed. The
schedules are designed for further progress from this level,
if one so desires. Increased speed and/or distance are not
prerequisites for good health—only for competition.

Progress from one level to another should be determined
not by the calendar, nor by what your friends or competitors can do, but always by the way you feel.

When you are perfectly comfortable at any level, and feel
the need of a further challenge, you can progress to a more

demanding schedule. Remember to make all transitions gradually. Depending on such factors as your initial condition, natural endowment, goals and expectations, you can spend anywhere from 3 months to a lifetime at the "beginner's" level of training. Twenty minutes of jogging, every other day, will keep most people in good condition— though they'll never be "distance runners"!

These schedules are not meant to be followed slavishly, but rather to suggest patterns which will lead to good progress at the various levels of running. You should choose the one which best fits your own needs, your ambitions, and the realities of your work schedule and family life. A 5/5 means a total of 10 miles, but two separate workouts. The easier way to do this is once in the morning and once at night.

BASIC FITNESS TEST—THE 1½-MILE RUN

This test, derived from Dr. Kenneth Cooper's famous "twelve-minute-test," helps you determine your initial fitness level and subsequent improvement. All you need is a standard ¼-mile track and a watch, so you can time yourself for 6 laps, equivalent to 1½ miles. The elapsed time determines fitness level.

Since this test should represent a *maximal effort,* do not try it unless you have been exercising regularly or have been checked by a doctor. Also, do not try such a hard, timed run more frequently than once every 6 weeks—it's uncomfortable, and merely a testing device.

DR. KENNETH COOPER'S AEROBIC STANDARDS FOR WOMEN

Category	Below Age 30	Ages 30-39	Ages 40-49	Ages 50-up
Very poor	above 17:30	above 18:30	above 18:30	above 20:30
Poor	15:31-17:30	16:31-18:30	17:31-18:30	18:31-20:30
Fair	13:31-15:30	14:31-16:30	15:31-17:30	16:31-18:30
Good	11:01-13:30	11:31-14:30	12:31-15:30	13:31-16:30
Excellent	below 11:00	below 11:30	below 12:30	below 13:30

BASIC FITNESS TEST

	S	M	T	W	Th	F	S	Total
1. Beginning								
Jog a.	20 min.	0	20 min.	0	20 min.	0	15 min.	1 hr. 15 min.
or								
Jog/walk b.	0	1 hr.	0	1 hr.	0	0	1 hr.	3 hr.
2. Intermediate	8	2	5	7	3	0	5*	30 miles
can be a race	12	3	5	10	5	0	5*	40 miles
3. Advanced	20	7	3/12	5/5	3/12	3	10	80 miles
or	20	5/5**	5/5**	5/5**	5/5**	5/5**	10	80 miles
or	20	5	3/7***	5/5	3/8***	7	Race or 7 hilly	70 miles
4. Pre-Marathon Week a.	20	12	2-3 mile time-trial + striding	10	long walk	5	0	49–50 miles
or								
(race on Sunday) b.	15	10	5	8	5	5	2	50 miles

*can be a race   **to and from work   ***with Interval workout

RRCA Women's Time Standards.

These standards were developed by statistician Ken Young for the Road Runners Club of America. By matching some of these marks in races, you can qualify for a national award, or simply measure yourself against other competitors. Note that these standards, unlike Cooper's Fitness Test, make no allowance for different age groups. So if you're over 40, I'd suggest moving yourself up one class, mentally. If you can run Class A times after 40, you're definitely Champion level!

Event	World Class	Champion	Class A	Class B	Class C
6 miles	33:00	35:30	38:00	41:30	45:30
10 kilometers	34:00	36:30	39:30	43:00	47:00
15 kilometers	52:30	56:00	1:00:30	1:06:00	1:12:00
10 miles	56:30	1:00:30	1:05:00	1:11:00	1:17:30
One hour	10m 1100yds.	9m 1600yds.	9m 400yds.	8m 900yds.	7m 1500yds.
20 kilometers	1:11:00	1:16:00	1:22:00	1:29:00	1:37:30
15 miles	1:26:30	1:33:00	1:40:00	1:49:00	1:59:30
25 kilometers	1:29:30	1:36:30	1:44:00	1:53:00	2:04:00
30 kilometers	1:49:00	1:57:00	2:06:30	2:18:00	2:31:00
20 miles	1:57:30	2:06:30	2:16:30	2:28:30	2:43:00
Marathon	2:38:00	2:50:00	3:04:00	3:20:00	3:39:30
50 kilometers	3:10:30	3:25:00	3:41:30	4:01:30	4:25:30

Race Pacing Tables

Proper pacing is vital in long-distance racing. Most record times—whether "personal," or "world"—are set when the effort (and speed) are consistent throughout the race. The tables below can help you distribute your efforts most efficiently. Thus, if you wish to race 10 miles in 70 minutes, you should try to run each half in 35 minutes. Or if you aim to break 3:20 in the marathon, and "qualify for Boston," you can see from the table that a steady 7:30-minute/mile pace will bring you in under the wire, and that you should try to run the first 5 miles in 37:30. Many expert marathoners refer to this chart before each race, and write their desired intermediate times, or "splits," on their arm. It's easier to check your arm, during the marathon, than to try to calculate anything in your head!

If you're running in Europe, or in metric-distance events, you can do your pre-race planning the same way, using the mile-kilometer comparison and metric pacing tables.

RACE PACING TABLE

Mile	5 Miles	10 Miles	15 Miles	20 Miles	Marathon	50 Miles
4:50	24:10	48:20	1:12:30	1:36:40	2:07:44	
5:30	25:30	55:00	1:22:30	1:50:00	2:24:12	
5:40	28:20	56:40	1:25:00	1:53:20	2:28:34	
5:50	29:10	58:20	1:27:30	1:56:40	2:32:56	
6:00	30:00	1:00:00	1:30:00	2:00:00	2:37:19	5:00:00
6:10	30:50	1:01:40	1:32:30	2:03:20	2:41:41	5:08:20
6:20	31:40	1:03:20	1:35:00	2:06:40	2:46:03	5:16:40
6:30	32:30	1:05:00	1:37:30	2:10:00	2:50:25	5:25:00
6:40	33:20	1:06:40	1:40:00	2:13:20	2:54:47	5:33:20
6:50	34:10	1:08:20	1:42:30	2:16:40	2:59:09	5:41:40
7:00	35:00	1:10:00	1:45:00	2:20:00	3:03:33	5:50:00
7:10	35:50	1:11:40	1:18:20	2:23:20	3:07:55	5:58:20
7:20	36:40	1:13:20	1:50:00	2:26:40	3:12:17	6:06:40
7:30	37:30	1:15:00	1:52:30	2:30:00	3:16:39	6:15:00
7:40	38:20	1:16:40	1:55:00	2:33:20	3:21:01	6:23:20
7:50	39:10	1:18:20	1:57:30	2:36:40	3:25:23	6:31:40
8:00	40:00	1:20:00	2:00:00	2:40:00	3:29:45	6:40:00
8:10	40:50	1:21:40	2:02:30	2:43:20	3:34:07	6:48:20
8:20	41:40	1:23:20	2:05:00	2:46:40	3:38:29	6:65:40
8:30	42:30	1:25:00	2:07:30	2:50:00	3:42:51	7:05:00
8:40	43:20	1:26:40	2:10:00	2:53:20	3:47:13	7:13:20
8:50	44:10	1:28:20	2:12:30	2:56:40	3:51:35	7:21:40
9:00	45:00	1:30:00	2:15:00	3:00:00	3:56:00	7:30:00
9:10	45:50	1:31:40	2:17:30	3:03:20	4:00:22	7:38:20
9:20	46:40	1:33:20	2:20:00	3:06:40	4:04:44	7:46:40
9:30	47:30	1:35:00	2:22:30	3:10:00	4:09:06	7:55:00
9:40	48:20	1:36:40	2:25:00	3:13:20	4:13:28	8:03:20
9:50	49:10	1:38:20	2:27:30	3:16:40	4:17:50	8:11:40

METRIC PACING TABLE

1 km.	10 kms.	15 kms.	20 kms.	25 kms.	30 kms.	50 kms.
3:00	30:00	45:00	1:00:00	1:15:00	1:30:00	2:30:00
3:10	31:40	47:30	1:03:20	1:19:10	1:35:00	2:38:20
3:20	33:20	50:00	1:06:40	1:23:20	1:40:00	2:46:40
3:30	35:00	52:30	1:10:00	1:27:30	1:45:00	2:55:00
3:40	36:40	55:00	1:13:20	1:31:40	1:50:00	3:03:20
3:50	38:20	57:30	1:16:40	1:35:50	1:55:00	3:11:40
4:00	40:00	1:00:00	1:20:00	1:40:00	2:00:00	3:20:00
4:10	41:40	1:02:30	1:23:20	1:44:10	2:05:00	3:28:20
4:20	43:20	1:05:00	1:26:40	1:48:20	2:10:00	3:36:40
4:30	45:00	1:07:30	1:30:00	1:52:30	2:15:00	3:45:00
4:40	46:40	1:10:00	1:33:20	1:56:40	2:20:00	3:53:20
4:50	48:20	1:12:30	1:36:40	2:00:50	2:25:00	4:01:40
5:00	50:00	1:15:00	1:40:00	2:05:00	2:30:00	4:10:00
5:10	51:40	1:17:30	1:43:20	2:09:10	2:35:00	4:18:20
5:20	53:20	1:20:00	1:46:40	2:13:20	2:40:00	4:26:40
5:30	55:00	1:22:30	1:50:00	2:17:30	2:45:00	4:35:00
5:40	56:40	1:25:00	1:53:20	2:21:40	2:50:00	4:43:20
5:50	58:20	1:27:30	1:56:40	2:25:50	2:55:00	4:51:40

MILE-KILOMETER TIME COMPARISONS

Mile	Kilometer	Mile	Kilometer
4:00	2:29:16	7:00	4:21:03
4:10	2:35:37	7:10	4:27:24
4:20	2:41:59	7:20	4:33:46
4:30	2:47:80	7:30	4:39:67
4:40	2:54:02	7:40	4:45:89
4:50	3:00:23	7:50	4:52:10
5::00	3:06:45	8:00	4:58:32
5:10	3:12:66	8:10	5:04:53
5:20	3:18:88	8:20	5:10:75
5:30	3:25:09	8:30	5:16:96
5:40	3:31:31	8:40	5:23:18
5:50	3:37:52	8:50	5:29:39
6:00	3:43:74	9:00	5:35:61
6:10	3:49:95	9:10	5:41:82
6:20	3:56:17	9:20	5:48:04
6:30	4:02:38	9:30	5:54:25
6:40	4:08:60	9:40	6:00:47
6:50	4:14:81	9:50	6:06:68

Annotated Bibliography

Anderson, Bob, *Stretching*. P.O. Box 2734, Fullerton, Ca. 92633. $7.00 plus 50¢ postage. Paper. 1975. A useful, complete guide to loosening up your body in a comfortable and enjoyable fashion. No pain! Recommended to the tight and stiff in all sports. An excerpt from this book, "The Perfect Pre-Run Stretching Routine," was widely distributed in May, 1978 as a *Runner's World* flyer.

AÅstrand, Per-Olof, M.D., and Kaare Rodahl, M.D., *Textbook of Work Physiology*. McGraw-Hill Book Co., New York, 1977. $21.00. The classic and often revised "Bible" for exercise physiologists and all those interested in studying the processes by which the body moves, breathes and plays. Scholarly and detailed, this is the technical counterpart to Dr. Kenneth Cooper's *Aerobics* (see below).

Bailey, Covert, *Fit or Fat*. Houghton Mifflin Co., Boston; $6.95, cloth, or $4.95, paper, 1978. A lucid and entertaining discussion of body composition, the difference between fat and weight, and the uselessness of diets. Bailey advocates aerobic exercise to reshape the body and its metabolism.

Bishop, Bob, *The Running Saga of Walter Stack*. Celestial Arts, Ca; $4.95, paper, 1978. The biography of an unusual and inspirational 70-year-old runner, who is also perpetual President of San Francisco's Dolphin South End (DSE) Runners, and a long-time promoter of women's running.

Burger, Robert, *Jogger's Catalog*. M. Evans, New York; $5.95, paper, 1978. Subtitled "a sourcebook for runners," this eclectic collection of reviews, helpful hints, addresses, biographies, and sound advice can be both useful and amusing for all runners. The flavor of both text and photos is lighthearted.

Cooper, Kenneth, M.D., *Aerobics*. Bantam Books, Inc., New York; $1.75, paper, 1968.

————*The New Aerobics*. Bantam Books, Inc., New York; $2.25, paper, 1970.

————*Aerobics for Women* (with Mildred Cooper). Bantam Books, Inc., New York; $2.25, paper, 1972.

————*The Aerobics Way*. M. Evans, New York; $10.00, 1977.

All of these "classics" are now available in paperback. *Aerobics* describes lucidly the physiological effects of training and gives the original testing system and exercise schedules, with point values. Later books modify and expand the system for various ages, women, and medical skeptics. Especially good for beginning fitness buffs.

Costill, David L., *A Scientific Approach to Distance Running*. Tafnews Press, Los Altos, Ca.; $5.00, paper, 1979. A leading exercise physiologist tells of the facts and research behind the sport.

Daws, Ron, *The Self-Made Olympian*. World Pubns., Mountain View, Ca.; $3.50, paper, 1976. An ideal book for the thinking runner who is ready to train systematically and develop her potential. Entertaining and lucid explanation of the Lydiard System, as utilized in the author's own 28-year running career.

Fixx, James, *The Complete Book of Running.* Random House, Inc., New York; $10.00, 1977. The best-seller of the 1970s running boom. An interesting potpourri of practical advice, personalities, and information about running.

Frederick, E. C., *The Running Body.* World Pubns., Mountain View, Ca.; $1.95, paper, 1973. This little booklet is worth back-ordering if necessary. In forty-eight pages, exercise physiologist Frederick explains what happens when you run—biochemical reactions, metabolic pathways, and the physiological basis for different types of training. Detailed, but clearly written.

Glover, Bob and Jack Shepherd, *The Runners Handbook.* Penguin, New York, $3.95, paper. 1978. A broad-spectrum, "how-to" manual especially useful for "do-it-yourself" runners who don't have access to a coach like author Glover. Contains lots of helpful advice for beginners.

Henderson, Joe, *Long, Slow Distance.* Tafnews, $2.50. 1970.

———*Thoughts on the Run.* World Pubns., Mountain View, Ca., paper, 1972.

———*Run Gently, Run Long.* World Pubns., Mountain View, Ca., $2.95, paper, 1974.

———*The Long-Run Solution.* World Pubns., Mountain View, Ca., paper, $3.95, 1975.

———*Jog, Run, Race.* World Pubns., Mountain View, Ca., paper, $3.50, 1977.

———*Run Farther, Run Faster.* World Pubns., Mountain View, Ca., paper, $4.95, 1979.

Except for *Jog, Run, Race,* which gives specific training schedules for runners at various levels, Joe Henderson's books are for browsing. The former editor of *Runner's World* has developed, over years of running, a philosophical, humorous, wise approach to the sport as recreation and self-discovery. His books are enlightening as well as instructive.

Higdon, Hal. *On The Run from Dogs and People*. P.O. Box 372, Michigan City, Ind. 46360. Long out of print, this amusing collection of tales from the early years of running has been reissued. Hordes of new runners can now be assured of some good laughs about their chosen idiosyncracy.

——*Fitness After Forty*, World Pubns., Mountain View, Ca., $3.95 paper, 1977. Of interest to all older runners. Higdon explores the effects of age on performance, discusses health hazards and means of maintaining fitness, including sports, diet and habits.

Jackson, Ian. *Yoga and the Athlete*. World Pubns., Mountain View, Ca., $2.50 paper, 1975. The odyssey of a young runner, from surfing to swimming, through competitive running, into contemplative running, yoga and vegetarianism. An "underground classic."

Kostrubala, Thaddeus, M.D., *The Joy of Running*. Lippincott, Philadelphia, Pa., $3.95, 1976; Pocket Books, New York, paper, $1.95, 1977. Confessions of a psychiatrist who was once a coronary-courting middle-aged fat boy, but transformed himself into a marathoner who now uses running as therapy for psychotics. A fascinating story, enhanced by psychological insights and speculation.

Lance, Kathryn, *Running for Health and Beauty*. Bobbs-Merrill, Inc., Indianapolis, In., $8.95, 1977. Good first-person account of the author's self-cure, through running, of high blood pressure, chain-smoking and weight problems. Helps to encourage non-runners to try the sport and guides them up to 1- to 2-mile runs, with a variety of hints for beginners.

Lydiard, Arthur, *Run to the Top,* (out of print), New Zealand, 1962.

————*Running the Lydiard Way.* World Pubns., Mountain View, Ca., $7.95, 1978.

The first book is an inspirational classic, if you can lay your hands on it. The second is a recent update and expansion of training advice by the renowned New Zealand coach whose methods have revolutionized long-distance running around the world.

Milvy, Paul, ed., *The Long-Distance Runner.* Urizen Books, New York, $15.00 1978. Subtitled "A Definitive Study," this book collects papers presented at the New York Academy of Sciences symposium, "The Marathon," in 1976. It includes physiological, medical, epidemiological and psychological studies. Authoritative and fascinating.

Mirkin, Gabe, M.D., and Marshall Hoffman, *The Sportsmedicine Book.* Little, Brown & Co., Boston, $12.50, 1978. An authoritative tome, useful to all athletes concerned about the body and its needs. Debunks myths and offers common-sense advice about diet, injuries, and training.

Osler, Tom. *The Conditioning of Distance Runners.* Tafnews Press, $1.50, paper, 1970. A little gem by an ultramarathoner and mathematics professor, pointing out patterns of training and ways to achieve your best performance at the proper time, called "peaking."

Sheehan, George A., M.D., *Dr. Sheehan on Running.* World Pubns., Mountain View, Ca., $3.50, paper, 1975.

————*Running and Being.* Simon and Schuster, New York, $8.95, 1978. Dr. Sheehan is both a humorist and a philosopher, who views running as a means of self-discovery and self-expression. Anyone to whom running is important will enjoy these well-written reflections on the sport. Reading them is a pleasure in itself.

————*Dr. George Sheehan's Medical Advice for Runners.*

World Pubns., Mountain View, Ca., $10.95, 1978. In his physician's role, Dr. Sheehan dispenses medical advice to ailing athletes in his monthly *Runner's World* column. Questions sent in by despairing, grounded runners throughout the country inspired this collection of sensible recommendations for restoring health and mobility.

Steffny, Manfred, *Marathoning*. World Pubns., Mountain View, Ca., paper, $5.95, 1979. Training advice from the German Olympian who coached Christa Vahlensiek to a world-record marathon, and is the editor of *Spiridon*, the German road running magazine.

Subotnick, Steven, D.P.M., *The Running Foot Doctor*. World Pubns., Mountain View, Ca., $3.95, paper, 1977. Addressed to the layman rather than experts, this book utilizes case histories to illustrate the most common "overuse" problems of runners, and their treatment.

Ullyot, Joan, M.D., *Women's Running*. World Pubns., Mountain View, Ca., $3.95, paper. 1976. This is a "how-to" manual of practical advice for runners at all levels from first steps through marathoning. Though the book is addressed particularly to women, nearly all of the training and medical material is equally valid for men.

Van Aaken, Ernst, M.D., *The Van Aaken Method*. World Pubns., Mountain View, Ca., $3.95, paper, 1976. The only work available in English, this book is a collection of advice on diet, training and health by the famous German physician/coach. It is far shorter and less comprehensive than the original book and its sequels, listed below, which are fascinating reading for those who know German:

————*Programmiert Für Hundert Lebensjahre,* Pohl-Verlag, 3100 Celle, Germany, 1974.

————*Die Schonungslose Therapie,* Pohl-Verlag, 3100 Celle, Germany, 1977.

————*Schonungslose Behandlung,* Pohl-Verlag, 3100 Celle, Germany, 1978.

RECOMMENDED PERIODICALS

On Running

$13.00/yr. *Runner's World,* P.O. Box 366, Mountain View, Ca. 94042. Monthly.

$18/yr. *The Runner,* P.O. Box 2730, Boulder, Co. 80322. Monthly.

$7/6 issues. *Running,* P.O. Box 350, Salem, Oreg. 97308. Quarterly.

Foreign Language

$15/yr. (airmail) *Spiridon* (French) 1922 Salvan, Switzerland, 6 issues/yr.

$15/yr. (airmail) *Spiridon* (German) Postfach 8901, 4000, Düsseldorf, Germany. 8 issues/yr.

On Physiology and Sportsmedicine

$26/yr. *The Physician and Sportsmedicine,* McGraw-Hill, 4530 West 77th St., Minneapolis 55435. Monthly.

$18/yr. *Medicine and Science in Sports,* 1440 Monroe Street, 4002 Stadium, Madison, Wis. 53706. Quarterly.